Work From H

463 Ways To Make Money From Home.

Moneymaking Ideas & Home-Based Business Ideas.

Includes Online And Offline Ideas For All Ages.

by

Christine Clayfield

Christine Clayfield is the author of:

"No Fourth River" A novel based on a true story.
Available on Amazon or buy it as an eBook on
www.ebooknofourthriver.com

"From Newbie To Millionaire"
Available on Amazon or buy it as an eBook on
www.FromNewbieToMillionaire.com

"Drop Shipping and eCommerce. What You Need and Where to Get It"
Available on Amazon or buy it as an eBook on
www.DropshippingAndEcommerce.com

"Finding Niches Made Easy"
Available on Amazon or buy it as an eBook on
www.findingnichesmadeeasy.com

"Design Free Websites"
Available on Amazon or buy it as an eBook on
www.designfreewebsites.com or Get a Free Copy on
www.fromnewbietomillionaire.com

"Work From Home Ideas"
Available on Amazon or buy it as an eBook on
http://www.makemoneyfromhomebook.com

Creator of www.WorldwideSelfPublishing.com Video Tutorials

Table of Contents

Table of Contents

Table of Contents

Acknowledgments

My biggest thank you goes to my darling husband. Thank you for supporting me in all that I do. You are my rock and my world. I will always love you.

A second huge thank you goes to my twin daughters for being respectful young adults. I hope your dreams may come true. I love you with all my heart.

A third thank you goes to my stepchildren for accepting my daughters into your worlds.

Thank you to you, the reader, for putting your trust in me and buying my book. I hope that you will create some extra income with one or more ideas from this book.

Other than the above, I don't really have a lot of people to thank as all I've learned in business comes from hard work, making mistakes and learning from them.

Introduction

You probably have a million dollar idea! Everyone has at least one! The problem is that not everyone takes action to put their idea into practice. If you *do* have an idea: put it into action! Start small by working from home. If you *don't* have an idea to make money, there's plenty of thinking material for you in this book.

Our conversations at the dinner table are often about moneymaking opportunities. My children often start the conversation with: "I thought of something to make money with". Although they are still at university at the time of writing this book, I believe they already possess the entrepreneurial spirit. I can see them owning a home-based business at some time in the future. Could you see yourself owning a home-based business? Why not? In fact, welcome to the club!

I have been working from home for the last 8 years and I totally love it. In fact, in the part of this book called: "My other products", you can see the type of products that I have created working from home and you can read the sort of things I have been doing to make money online.

Let me be one of the first to congratulate you. You are probably very excited about your decision to earn some extra money or to work from home or perhaps you are even a little bit scared. Don't worry, being scared is perfectly normal. Let me just reassure you: yes, you can do this. With some guidance, good advice and hard work, you will be well on your way to successfully being self-employed in a home-based business. And trust me, being self-employed in a home-based business is the greatest feeling in the world. The benefits include the following:

- You make the rules (ice cream at noon)!
- You set your work schedule.
- You can take your kids (or your pets) to work.
- You can spend more time with your family (or not; it's your choice).
- You can call your ex-boss an idiot and get away with it.
- No expensive premises to rent/buy
- Save time and money spent commuting
- Less stress therefore better health
- Freedom to do what you want and when you want it

- You can create passive income with some methods mentioned in this book, which means that even when you don't work, you will earn money
- You can't get fired
- Big savings on work clothes as you can wear your jeans or comfy trousers every day
- You are your own boss - nobody tells you what to do and when to do it
- You can earn what you are truly worth, not what someone else thinks you are worth. (And they never seem to think you are worth all that much, do they?) If you succeed, you will certainly earn more than you would at a regular job.

No matter what type of home-based business you want to start, this guide can really help you. It doesn't matter if you want to work from home using a computer, making a product and selling it, running a business servicing the local area (like a contractor, computer service professional, etc.) or you want to have a business in your home (like child care) – this book can help you become successfully self-employed.

The key is actually doing the right things and knowing which mistakes to avoid. This guide will help you by showing you both what to do and what not to do. If you're serious about owning a home-based business, then this book is for you.

In this book you'll find:

- Some ideas that you can do without having a computer

- Some ideas where you'll need to have a computer but won't need to have your own website

- Some ideas where you'll need a computer *and* your own website.

Why this book?

I already have a home-based business so why did I write this book? Well, 2 main reasons:

- Countless people I speak to ask me all the time how they can earn money working from home without spending a lot of money.

- Millions of people are struggling financially and are always looking to earn some extra cash.

I hope that I will be able to help some people to earn extra money so they can improve their financial situation.

Not all the ideas in this book involve just sitting at home, though. You'll find plenty of ideas for making money that you can do outside the home while still being your own boss and others that are just quick and easy ways to make money, which you can use at any time – whether you're running your own business or not.

Who is this book for?

There are people in all walks of life who dream of earning a living whilst working from home. It is, of course, for these people that this book is written. In the last 10 years I've met a lot of people who I know had the strong desire to work from home but just didn't know where to start. Working from home is especially interesting for these types of people:

-   People who are forced to stay at home to take care of their children or their parents

-   O.A.P (Old Aged Pensioners) who would love to earn some extra income

-   Parents who want to spend more time with their children

-   Parents who don't like taking their children to day-care

-   People who are not happy in their current job

-   People who have been looking for a job for many years and can't find one

-   Teenagers and young people who want to earn some money

-   Students who want to earn some extra money

-   Disabled people, often forced to stay at home a lot due to poor mobility

-   Self employed people who would like to supplement their income

-   etc.

So, in other words: for everyone, young and old.

My Other Products

My novel "No Fourth River". A Novel, based on a true story; my own personal story.

Buy the **eBook** here: www.ebooknofourthriver.com
Buy the paperback book on Amazon or other book websites.

My Bestselling Book "From Newbie To Millionaire"

Buy the **eBook** here: www.FromNewbieToMillionaire.com.
Buy the paperback book on Amazon or other book websites.

My Drop Shipping and eCommerce Book

"DropShipping and eCommerce. What You Need and Where to Get It"
Buy the **eBook** here: www.dropshippingandecommerce.com.
Buy the paperback book on Amazon or other book websites.

My Finding Niches Made Easy Book

"Finding Niches Made Easy"
Buy the eBook here: *www.findingnichesmadeeasy.com*

Buy the paperback book on Amazon or other book websites.

My Design FREE Websites book

Buy the **eBook** here: www.designfreewebsites.com or Get a Free Copy on
www.fromnewbietomillionaire.com

Buy the paperback book on Amazon or other book websites.

My Self Publishing Success System Explained Step by Step in Video Tutorials

I publish a new book, on average, every 2 weeks. These books are all in different niches, and I outsource all aspects of the book, including writing and cover design, except for the publishing, which I do myself. I explain EVERYTHING I do, from finding a niche to publishing the book worldwide in watch-over-my-shoulder style video tutorials: www.WorldwideSelfPublishing.com.

My Break Reminder Software

I have to try to reduce the time I spend on my computer due to a neck injury (you will read about it later). I used to use www.workpace.com, which is software that forces you to take breaks while on your computer. I had my own simplified version developed, which you can buy here: www.BreakReminderSoftware.com.

My Repetitive Strain Injury Book

The real-life stories in the book will make you think and will, hopefully, make you take regular breaks on your computer/mobile phones, etc. The book is aimed at anyone who use our much-loved electronic gadgets too often, too long, without taking breaks. Nobody warns people about the permanent damage it can do to your body.

Buy the **hard copy boo**k: search for it on Amazon by author Lucy Rudford (pen name)

My Print Screen Software

When I was looking for a very simple print screen software application, without all the bells and whistles, I couldn't find it, therefore I had my own developed. I use it every single day and don't know how I could ever be without it.

You can buy it here: www.PrintingYourScreen.com.

Print a Kindle eBook

I don't like reading from a screen and searched A LOT for a reliable solution to print a Kindle book. You can grab your copy here free: www.HowToPrintAKindleBook.com. How to print a kindle book from your PC. If you are like me and you prefer reading books from paper, this is for you. Before I knew how to print a Kindle book, I never bought any Kindle books, now I do because I print them and read them.

Please note there is a one-time charge of $29.99 / £19.00 to buy the Kindle Converter that I recommend in order to convert your Kindle to a pdf format that you can print. However, you have 5 days to test the product free. This converter is not my product and I don't earn any money from it if you buy it but it is a product that actually works.
Works on PC, windows explorer. I have not tested it an Apple computer.

More Information About Me:
www.ChristineClayfield.com
For more information about how you can make money as an affiliate selling my products, please refer to the end of this book.

Important To Mention

There are a few important things to mention.

This book is about IDEAS. As there are so many ideas in this book, it is impossible to explain each one in detail. You will find a brief explanation of what the idea is all about. If a particular idea is of interest to you, you will have to investigate that topic in more detail to see what is involved to put that idea into practice and to find out how much money you will need in advance (if any).

Although these methods are all called "home-based business ideas", some of them do involve you leaving your home, but with all the methods you can work from your own home. What I mean here is you don't have to rent big warehouses, have lots of stock or have huge overheads.
With some ideas, you will be able to earn money sitting in your pyjamas all day but with other ideas you'll have to put in some more effort and leave your home.

Important to note: nothing in this book will work if you don't!

- Some of the moneymaking methods detailed in this book may appear in more than one section e.g. Offline ideas and Online ideas.

- Whatever you do to earn money you MUST provide good quality products and have brilliant customer service. You must go the extra mile to provide your customers with a pleasant experience when they deal with you.

- My mother tongue is not English, and for the first 30 years of my life I spoke only Flemish (I am from the Flemish part of Belgium, not the French part), until I met an English gentleman who is now my husband. For that reason, if you do find some grammatical errors in this book, I apologise. This book has been proofread, but perfect proofreaders are very rare to find. In my experience, even the very expensive proofreaders leave mistakes! It is not my goal to write a "perfect English" book; instead, it is my goal to write an informative book that will help you.

- Readers who have read my other books: you will find that I repeat some of the same information in this book, but not much.

- Internet marketing is really well explained in my book "From Newbie To Millionaire". If you can afford it, get yourself a copy. People call it The Internet Marketing Bible. Check out the reviews on Amazon: it's not me saying it is a really good book!

- I live in the UK, so this book is written in English spelling, therefore you will see colour instead of color, optimise instead of optimize, socialise instead of socialize, etc.

- At the time of printing this book, all websites were fully functional. If you come across a website that is no longer available, as the Internet changes constantly, sorry.

- This is NOT a book about how to set up a business. The largest part of this book is simply to give you ideas to earn extra money. You will have to do some thinking or research on how to best put the idea into practice and earn you money.

a. You need to look after your health! Believe me, I know!

If you are planning to work from home and spend a lot of time on a computer, consider this a very important message. Believe me, I have learned the hard way.

For years I sat working on my computer for hours and days in the wrong position, in the wrong chair, without any breaks. On some days, I would switch my computer on at 8 am and work on it until 1 am the next morning. My punishment for this: I have been diagnosed with cervical spondylosis (a non-curable condition) in my neck, with disc space between C5, C6 and C7 most affected. Want proof? Here it is. As I always like to prove what I say, here are an X-ray and MRI scan of my neck. You can see on the first picture that the space between disc C5 and C6 is thinner than all the other spaces. The second picture shows a bulging disc putting pressure on the spinal cord and its nerve fibres. Permanent damage can be caused when a bulging disc in the neck is compressing a nerve for a long period of time.

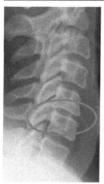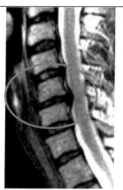

Now I cannot work on the computer as much as I would like to because when I do, my neck starts to hurt, my arm goes "dead", and I lose part of my grip and feelings in my arm. I have two choices: work a long time and give myself pain, or work less and have no pain. As health is more important than money, I obviously choose to work fewer hours. I can still work long hours on the computer but certainly not as long as I would like to, in order not to make my condition worse. I am not telling you this out of self-pity, as I am very happy with what I have achieved. *I am telling you this so you don't make the same mistake.* I am a professional, full-time Internet marketer and always will be; I love it. The fact that I cannot work as much as I would like to is not a major disaster for me, because a lot of my sites/products will provide me with income on autopilot for many years to come, and I do have staff members. *Please, please pay attention to the following. What I am about to say truly is very important for your health.*

I feel that it is my duty to tell everybody in an office environment about the dangers of working constantly on a computer. I would not want you to make the same mistakes as me. If somebody had told me seven years ago what I am going to tell you, I would not have a problem with my neck now.

Most people think that an office environment is a place with very low risk of injury. I thought the same until I had excruciating shoulder pain (caused by pinched nerves in my neck) when I woke up one day. The truth is, a lot of musculoskeletal disorders are caused in office environments. These disorders develop because of repetitive strain to the body's muscles, tendons, ligaments, joints and nerves. The back, shoulders, neck, arms and hands are the most commonly affected from computer injuries (work-related musculoskeletal disorders).

The two most important things that you need to know:

1. Make sure that you are sitting in the correct position on your computer. Search for "correct posture at a computer" and you will find a lot of information. Search for "ergonomic office chair" and change your office chair if you have to.

2. Make sure you take regular breaks. Staring at a computer screen with your head and neck always in the same position is very straining for your neck.

I use the software that I have had developed: www.breakremindersoftware.com. In my opinion, this should be installed on each computer that is sold anywhere in the world. It is not available for Apple computers.

www.workpace.com is similar, more sophisticated software and I believe it is available for Apple computers. The software monitors the time you work on the computer and it alerts you when you need to take a break. It shows you general exercises that you can do while sitting on your chair. You can set it to block your keyboard during breaks so that you cannot work. My settings are as follows:

-   I have a break for 20 seconds every 10 minutes, and I've set the software so that my keyboard is blocked. Therefore, every 10 minutes I do some gentle neck exercises.

-   I have a 10-minute break every hour, and my software is set so my keyboard is blocked, which forces me to get up and do something else for 10 minutes.

If you can afford it, invest in www.breakremindersoftware.com. It is the best piece of software available for an office environment. You have been warned: install it as a matter of urgency. If you cannot afford it, force yourself to take regular breaks. There are similar programs on the market. Simply search for "office timers" or "office break timers". Since I installed break reminder software on my computer, I am happy to say I have no more pain at all, anywhere. I'm sorry to be the one to tell you this, but iPads, laptops and mobile phones are a lot worse for your neck than a normal computer screen. This is because your face is always pointing downwards, so your neck has a lot more strain on it. In addition, finger arthritis is predicted to be a major worldwide problem in years to come, as people use their phones for too long. The finger movement involved in texting and moving a mouse causes repetitive strain injury, resulting in arthritis for a lot of people.

Correct and bad posture at the computer:

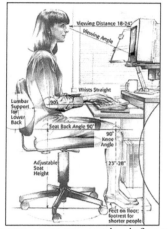 

(Source: www.ergonomics-info.com)

Please do not ignore this message — it really is very important!

****

b. About your products or services.

Whatever you do, you absolutely MUST provide a product or service that is worth the price you ask for it! You might decide to start practicing an idea from this book. Whatever it is that you are planning to do, these messages are important for you to remember:

> **If you have put the effort into creating a product to sell or providing a service and you deliver a poor product or a poor service, all your efforts will be totally wasted!**

Impress your customers with great products or services!

> **People might not remember what you said but they WILL remember how you made them feel! So... make them feel good by impressing them with your product or service!**

Part 1) Starting a Home-Based Business

In this part you will find important issues about having a home-based business.

Chapter 1. Being An Entrepreneur

Working from home in order to try to earn money in essence means that you are going to be an entrepreneur, as anybody selling anything anywhere is, in a way, an entrepreneur.

The word "entrepreneur" comes from the French verb "entreprendre" meaning "to do" or "to undertake." An entrepreneur is someone who "does", someone who acts. Generally, this means putting their time, energy and money into starting up a business, and being willing to take the risks that come along with it.

> Most people see problems, entrepreneurs see opportunities.
>
> Most people complain about problems, entrepreneurs create solutions.

Small businesses are the lifeblood of the economy. Nearly two-thirds of all new jobs created in the past fifteen years have come from small businesses, and over half of these businesses are run from home!

About one in ten working people work for themselves or for a small business. We're all very fortunate to live in a world that encourages the creation and growth of new businesses. The process of opening your own company is relatively easy. There are agencies that exist solely to help small companies, tax benefits available for start-ups, and not too many regulations to deal with to start your business and keep it functioning.

One of the most important things you need to be able to do if you are starting a side business, or any business, is to be able to explain to people in one sentence how you are going to make money.

Studies have shown that people who work from home are happy to earn up to 30% less for the convenience of being able to work at home.

Another study has shown that the vast majority of people in the rat race are totally exhausted at the end of the week and therefore don't enjoy their free time with the family as much as they should.

Millions of people are happy with a 9 to 5 jobs and that's perfectly fine. There's absolutely nothing wrong with being an employee all your life, if that's what you feel happy with. But perhaps you want something more? You want to quit the rat race? I always look at it this way:

1) As an employee:

- You earn a salary

- You pay taxes on that salary

- You can spend what is left over

2) As an entrepreneur, or self-employed person:

- You earn money

- You spend money e.g. company expenses, phone bills, furniture, computers, etc.

- You pay tax on what is left over

The big difference here is that, as an employee, you pay tax *first* and as an entrepreneur, you pay tax *last*.

I have chosen the latter option.

Nothing that is worth having is easy to get!

a. Who Can Be an Entrepreneur?

Anyone can be an entrepreneur. You don't have to be old to create a business: Google, Facebook, and Dell are all examples of companies that were started by students. You don't need a lot of money, either: Microsoft, Nike, Domino's Pizza, Hewlett-Packard, and Eastman Kodak are all examples of companies that started with little money. Don't think that setting up a business is an intimidating task that requires money, and special talent. Personally, I started with nothing! I never did well at school! Just shows, you don't need a diploma to earn money or to start your own business.

The question "Who can be an entrepreneur?" wasn't really a fair one, was it? If I'd asked "Who can play golf?" and you answered "Anyone," you'd be technically right - just about anyone can pick up a club and hit a ball. The real question should be, "Who can play golf well?" Just about anyone can start a company, but being a successful entrepreneur requires a particular type of person, a lot of hard work and a good measure of luck.

Many people think that today's entrepreneurs were always entrepreneurs, and that they were born with some "entrepreneurial gene" that directed them into starting up companies from an early age. In reality, many of the most successful entrepreneurs were people who worked for large companies for many years, gaining experience, saving money, testing ideas and making business contacts before venturing out on their own. Every large company or corporation you see today was at one time nothing more than an idea in some entrepreneur's mind.

> **Entrepreneurship is working a few years of your life like most people *won't*, so that you can spend the rest of your life like most people *can't.***

b. Optimism

Optimism is a great characteristic of many business people. Most entrepreneurs have an abundance of optimism and young people, in particular, seem to have vast reserves of it.

Optimism is a fuel. It can propel you through obstacles that would stop the average person. When the average person is slumped with his head in his hands, wondering why he can't get anyone to see the genius of his product and hand over their credit card, the optimist will think past the moment, visualising the day when his product is in every home and he's become a rock star of the business world. That ability to think positively, what less optimistic people might call "the ability to convincingly and repeatedly delude one's self into persevering against all odds" is perhaps the entrepreneur's greatest asset, though you'll never find it on a balance sheet.

Optimism is a double-edged sword. Optimism can be fuel, but it can also act like blinkers. Optimists have a knack for glossing over risks and making forecasts and plans that are wildly unrealistic.

> **Be an optimist but always take an umbrella with you!**
>
> **Optimists have twice as many good days as pessimists!**

If you make statements like "there are seven billion people on Earth; I expect to sell my product to only 10 per cent of them, meaning that I will sell 700 million units," you will be treated as a fool. (Making the "the-potential-market-is-so-large-that-I-only-need-a-small-percentage-of-it-to-succeed" argument is a very common mistake that entrepreneurs make). It's much better to be a realistic optimist!

c. Character-Based Weaknesses and Skill-Based Ones

The reason that others will judge you harshly is because unchecked optimism can appear to be a character flaw. If there's something wrong with your character - you're careless or prone to not considering risks - it can be a very difficult thing to change. If your optimism continually gets the better of you, leading you to paint overly rosy pictures of what you and your business can deliver, you risk losing credibility with people you need to have on your side. Don't let your optimism - a great strength for an entrepreneur - run riot. Always be able to highlight risks to your scenarios and ideas and explain how you intend to circumvent or overcome these risks.

At the opposite end of the weakness spectrum to character-based weaknesses are skill-based ones. Skill-based weaknesses are judged less harshly because they are easier to overcome. That is why if an interviewer ever asks you for a strength and weakness, give them a character-based strength and a skill-based weakness.

What does that mean? It means that the strengths you identify are things rooted in your character: honesty, dependability, loyalty, intelligence, creativity, and so on. On the other hand, when you discuss a weakness, make sure it's a skill-based one: you're not good at typing or have problems using Excel, for example. You tell an interviewer a skill that you're weak at, and then explain what you're doing to address that weakness: "I know this position requires that I be proficient in Excel, and my weakness is that I don't have very much experience at using that kind of program. I've signed up for an online course in using Excel, though, and I'm a very fast learner."

Remember, the reason you highlight character-based strengths and skill-based weaknesses is that you can erase any skill-based weakness fairly easily. If you have a character-based weakness, that's a hard thing to fix.

Similarly, if you don't have a credit history, you can create one. If you can't get a loan from a bank, you can find other sources of capital. In comparison, if you have a character flaw - if you let your optimism impair your judgment and lead you to ignore risks and create unrealistic plans - that's a deep-rooted problem.

d. Impatience

Impatience is another double-edged sword. Impatience can lead to action and an insistence on change. These can be good things, but you need to understand when the walls you're charging into are going to give way and when they're not. Energy, enthusiasm, and demand for change can remove many obstacles in an entrepreneur's way, but some things require a more subtle approach. Sometimes the world's not going to move at the pace you want it to, but you can't let that stop you.

You can't control the waves but you can learn how to surf!

e. Drifting From The Target

Another negative of impatience is that you can lose focus if the results you expected aren't materialising. You and your friends may start a business designing websites for local restaurants. You figure you can sign a few customers pretty quickly and be making a couple thousand dollars a month by the end of your third month of operations. Five months in, though, you find that a lot of restaurants just don't have the money to pay you to make a website, or think they can make their own. Your partners start drifting, spending less time on the business. Pretty soon, your interests start to drift, too, and the business goes into limbo.

There's a balance between being slow, cautious, and contemplative and being aggressive, fast, and action-oriented. The more you can maintain that balance, the greater your likelihood of success. Set realistic goals and anticipate slow starts. Plan for the worst-case scenario, then, if something good does happen, it's more of a motivator.

Aiming low and beating expectations - at least when you're starting out - can be a better path than aiming really high and continually underachieving.

f. Reality

Potential entrepreneurs should ask themselves why they are taking the start-up path. Are you doing it for money? For freedom? For glamour? Are you going to be a part-time or a full-time entrepreneur? Do you have romanticised ideas of what being an entrepreneur means and are you prepared for the trade-offs, sacrifices, and possible setbacks?

If you have realistic expectations of yourself, your partners, and your business idea, it's far less likely you'll be disappointed with your results. A big reason many entrepreneurs give up on a business is that they are disappointed that their too lofty expectations weren't met in a short period of time. Success takes time. The chances of you coming up with the next big thing and striking it rich overnight are about the same as winning the lottery. Maybe less.

Know what you're getting yourself into, set realistic expectations and be persistent. Of course, if you don't have a good business to begin with, all the character- and skill-based strengths in the world won't matter.

g. Avoiding Pitfalls

Common mistakes and misconceptions of new entrepreneurs:

- Focusing solely on invention and ignoring innovation

- Not asking yourself why your product or service doesn't already exist

- Being too optimistic about your budget

- Expecting other people to make the business a success

- Focusing on too narrow a customer group

- Getting into very labour- or capital-intensive businesses

- Coming up with far-fetched business ideas

- Not working hard enough

- Not watching cash-flow

- Not setting a goal

- Falling for the scams

- Listening to the whiners or the people who will tell you that you can't do it

Let's have a look at these in more detail.

Focusing solely on invention and ignoring innovation

Entrepreneurs and inventors are two very different groups of people, but many people tend to believe that if they don't invent some new product or service, they can't be successful entrepreneurs. That's far from the truth.

Rollin King and Herb Kelleher didn't invent the aeroplane or any part that goes in it, but they did create one of the most efficient and profitable airlines in the world: Southwest Airlines. King and Kelleher's genius lay in changing the business model of airlines, streamlining costs, and focusing on the customer. (That may not sound revolutionary, but many of the "big name" airlines treat their customers almost as annoyances).

Similarly, Michael Dell didn't invent the personal computer, but he created an approach to building and selling PCs that customers loved, and Dell has built the company into a very successful one.

Craig Newmark didn't really invent anything when he started Craigslist, but he changed the way that classified ads, once the domain of print newspapers, could be posted and viewed.

The message should be obvious: you don't have to invent something new to make a great business. Identifying and filling a need can lead to great success. A related myth is that your product has to be a fantastic, revolutionary one in order for the business to be successful. You don't have to start with a grandiose idea. Rather than launching a business that will try to take on Amazon or eBay, why not start with one that tries to be the best in a narrower field, or launch in an area that isn't served by someone else (as Craigslist, LinkedIn, and Wikipedia all did)?

Not asking yourself why your product or service doesn't already exist

Some good ideas are truly unique. Others might not be unique, but you can make them a success by getting them to market quickly, offering great service, or otherwise differentiating your product from others out there. Some good ideas have been tried and tested, though, and are still found to fail.

Being too optimistic about your budget

A budget is composed of inflows (revenue from sales) and outflows (money spent on setting up and running the business). Most entrepreneurs make two budget mistakes, the effects of which compound and create real problems for the company. First, they overestimate their revenues (remember earlier, when we talked about tempering your optimism and setting targets that were easy to hit or surpass at first)? Second, they underestimate their costs. My advice in regard to estimating costs is the mirror image of the advice regarding revenues: make low estimates about how much money your firm will take in, and high estimates about how much you'll spend.

In essence, you'll be making a worst-case scenario for your business. If you can stand the results of that scenario—that is, if you and your business can endure under those bad circumstances—then you're in a good position. Chances are, your company will do better than your worst-case scenario assumes. Overestimate your costs and underestimate your revenues. You'll be doing the opposite of what most entrepreneurs do, and saving yourself a lot of heartache and stress by doing so. One final thing: go out and investigate what the real costs are. If you want to rent an office, don't assume you can get one at $500 (£300) just because that seems like a reasonable price to pay. Go and find out exactly what an office would cost (rent, deposit, improvements, and other costs).

Expecting other people to make the business a success

There are two types of new entrepreneurs: those who intend to build the business themselves (or with people they have on board already) and those that expect to bring others into the business in the future. The problem with this second group of would-be entrepreneurs is that they tend to overestimate their own importance and the ease with which they can recruit others. There are several entrepreneurs who create business ideas in which the critical success factor is in the hands of someone else, usually some professional engineer that they hope to find, somewhere and somehow, without thinking of things from that person's view. There are always whiners who blame the government, the recession, the high level of taxes, and the lack of this or that...but ultimately YOU are responsible for your success!

People who blame others, the environment or the economy, just don't want it bad enough!

Focusing on too narrow a customer group

Your customers might not be the people you expect them to be, or even people at all. No, I'm not talking about businesses aimed at pets (though that might be the best market for your company) - your target market might be other companies, government organisations, non-profit organisations or other countries. If you're thinking of starting a company that will turn VHS tapes into DVDs, rather than hoping to find individuals that will be your customers, you could approach your local library or school. If your company sells sunglasses, perhaps you should try selling to a local skateboarding or sports shop, a place that would buy your glasses by the case, rather than to kids at school, who'll buy only one pair at a time. Don't assume that the best customer for your product is a person like you. It might be someone, or something, very different.

Getting into very labour- or capital-intensive businesses

If you want to grow the business, it often means hiring someone else. Keep in mind that bringing in an employee means doing payroll, adding a lot of tax work, paying social security and other costs for the employee, and a host of other work for you. Scaling up by adding people isn't a very efficient way to grow your business. Use your mind rather than your muscle or time. Be a manager rather than an employee or labourer. Try to set up a business that can grow to ten times its initial size without requiring ten times the capital or labour needs. I decide to hire an employee:

a) When I have the monthly profit to pay for the new employee, based on the profits of the last year. Example: if I have made $2,500 (£1630) profit per month over the last year, I clearly have the money to pay for the employee, although it means I can draw less money myself, as a large part of my profit will be used to pay for the new employee. If I would only have made $600 (£391) profit per month, I would not have the money to pay for the employee, therefore I can't hire one.

Of course, the whole idea when hiring an employee is that extra profits will be generated because of the work that the employee will do e.g. you will have more time to create sales as the employee will do more administrative tasks.

b) When I think the employee will pay for himself/herself. I might take on an employee to set up a website selling products. The profit of the sales from that website will pay for the employee. You will still need the money for the first few months to pay the employee's wages as time will be needed to set up the websites, source products, etc. before sales will kick in.

c) When I know I will have tons more time to generate profits if I would have an extra employee. Example: when all my time is consumed doing administrative tasks rather than selling and creating products, I know that, if I would have an employee, I would make the extra profits to pay for him/her.

Hiring an employee is not easy though: sometimes it will work and other times it won't. Potential candidates can be very good at selling themselves during an interview but useless when you actually hire them. It's a change you need to take to grow your business.

Coming up with far-fetched business ideas

Try to identify a business that you could set up and run in realistic time frames while requiring no more money than you have available to you right now or can get within a few weeks.

Not looking after your customers

Never forget that "Customer is King".

If you don't look after your customers, they won't look after you! In my opinion, you don't build your business - you build customers - and then your customers build your business.

Treat your customers like you want to be treated yourself.

Let me give you one simple example: I was in need of a plumber and called one. I made an appointment with him on a Monday at 2pm. Nobody turned up, no phone call to say he wasn't coming either. I called him and re-scheduled another appointment for Wednesday at 4pm. Same thing: he did not turn up or didn't call. Will I use this plumber again? No way! He doesn't deserve my business!

Find out if your customers are happy - customers will leave if you don't look after them and they will not tell you when they leave or why they leave. You just have to make sure that they DON'T leave!

Not working hard enough.

Lots of people expect to set up a business and think the customers will just come knocking on their door. YOU have to attract and find customers! This is hard work, definitely if you just start with your business.

People who are successful are people who work hard!

Not watching cash flow.

Cash flow is the flow of money in your company: money going out, money coming in. Bad cash flow means a shortage of funds, liquidity problems, e.g. no money in the bank to pay your rent or your suppliers. If a business is out of cash, it will become insolvent. A cash flow forecast shows you the likely movement of cash in and out of the business.

Cash flow is a killer in any business!

There are a lot of businesses going under, and very often it is because of one or more of these reasons that affect the cash flow:
- Growing too quickly

- Bad management
- Not enough customers
- Not controlling expenses
- Too much competition
- Cash flow problems
- Drawing out too much money too quickly

Here are a few things you can do to keep a positive cash flow or to improve your cash flow:

- Your stock or your inventory (same thing) is money transformed into products. This means when you are holding stock, which could be turned into cash, you are stopping cash flowing into your company. Sell all your slow-selling stock FAST. Even if you have to sell it at a loss; at least you will get the money in your bank, thus improving your cash flow situation.

- In case you are running an online store, you will be collecting money online with your eCommerce business, thus you will receive the money immediately when you have a sale. Try to get a credit account with your suppliers where you pay your supplier 30 days after their invoice date. This will create positive cash flow.

- If you do give credit facilities to your customers, you MUST have a strict payment policy and follow up to make sure the customer pays you ON TIME. Never give a customer more than 30 days to pay, and try to get credit from your suppliers for 60 days.

- Reduce your costs, wherever possible. Costs means money going out. Look constantly for ways to lower your expenses.

- Delay payment of suppliers if you really have to. However, this is not a good idea if you want to work with that supplier in the future, as next time he might demand payment in advance.

- Don't expand—solve your cash flow problems BEFORE you expand.

- Minimise the wages you draw from your company for a while.

- Improve your profit margins.

Go to www.microsoft.com and search for "cash flow forecast". You will find a few

31

examples of cash flow forecast to study and learn from.

Falling for the scams

The Internet is full of scam artists, like people selling you a Get Rich Quick Scheme that does NOT work. The only ones who get rich quick are the scammers because thousands of people buy the stuff they sell.
Often, these sites have testimonials from stay-at-home mums who made a lot of money. The truth is, almost all the time, these are actors paid by the scammers and because they are actors, they can make it sound like they really DID make a lot of money. Don't fall for these!
Just remember: if it sounds too good to be true, it probably is.
Scammers can and have fooled lots of intellectual people as their offers are so well presented.
Make sure you check out every company if you are thinking of buying something. Always search for "reviews xyz product" and you might find out that it is a scam before you've spent money.
If you are promised unlimited wealth with little work: run a mile! If you believe in these companies promising you your dreams: sweet dreams!

Not setting a goal

Whatever business you are going to set up or whatever method you are going to use, you must set yourself realistic goals and don't stop until you've reached your goals.

So, get a piece of paper and set some goals and focus to reach those goals. Everything you think, everything you say, everything you dream should be about reaching your goals.
Set yourself a realistic goal/target and remember:

Missing a target is NEVER the target's fault!

Listening to the whiners or the people who will tell you that you can't do it

Do NOT surround yourself with the whiners of this world. There will always be people who will tell you that you can't do it or it will never work.
IGNORE THEM.
PROVE THEM WRONG!
BELIEVE IN YOURSELF AND DO IT!
Surround yourself with people who DO believe in you and who will support you.

Chapter 2. Home-Based Business Basics

1) What Kind Of Business Can You Run From Home?

What kinds of businesses are being run from home? The simple and easy answer is that almost any business can be run from home. Exceptions to this, to name but a few, are: businesses that need a manufacturing plant, businesses that need warehouses full of stock, businesses that have over 5 or more employees, etc.
Professionals—doctors, lawyers, accountants, architects—continue to swell the ranks of home-based business owners but traditional home-based businesses such as child care, music lessons, interior design, crafts and freelance writing are also growing.

New types of businesses are also being run from home. Kitchen table-based consultants can be found in just about every field, including computers, marketing, and public relations. Mail-order selling, travel agencies, and network marketing of all kinds are just some of the newer enterprises to move into the home office. E-commerce (online shops)—from selling at online auctions to web page design—has become all the rage.

About 30 per cent of home-based business owners are likely to be part of a two-income family. A recent study indicates that women start home-based businesses at twice the rate of men. Because many of these businesses use the Internet for distribution, the number of home-based businesses in rural America, for example, is exploding. The growth of home business has been made possible by technology. The personal computer, photocopier, high-speed broadband Internet access, and of course the mobile phone allow any Jack in a bedroom in a city apartment or Jill in a den in the suburbs to become an entrepreneur.

We live in the information age. Manufacturing is no longer the driving force of our economies. Instead, we share information via the computer and other technologies. The person running a home business can get just about the same information as any FTSE 100 (Financial Times Stock Exchange) or Fortune 500 Company can. Computers themselves have spawned more business opportunities than Edison's light bulb. Computer consultants now advise individuals and businesses on software applications. There are others who are into software development, and there are some who offer repair services for hardware and software problems.
Even if the business isn't technologically oriented (for example, craft or house cleaning

businesses), computers have become an integral part of keeping a business afloat. Computers are being used for bookkeeping, marketing products and services, finding supplies, e-mail, getting information and more.

The vast majority of home-based business owners who succeed continue to operate from home. However, a number of hugely successful enterprises had humble beginnings in a spare bedroom or garage-turned-office. Here are some examples:

- Martha Stewart started a catering business out of her kitchen.

- FedEx's first packages were sorted on the founder's kitchen table.

- HP, Apple and Google all started in garages.

- Michael Dell started his computer company from his college dorm room.

- McDonalds started with one restaurant and they now have almost 34,500!

- Calvin Klein and his partner started their clothing line in Klein's living room.

- Guy Laliberte was a homeless street performer. Someone told him, when performing in the streets: "You are good at this, you should do it in a show".
He created Cirque de Soleil, which now has over 4,000 employees in 40 countries, and the show is a massive hit everywhere. His net worth is now $2.6 billion! It all started with an idea.

- Chad Hurley launched YouTube after he went to a party. He wanted to share his videos from the party with his friends.

- Gary Kremer, founder of www.match.com, started the dating site when he was trying to find love for himself at the age of 30. He imagined having a list of women on his computer from which he could just select the best one. Match.com is now one of the world's leading dating sites, with over 20 million members, 1.3 million of whom are paying subscribers!

- In 1999, Stephen Kaufer wanted to go to Mexico but couldn't find a lot of good reviews. He started www.tripadvisor.com. Tripadvisor.com is now the world's largest travel website, with subscribers in over 30 countries. It has 50 million visitors a month, reading reviews in 21 languages.
- In 1886, John Pemberton was experimenting in his backyard with some ingredients and a

caramel-coloured liquid. John claimed it would cure diseases and convinced a pharmacy to start selling it. He sold an average of 9 glasses per day. The recipes changed a bit, adding sugar and taking away the alcohol, and his bookkeeper called it Coca-Cola. The name came from the leaves from the coca plant and from the caffeine-rich kola nut. More and more pharmacies started selling the drink. John died in 1888 and a businessman from Atlanta bought the rights to the drink for $2,300!

- After having done lots of jobs, Harland Sanders opened a gas station in Kentucky. His customers kept asking him if they could get food nearby. He started to cook some food, and opened a tiny restaurant, as part of his gas station. The restaurant had 1 table and 6 chairs. That tiny little place became known as Kentucky Fried Chicken!

- The list of businesses launched from home also includes Microsoft Corp. and Amway Corp.

I could search for more companies online, and probably find thousands more, but I think you are getting the message: think, analyse and look around you. EVERY SINGLE company, big or small, started from a simple idea.

The lesson: even if you don't intend to remain there forever, and whatever room you put your desk in, home is still a good place to get started.

Home-based businesses aren't a fad. They're here to stay and the ranks should continue to swell. All age groups are represented in home businesses. People reaching their 50s are ripe for starting their own businesses. If these hard workers are laid off from their high-paying jobs, they are, for the most part, too old to re-enter the ever-shrinking pool of high paid jobs. What's more, there's a desire to be your own boss that's stronger than the instinct of salmon to swim upstream. And even those who continue to work for a pay cheque may be inclined to start a side-line business to get extra cash to meet living expenses, pay for a child's education, or save for retirement. Those already in retirement may run businesses from home to supplement their retirement income. And even some teenagers, who find the computer no more technologically complex than the telephone, have started up businesses from home to help older computer-illiterates learn the ropes.

Seniors who want or need to earn additional income, to feel productive, or to channel their creative and entrepreneurial impulses are starting businesses from home. Many are into their second or third careers!

Increasingly, people in their 20s and 30s are turning to home businesses in surprising numbers. They've seen the writing on the wall and know that job security is a contradiction in terms. Instead of waiting to be made redundant by a corporate employer, they're launching their own business ventures from home. Their youth makes it easier to take the risk of business ownership and still have time to run back to the corporate fold if things don't work out.

Being computer literate is almost as essential to succeeding in a home-based business as is being able to dial a telephone. If you're not computer literate, you can get the training you need at computer stores offering training courses, special computer-training schools, adult education classes, your local community college, or even on the web.

Teens are teaching older generations a thing or two about entrepreneurship from their home computers. Before they even leave school or college, some are already earning money from their computer skills.

2) What Distribution Channel Do You Choose?

A distribution channel or trade channel is the path a product takes to end up in the hands of the consumer (also called the buyer, the customer or the end-user). If you will be selling physical products, it is important to understand the models. To understand a distribution channel, you first need to understand the parties involved. These are:

- **The manufacturer:** the company that actually produces the goods.
- **The importer:** the company that imports a product from one country to sell it in another country.
- **The wholesaler:** the company who does the distribution of the goods towards the retailer. The importer and wholesaler are often the same company so in the examples given below, I will only talk about the wholesaler.
- **The retailer:** a shop or outlet e.g. market, online shop, high street shop, that is selling the goods. Anybody selling products directly to the consumer can be considered a retailer e.g. Amazon, eBay shops, supermarkets, shops in the high streets, garden centres, airport shops, etc.
- **The consumer:** the person who buys the product e.g. in a shop or at a market.
Each party will, of course, earn some money on the path from manufacturer to consumer.

Let's have a look at the most used distribution channels. I will explain this with an example of the distribution of biscuits.
- One pack of biscuits costs 0.20 to produce

- 2.50 is the RRP (Recommended Retail Price) or the price the consumer pays for the biscuits in a shop
- There are 20 single packs of biscuits in one case of biscuits.
- In our example, we look at selling 1000 single packs, so 50 cases

It is irrelevant whether I am talking here in $ or £ therefore I am not giving $ and £ prices.

a) Manufacturer direct to consumer.

This is the shortest distribution channel where the manufacturer sells directly to the consumer, with no other parties or middleman involved. This is how the profit looks:

200.00	Cost to produce 1000 packets of biscuits (0.20 per pack x 1000)
2,500.00	Price consumer pays per biscuit: 2.50 x 1000

2,300.00	Profit for the manufacturer

This model will create the most profit for the manufacturer, as there are no other middlemen. However, the manufacturer will also need to take care of all marketing, distribution and selling activities, therefore needing a lot of staff to do all of this. For this reason, many manufacturers choose to work with wholesalers, which brings us to the next distribution model.

b) Manufacturer - Wholesaler - Retailer - Consumer

In this scenario, the manufacturer points out one or more wholesalers who will sell the products to retailers and the retailer will sell the product direct to the consumer. This is the most commonly used distribution channel. Here's the path the product will take:

- Wholesaler will buy 50 cases of biscuits from the manufacturer. A wholesaler needs to buy in bulk so cannot buy 10 single packets of biscuits. One case contains 20 single packets of biscuits therefore the wholesaler buys 1000 (50 cases X 20 single packs) single boxes of biscuits.

- The wholesaler finds retailers and sells 1 case of biscuits to the retailer, so the retailer buys 20 single packs of biscuits.

- The retailer will sell the single packs of biscuits to the consumer.

Here's how the profit will look for each channel, assuming that the manufacturer sells the biscuits for 0.40 per single biscuit box or 8.00 per case (0.40 x 20 biscuits per case).

200.00	0.20 (price to manufacturer one packet) x 1000 (wholesaler buys 1000)
400.00	0.40 (price the wholesaler pays for one packet) x 1000

200.00	Profit for the manufacturer

Now the wholesaler too needs to earn some money and he will sell a single biscuit to the retailer for 0.80, so the retailer will pay 16.00 per case of 20 single biscuits (0.80 x 20). The wholesaler has bought 50 cases of biscuits or 1000 single packets.

400.00	0.40 (price the wholesaler pays for one packet) x 1000
800.00	0.80 (price the wholesaler sells the biscuits to the retailer) x 1000

400.00	Profit for the wholesaler

The retailer now has the stock in the shop to sell to the consumer. Assuming the retailer will sell the biscuits at 2.50 per single pack:

800.00	0.80 (price the wholesaler sells the biscuits to the retailer) x 1000
2,500.00	2.50 (price the retailer sells the biscuits to the consumer) x 1000

1,700.00	Profit for the retailer

Note: a retailer is unlikely to order 1000 packets of biscuits in one order, so the wholesaler will likely sell 1000 packets to 20 or so different retailers. Not to make things too complicated in this example, I have put 1000 sold.

Note: there is no VAT on lots of biscuits in the UK so if VAT does apply, the retailer needs to deduct the VAT of the profits so the profit would be 1,360.00 instead of 1,700.00, assuming VAT is 20%, which it is in the UK.

A manufacturer will usually point out several wholesalers but if you are a good negotiator, you can try and obtain an exclusive distribution agreement. This means the manufacturer will ONLY supply you and other wholesalers will have to buy from you if they want to sell the product. In this case, you would supply other wholesalers but give them a discount so they too can earn money selling to retailers.

c) Manufacturer-Retailer-Consumer.
This distribution channel is mostly used for buying very large quantities. Example: a well known supermarket will sell 50,000 packets of biscuits per week. Because they sell so

many, they can squeeze a very good price from the manufacturer and often supermarkets refuse to buy from wholesalers, as they know that is an extra middleman. They often buy direct from the manufacturers at very discounted prices.

There are other distribution models e.g. where an agent sits in the middle of the manufacturer and the wholesaler or there is an agent between the wholesaler and the retailer.

Which distribution channel you choose will depend on your set-up, the space you have for stock, your preferences and how hard you are prepared to work. One thing is sure: all of the models will require hard work.
Personally, I think model **b) Manufacturer - Wholesaler - Retailer - Consumer** is a great model, where you can be the wholesaler and find retailers to sell to. The big advantage here is that, once you have found retailers that will sell your products in their shop, they will automatically buy more from you once they need new stock.
The biggest problem will be finding products to sell and negotiating your prices and payment terms with the manufacturer. That's where being an entrepreneur is essential for this model.

These distribution channels are also sometimes called one level channel, two level channel, three level channel, depending on how many middlemen there are involved in the product path.
Here's an overview where I want to show you that each channel buys less and less from the channel above it. I also show typical profit margins for each channel.

Who	Quantities	Typical Profit Margins
Manufacturer	Produces 10,000 products	50 to 200%
Wholesaler	Buys 1,000 products from manufacturer	30 to 100%
Retailer	Buys 50 products from wholesaler	30 to 200%
Consumer	Buys one product from retailer	NA

Note: There are no strict rules for profit margins, I just want to give you some ideas; often the manufacturer earns the most. There are companies who are happy selling products with 20% profit margins but that is something that I don't practice myself and also don't recommend. The rule is simple: sell with as many profit margins as possible, whatever channel you are in.

Chapter 3. Advantages And Disadvantages Of Working From Home

Starting any business costs money, but the amount you need to launch and run a business from home is less than if you had to rent a space in the local office complex. You're already paying rent or the mortgage on your home. You're already heating it. It generally doesn't cost you any more to use a portion of your home for a business.

Low overheads may be the prime reason why home-based businesses are so successful. They can afford to be! Low overheads (what it costs to pay for space and utilities) means that you don't need to earn as much to cover expenses. The earnings from your home business that don't go into office overheads can go into your pocket. You can reinvest that money in the business in the form of advertising, travel and entertainment expenses, equipment and stock.

When you run a business from home, you don't board a train or bus or get caught in gridlock on the way to work. You simply get dressed (if you want to) and go down the hall or up the stairs to your office when you're ready to get to work.

Eliminating the commute is a saving in several ways. First, you save time. Many who hold jobs outside the home commute 30 minutes, an hour, or more each way every day. The commuting time you save can be used in other ways. You can use it in your business or for some personal stuff.

Second, you don't have the stress and strain of missing your bus or bumper-to-bumper traffic to contend with when you work from your home. The savings to your psyche can't be easily quantified, but eliminating the stress of commuting can add substantially to your health and personal wellbeing.

Getting rid of the commute also saves you money. The cost of commuting—the commuter ticket, fuel for your car, parking, tolls, taxi rides—can be steep, not to mention the aggravation of choice words and gestures from less-than-polite drivers. You paid for the cost of commuting while you were working outside your home with a portion of each pay cheque. And you couldn't even deduct it on your tax return!
The money saved by not commuting, just like the time saved, can be used in other ways. You can put it into your business, take the family out to dinner once a week or save it for a rainy day.

a. Taking Care of Others

A lot of people find it difficult to leave home for work when there are children or elderly parents to care for. Either they don't choose to leave such care in the hands of others or, even if they would like to share the responsibility, just can't afford to pay for such care.

Child's Play

When both parents work, they have to deal with the emotional and financial costs of day care. Some may be lucky to have a parent or in-law available to come and watch the kids during the day, but many don't. Most are forced to hire private help to care for their children. The cost of good childcare runs from substantial to outrageous. Some people simply can't afford to work because of the high cost of day care. When that cost is added to the cost of commuting, working outside the home just doesn't make much sense. According to some surveys, the majority of people working at home —female and male— say they do so in part because of the kids.

Even if you're not required to stay at home to watch the children because they're old enough to fend for themselves, you may prefer to work from home. You'll be there to see them onto the bus in the morning and welcome them back when they return from school. Working at home may even allow you the flexibility to see your son or daughter in the school play or in a sports team.

Role Reversal

Taking care of children is not the only at-home responsibility faced by the modern working man or woman. Increasingly, there are elderly parents to care for. In fact, statistics show that women spend on average not only 17 years as caregivers for their children, but also 18 years as caregivers for parents.

With the greying of our population, this parent-care bomb will explode. According to a Genworth Financial survey, 77 million baby boomers are entering retirement age and costs for caring for them (and in some cases their parents) will be substantial. The average caregiver will lose nearly $660,000 (£407,000) in lifetime income due to care giving. The cost of hiring someone to care for an elderly father or aunt can be much more than the cost of childcare. People who can't afford to pay this high cost might be forced to quit a job to help out mum or dad. If you have to provide care for an ill or infirm parent, working from home might just be a great way to have it all.

An estimated 16 million Americans, mostly women, are caught in the sandwich generation. This growing group (currently larger than the population of New England) has the double whammy of caring for both their own children and their parents at the same time. These aren't easy situations, but you may just be able to juggle all this and relieve some financial pressure by working from home.

b. Flexibility

Working from home usually gives you greater flexibility in your schedule. You can work when it's convenient for you and take care of your life when and how you want. Of course, the demands of your home business don't always permit this kind of freedom. Many people find they work longer hours when they run a home business. This is especially true when you are just getting started. But generally speaking, even if you work long hours, you can pretty much schedule your time the way you want to.

Working from home might also give you the time you need to stop and smell the roses. You may want to join a health club, take classes to improve your business skills, or do voluntary work—things that just wouldn't be possible for you if you held a 9-to-5 job. Flexibility means more planning, not less. Those with a 9-to-5 schedule know they have to clean the house and do the shopping after work. When you run a home-based business, what do you consider "after hours"? Be sure to give yourself separate times for work and family.

c. Starting Part-time

Starting any business is risky. Even with the success rate of home businesses, there's no guarantee against failure. But starting out part-time can offer you a leg up. You can begin your business on a part-time basis to see if you can cut it. Does somebody need your product or service? Can you provide it?

There's an important financial payback to starting out part-time from home. You still get your regular pay cheque to cover your personal expenses. This takes the financial pressure off. The nest egg you need to start your business is reduced considerably because you don't have to cover your rent or mortgage. You might even be able to use some of your pay cheque to cover the expenses of your home business.

Staying Part-time

Many people who start a home-based business have no intention of having it take over their lives. They look upon the business as a nice sideline. The part-time business can provide a little extra cash for those extra expenses.

A part-time sideline business can also be an outlet for something you like to do but can't do full time. For example, if you love kids, you might enjoy having a sideline day-care business at home with no intention of developing it into a full-time activity.

Some people will turn their nine-to-five job into a part-time home business. Scott was a computer repair specialist for a technology company. He wanted to open a home-based computer repair service, but he still wanted to keep the steady income from his employer. He cut a deal with his employer that he would work for them for 30 and then eventually 20 hours a week, freeing Scott to launch his home-based business so he could get more clients without having to worry about a drastic cut in his income. This approach is sometimes called a Tarzan. You don't let go of the vine you're swinging on until you've got a firm grip on the next one.

d. The Price You Pay For Working From Home

When you work from home, your house is no longer just your castle. It's also the place where you get calls from clients, create clutter with stacks of paper and go nuts when a project falls through. This means that your work life begins to spill over into your personal life. There are several consequences.

You may be bringing the business public—clients, customers, or patients—into your home on a regular basis. This means a certain loss of privacy. Your family, your pets, your lifestyle and even your dirty laundry may be visible to strangers. You have to be comfortable with this change. If you're the private type and the nature of your business brings people to your home, think twice about giving up your day job.

But giving up privacy is just one consequence of working from home. Another, for some, may be the loss of space. Before starting the business, your family had the run of the place. Now you have to use a room or two for business. Whatever was going on in the space before it became your office now has to be pushed into other parts of your home. If you convert a spare bedroom into a home office, where will the in-laws stay when they visit?

You may be the kind who thrives on a daily change of scenery. You may feel like living and working in the same place is like being in a very small closet. If so, you have to deal with the problem. Of course, just because your business is home-based doesn't mean you necessarily have to work at home all the time. For example, a plumber might use their home to schedule appointments, order supplies and bill for jobs. But basically, they're out in the field all day long, banging on pipes.

e. A Lifestyle Change ... for the Better?

When you work in an office, you basically have a nine-to-five focus on business. Of course, many jobs require travel and a lot more hours than just nine to five. But essentially, all jobs outside the home more or less stay outside the home. However, when you work at home, you're never far from your business. The work is always there. You can leave your office, but you can only go so far. A change in lifestyle involves not only you but also those nearest and dearest to you. Your family may know very well that you're in business, but they may continue to treat you as if you're on 24-hour call. You need to educate the people who live with you to the fact that during working hours you're basically not there.

Starting a business from home is like being a double agent. Firstly, you have to get used to working where you live and having the work always there. Secondly, the change from being someone else's employee to being your own boss can be a difficult transition. Because you're starting a business, you're now in charge. You have to get to know every aspect of running a business. This is more than just a technical orientation. It's a psychological one as well. You have to get used to the idea of shouldering all the responsibility for your business.

Learning to forego the social aspects of working outside the home is another lifestyle change to consider. No longer will you learn the latest scoop while at the office water cooler. Working at home means you're more or less alone for the greater part of the day. But with all the changes you'll go through, starting your home-based business can still be the most rewarding way to live and, if you want to do it, you can make it happen.

f. Be Realistic

Sure there are a lot of advantages to working from home: cost savings, an end to the commuting rat race, and greater flexibility. But it's not all gravy. If you want to run a business from home, go in with your eyes open. It'll save you from heartache down the road.

Chapter 4. About Your Skills

Wanting to run a business is just the first step in deciding whether you have the personality to give it a try. You must have the characteristics that will serve you well in business: a desire to succeed, leadership skills, being comfortable with risk-taking and the ability to tackle hard work.

Here's a list of other words that are often used to describe the entrepreneurial type. See how many of these words you think can be used to describe you:

- Confident
- Determined
- Disciplined
- Innovative
- Optimistic
- Positive
- Hard working

You may not have all of these traits, but don't let that stop you. You can pick up some of this stuff as you go along. For example, if you've never been a manager or supervisor, how can you know whether you have leadership ability? Obviously, you can't. But by assuming a leadership role you may be surprised to learn how well it suits you. Or maybe you've taken a leadership role outside of the business world—heading up the PTA (Parents Teachers Association) or running a community fundraising drive, for example.

There is also a chicken and egg part of this emotional stock. Starting off you may not feel disciplined, for example, but the challenge of achieving your weekly sales target forces discipline on you. Most of these traits are like muscles; the more you use them, the stronger they become.

Maybe taking risks gets your knees knocking and your heart pounding. Again, as you begin to run your business and learn to take setbacks in your stride, your tolerance for risks may rise.

Even if you're sure you'll never be a great communicator, you can always choose a business that plays down public contact. You don't have to go for selling a product where razzle-dazzle presentations are the order of the day. You may be able to perform a service—such as bookkeeping—out of the limelight, in the privacy of your kitchen.

a. Your Skills

If you think your current job has you wearing a lot of hats, be prepared to open a hat superstore when you start your own business. I will talk more about the hats you'll need later in the book.

Whatever business you run, you also need many other skills. You need to become an entrepreneur. You need to be able to market your business, whether it's a service or a product. You need to be able to juggle finances—raising capital to start up and grow, managing cash flow and purchasing. You need to work well with others—hiring employees or subcontractors, working with professional advisors and keeping customers happy.

b. Your Experience

You may know more than you think you know. What kind of experience do you have? Whatever business experience you have may prove helpful in starting your own business and the more experience you have, the better off you are.

Have you ever run a business before? Even if you've always worked for a weekly pay cheque, you may still have enough business experience to be successful. By simply working for a business, you may have picked up valuable information on how to run a business (or, as many disgruntled employees claim, how not to run a business). Even if you lack business experience of any kind, if you've run a household, budgeted to buy a new car, or coached a sports team, you've already picked up some important business skills in the areas of budgeting, purchasing, and personnel.

Even if you have general business experience, what do you know about the particular business you're considering? Have you ever worked in the field before? Obviously, the more you know about the field, the better off you'll be. Even if you've never been near someone who has done this kind of work, you may be able to translate your experience in a related area into valuable help for your business.

For example, you have experience in a retail-clothing store. Now you want to start your own mail-order business to sell clothes you design. You don't have experience in mail order, but you might be able to use your knowledge of selling clothes to research fashion markets and create a catalogue. You know clothes; you know selling.

c. Your Financial Picture

Your personal financial picture, rosy or not, will affect how you view your home business—how much you can afford to put into it and what you expect to get out of it. For example, if you're retired and living on a pension, then a home business may only have to supplement your income. The same is true if you have a full-time job and only expect the home business to be a sideline for generating extra cash. But if you've been laid off, your home business may be your bread and butter.

The kind of business you choose is influenced a lot by your bank account. How much do you have to invest? How much can you borrow? It may cost thousands of dollars to buy the equipment or stock needed to get up and running. Are you in a financial position to come up with the money you need to get going? Many other home businesses—day care services, cleaning services and even consulting businesses—can be started with a few hundred pounds/dollars.

Chapter 5. How To Find The Home-Based Business That Is Right For You

You want to start a business but you're not sure what that business should be? How do you find a business match made in heaven? Start with what you know. The idea for a business might be right in front of your nose. Your real-world interests and skills may easily translate into a business concept.

For example, you may love kids and be great at taking care of them. You might consider running a day-care business in your home. (This may make very good sense if you're already caring for your own children). Or, you may be a shrewd shopper and know the malls better than you know your in-laws. For you, a business as a personal shopper—for clothing, gifts, and home furnishings—might make sense.

If you've been laid off because the company you worked for relocated or downsized, you may already have chosen your business—even if you don't know it yet. Your old job may be the basis for your new business.

Suppose you worked in personnel and have been offered an early retirement package that you couldn't refuse. You might be able to use all the tricks you picked up in the corporate world to run your own business. Consider starting a personnel agency or a headhunting firm to find jobs for other people, or you might want to start a temp agency.

Consider the skills you've learned at a corporate job, and then look to apply those skills in your own business. If you were in marketing, maybe you should start your own advertising or promotions agency. If you were a secretary, you might be able to start your own virtual assistant business where you handle the same types of tasks for travelling executives. The opportunities are limitless.

With the Internet, your business has a worldwide reach. Don't limit your business ideas to the local market. You can still work as a headhunter in other markets via the Internet. In fact, starting a home-based Internet business is a great way to hedge your bets against the local economy. If your local market is depressed, you can get a virtual phone number in another market that rings in your home. To find a firm that is offering virtual phone numbers, contact your local landline, mobile, and broadband phone company or just search online.

Many of the skills learned in the corporate world lend themselves to consulting. As a consultant you're providing a service to others. Maybe you're a whiz at computers. You can offer your services in a variety of ways: helping people buy and set up equipment, teaching software programs, setting up websites and designing software applications. Consultants can command high hourly rates for their services but don't expect to be an overnight success. It may take months or even years to build up a consulting business to the point of equalling or surpassing corporate pay for comparable work. When you add in corporate benefits—health insurance, a retirement plan, and an expense account—it can take even longer for self-employment to match that weekly pay cheque. It takes time to develop business contacts. If you go into consulting, be prepared to use your savings or a spouse's income.

Some start their consulting work on a part-time basis, moonlighting with their day jobs. If you choose to begin part-time, you'll get the opportunity to develop your business contacts (which can take considerable time), without having to rely on the income from consulting to buy the groceries.

If you begin a consulting business as your full-time occupation, be prepared to work long hours—longer than when you had a full-time job. While it is easier and cheaper to eat a sandwich over your kitchen sink, networking is the name of the consulting game. Even though it is more expensive, try never to eat alone. Arrange breakfast, lunch, coffee and dinner meetings with people in your field. Be relentless. And again, it may take time before you'll see big money.

According to some experts, many people start home-based businesses so they can have more interesting work. And what is more interesting than doing what you love? If you have a hobby, it's an activity that you feel passionate about and already know. You may be able to turn your hobby into a full-fledged business.

Love antiques? You may be able to become an antique dealer without leaving home. The Internet allows you to buy and sell your wares virtually worldwide. Have a special craft skill? Produce your art at home and sell it at craft shows, flea markets, or in local gift shops.
I am a big believer in multiple streams of income. Don't put all your eggs in one basket.

Small amounts of money soon add up to a big amount of money!

You want to earn some extra money? Start cleaning some windows AND do some freelance writing. If one of them doesn't work out, you've always got the other one!

Look around you. There are business ideas EVERYWHERE you look. Analyse everything that you see and hear. Let me give you 2 examples:

1) My friend was looking for a company to install a new router in her house. She has a big house and in some bedrooms there was simply no Internet available. She searched for: "router installation Maidstone" (Maidstone is where she lives) but couldn't find anybody who installs routers. Here is an opportunity for somebody who can install routers.

2) Another friend wanted to install a new bathroom and searched for: "bathrooms Kent". She contacted 10 companies for a quote for a bathroom and only received 2 quotes! Big opportunity for more professional companies who actually respond to potential customers! In case you didn't know: people who ask for quotes already KNOW they are going to buy so they don't need convincing. They are dream potential customers. It's just a matter of finding a mutually convenient price point to get the order. If you are a handy man, you can install bathrooms and you live in Kent: here's an opportunity for you!

Chapter 6. The Importance Of Getting Prepared

Once you've determined that a home business is something you want and will be good at, you have to narrow down the field to find the business that's perfect for you. Here's where your creativity and ingenuity pay off.

Three quarters of start up businesses fail within the first three years. One third of these will go under during the first six months. So it is very important for you to prepare yourself. Here are a few important issues:

a. Fine-Tune Your Idea

You know you want to start a home-based business. Great. You may even know what type of business you want to run—a consulting business, selling products through catalogues, online or whatever. Even better. These vague ideas have to be fine-tuned before you can proceed. You have to work out all the particulars. So let's get specific.

You can't simply decide to be a consultant or start a catalogue or online business. You have to clearly define the service you'll be offering as a consultant or the products you'll be selling through a catalogue or online. If you plan to be a consultant, presumably you know the general area you'll be consulting in (for example, management advice or computers). But you have to get even more specific. For example, as a consultant for computers, will you be providing advice to individuals or to companies? Will you write a newsletter or blog about computers or service them door-to-door?

This might seem like a simple exercise, but give it a whirl. To help you focus your idea, try explaining it to others in 30 to 60 seconds. You might see that in your first few explanations you're about as clear as mud. Try to be specific. Try to address the four Ws: what, who, where and when.

- What will you be doing? What product or service will you be offering? Why would anyone pay good money for this? Can you actually make money doing this (after factoring in your costs and time)?

- Who will you be selling your product or service to once you run out of friends and relatives? The man on the street? Blue Chip companies?

- Where will you be selling your product or service? Are you going to bring every Tom, Dick, and Harry into your home for the sale? Will you put an ad in the paper? Will you sell through the Internet? Via mail order?

- When will you be selling your product or service? Are you starting part-time? Full-time? Are your sales seasonal?

The more concise you can be in your answers, the better off you'll be. As soon as you can describe your business concept in one or two sentences, then you have a place to begin.

b. Test Your Concept

After you think you've clarified your idea, make sure it will fly. Take the time to investigate the marketplace and find out whether there's room for you in it. It could take months to complete this phase of preparation for your business. But the time you take to do the legwork is time well spent. After all, why put the money and the effort into something that has no chance of succeeding? Find out at the beginning whether your concept is a winner.

c. But Will It Fly?

Your idea may sound great as a concept, but when you get into some of the specifics— looking at cost, how you'll reach the marketplace and other considerations—does the business really make sense?

Your business idea has to be one that's doable. You have to be able to have a realistic expectation of making a profit—if not immediately, then sometime in the foreseeable future. For example, initially you may be buying supplies and stock for your business at a loss or a very thin profit margin to build the business. Think long-term. Wal-Mart expects steep annual price reductions from its suppliers. Even though you're the smallest of businesses, you should try to do the same. Look at what economies of scale you can use to make your business more profitable. Use the Internet to shop around until you find the deal that will give you the highest profit margin. You may be surprised to find out that buying products or services (such as virtual assistants, etc.) from the other side of the planet may make your business much more profitable. Don't be afraid to go multinational right from the start.

d. But Will It Fit Into The Spare Room?

In figuring out if your idea is far-fetched or the real thing, be sure to take into account your base of operations—your home. Can this business succeed from a kitchen table? If your business involves a lot of people coming and going from your house, it may simply not be possible to accommodate that traffic because of planning laws or lack of parking. Here are some factors to consider:

- Space in your home. If, for example, you plan to run a stock-intensive business, do you have the storage space for the stock?
- Suitability of the space for the business. If you want to bring clients or customers into your home for business, is there a room that can be used for this? If, for example, you have young children, how will your major client react to squeaky toys underfoot and wet nappies in the bathroom?
- Planning restrictions. Local planning regulations might not allow the kind of business you want to run from home. For example, planning regulations might say you can't have employees (other than family members who live with you), you can't put up signs and you absolutely can't run certain types of businesses from home.
- Parking availability. If you need to have a constant flow of clients and customers coming to your home, are there enough parking spaces? Will you be violating any local planning regulations?

e. Finding Your Niche

Suppose you conclude that your idea would work. That's great. But now you have to go one step further and continue to refine your business concept so that you can find your niche or sub niche. A business niche is what sets you apart from everyone else in your area.

What is a niche?
Niche originally was a scientific term describing the role of a living thing. It can be defined as, *the way of life of a particular type of specie or the role of an organism or how it functions within an ecosystem*. Likewise, it applies to a person as well, meaning the role one plays in his or her community. In a marketing sense, it can also be thought of as a specific type of product or service an individual or business provides to their customers. Whether you're aware of it or not, niches are everywhere.

The first place you may look for niches is in your home. Many things around the house are things you love, or else you wouldn't have purchased them in the first place. For example, if you have a large DVD collection, it is likely that you love movies. More likely, your collection consists of mainly one type of movie: action/adventure, sci-fi, comedy, etc. If you own a sewing machine it is because you love to make or repair garments. These examples are all niches.

A second place to look is in your community. At any type of social gathering, be it with family or friends, you will notice that at least one person likes to ramble on about a particular subject. He or she may love to talk about current events, and another may talk about hunting. These are niches. If there is a certain topic you love to chat about endlessly and can educate others on it, whatever it is, it is a niche.

Furthermore, if there is something you love to build or repair, you have a niche. Auto mechanics have a niche – fixing cars. Those with table saws love building things out of wood. Women with embroidery sets enjoy sewing or making crafts. Again, these are niches.

Within a niche, there is a sub-niche. A *sub-niche* is a specific market within a market, or a restricted area within a niche. The term referred to as *niche market* is a *sub-niche*. *Niche market* means a market within a larger market, or a restricted market.
A niche is a small part of a topic or subject. A car market is a niche where all people are interested in cars. Mercedes is a sub-niche from the main niche (a niche within a niche), as it is a manufacturer of cars. You can keep digging deeper into a niche: a yellow Mercedes would be another sub-niche of the Mercedes niche. A yellow Mercedes with yellow leather chairs (digging deeper again) would be a micro-niche in that sub-niche.

Example:
Market or Niche: Car
Sub-niche: Mercedes
Micro-niche: Yellow Mercedes

Here's another example:
Market or Niche: Tennis
Sub-niche: Serving
Micro-niche: Serving left-handed

f. Your Competition

To help you define your niche, you must size up the competition. What are they doing right? What could you do better? What's the competition failing to do that you may be able to do?
The market research that you conducted to determine whether there'd be demand for your business may already have exposed the strengths and weaknesses of the competition. If not, you can size up the competition by becoming a consumer yourself and sampling

what's out there. For example, suppose you want to start a residential cleaning service. Call the competition and see how they respond. Did they get back to you promptly? Were they friendly? Helpful? Responsive to your needs? *Their negatives can be your positives.* Try out their service in your own home (even if you don't learn much, at least you'll get the windows cleaned). Did you like their work? Their price?

Where the competition failed to measure up to your expectations, you can design your business to shine. You may find that they're very good. In that case, you may have to specialise (offering only carpet and rug cleaning rather than general cleaning services or offering 24-hour scheduling).

Let's say, for example, you determine that your area can support another travel agency that you plan to run from your home. How do you plan to distinguish yourself from the competition? Are you going to offer lower prices? Are you going to offer better service? Are you going to confine your business to a particular type of travel, such as the cruise ship business or coach tours? Whatever you can do to separate yourself from your competitors will work to your advantage. Don't think that specializing, which trims your market size, is necessarily bad. There may be plenty of room for your specialization, and it might just help you target your potential customers much more accurately.

g. Pay Yourself

If you are going to start up a "proper" company, you need to think and analyse how you are going to pay yourself. Will you earn enough money to pay yourself all the money you will need to cover your costs of living: mortgage, car, food, etc.? A lot of companies put all the money they earn back into the business to expand and often, that's where things go wrong. You have to realise that, for a while, you might not be able to afford any luxuries. You might have to skip a meal once per week. You really need to keep a close eye on where your profits are going so you can pay yourself *and* expand.

h. Insurance

- By law, you are required to have employer's liability insurance if you have staff.
- You will also need to have public liability insurance if you are planning to meet customers or suppliers in your home or premises.
- If you will be driving around in your car/van with products, you need insurance to cover the contents of the van so as to insure the products.
This means that your costs to run your business will go up but it is crucially important that you DO have the appropriate insurance for your business, just in case things go wrong. Do **not** start a business before you have your insurance sorted!

i. Positioning Your Prices

Think about the last time you made a major purchase; say a car, some dining room furniture, or a TV. The price tag was important, but that wasn't all you considered. If it were, you wouldn't have had to spend three hours making your decision: you'd have just asked for the cheapest at the start. Pricing won't be the only thing that separates you from your competition either, but there's no doubt it's important. Most consumers today are price conscious. The price for your goods or services must be realistic; you have to be able to make a profit from what you sell.

If you charge lower prices than the competition—something that home-based businesses can often afford to do because of lower overheads—you don't want to come over as offering inferior goods or services. The public can become suspicious and worry that they're not getting quality merchandise. You may even have to explain why you charge lower prices. For example, if you can buy more economically than your competitor (because you have some special connection with a distributor), tell the public "we pass our savings on to you."
If you charge higher prices, make sure the public understands what additional benefit they're getting. Many people are willing to pay higher prices for something if there is added value, such as a personal service, a longer warranty, or a money-back guarantee.

Unless you're the only business offering a unique product or service, you have to be concerned about pricing, because the public certainly is. Whatever you offer, price is the first thing people look at.

Make your prices realistic. You have to charge enough to make a profit. You can't charge less than it costs you to sell the product or service or you'll be out of business before you know it. Divide your monthly expenses by your monthly units (the hours you expect to charge for your services or the number of items you plan to sell). This will give you a bare minimum to cover expenses (you'd lose money if you charged any less). Your profit margin—what you add on to each of your monthly units—depends on what you're selling and what the market will take. You don't want to charge so much that you turn off consumers. You need to be sure that the price for your product or service is not out of keeping with the competition.

After determining your minimum price (what you absolutely, positively cannot charge less than in order to stay in business), compare your price with your competitors. If everyone in your business offers the same price, maybe you have to do the same. For example, if you have a lawn-care business and the going rate in the area for mowing is $25 (£15) per week, you probably have to charge the same if you are to have any hope of getting customers.

If you see that your price is higher than the competition, you should have a very good reason for the higher price. Maybe you offer something more for the extra price—a special service or a guarantee that your competitors don't offer. Be sure that consumers know that they get a bonus for paying the higher price—"You pay more because you get more."

Continue to monitor your prices as your business develops so you can adjust them to allow for shifts in the marketplace or other changes.

I strongly believe in this:

> **The price is too high when the value is too low!**

From the table below you can see why I always advise people not to sell their products TOO low.

I've put the product profit on the spread sheet below as 50%, for ease of calculation. You can see that if you sell a product for 2.99 and sell 10,000, you will earn 14,950 but if you sell a product for 19.99 and you sell the same amount, your profit will be 99,950! Big difference! By the way, I have intentionally not put a $ or £ sign in front of these prices, as it doesn't matter if the prices are in $ or £, it's the principle I want to get across.

Selling Price	Profit per product	Qty sold	Total Profit

Sell at 2.99:

Selling Price	Profit per product	Qty sold	Total Profit
2.99	1.50	10	14.95
2.99	1.50	50	74.75
2.99	1.50	100	149.50
2.99	1.50	1000	1,495.00
2.99	1.50	2000	2,990.00
2.99	1.50	5000	7,475.00
2.99	1.50	10000	14,950.00

Sell at 8.99:

Selling Price	Profit per product	Qty sold	Total Profit
8.99	4.50	10	44.95
8.99	4.50	50	224.75
8.99	4.50	100	449.50
8.99	4.50	1000	4,495.00
8.99	4.50	2000	8,990.00
8.99	4.50	5000	22,475.00
8.99	4.50	10000	44,950.00

Sell at 19.99:

Selling Price	Profit per product	Qty sold	Total Profit
19.99	10.00	10	99.95
19.99	10.00	50	499.75
19.99	10.00	100	999.50
19.99	10.00	1000	9,995.00
19.99	10.00	2000	19,990.00
19.99	10.00	5000	49,975.00
19.99	10.00	10000	99,950.00

To put it very simply, look at this:

Selling Price	Quantity Sold	Total Profit
2	100	200
100	2	200

Selling a product for 2 and selling 100 gives you the same profit as selling 2 products at a price of 100!!
Very often selling a product for 2 requires the same effort as selling a product for 100!
So, which one would you choose: sell 2 products or sell 100? I know I would choose to price my product at 100 at only sell 2!

I assume, in the above example, that you have 100% profit, which is perfectly do-able if you sell an eBook or downloadable videos as selling these products from your own website means you are selling at 100% profit.

j. Put Your Idea in Writing With a Business Plan

The best way to formulate your business concept is to put it in writing. This means writing a business plan.

A lot of people start a home-based business as a casual sideline. This is a mistake. If you fail to take the business seriously, others may not take you seriously. Writing a business plan shows serious intent. There are several other important reasons for writing a business plan:

- Organize your ideas. You may think you have things straight, but until you put them in writing you can't be sure. For example, you may have thought about how you'll sell your services, but maybe you haven't thought through how much money you'll need to meet your advertising budget. To complete your report, you may even have to do additional research on your idea.

- Learn the strengths and weaknesses of your business concept. As you develop your plan, you'll find what aspects of your concept are real winners. You'll also learn where your idea just doesn't hold water. In the plan, you'll be addressing all aspects of business operations: personnel, marketing, finance. By writing the plan, you'll find out what areas you need to learn more about. For example, when you put everything in writing you may discover that you just can't do it all yourself. You may have to hire a clerk or an assistant, subcontract out, or bring in a partner.

- Have a road map for the future. You wouldn't drive without a map, so why venture into the world of home business any less prepared? Having an idea will only bring you so far. You have to be able to put that idea into action. How will you take your idea and turn it into a working business? What will you do first? What will you do next? A business plan can serve as your road map, getting you from point A to point B. The business plan will not only serve to get you started; it can also help you grow your business in the first few years.

- Have a presentation package to raise money. Banks and just about anyone else who's thinking about loaning you money or investing in your business will want to see that you know your business, have thought about your needs, have considered your problems and have put it all together in a business-like way.

I am not going to show you how to do a "proper" business plan, as I assume you are trying to earn money whilst working at home without needing a big bank loan. In that case, you are not going to have massive overheads like most businesses have that are not home-based.

The absolute minimum you must do is make a simple spread sheet and see how much profit you can realistically make and when you will start to make a profit. A mini business plan will show you how long you will have to invest money before you will start to make a profit.

Even if you don't need money from the bank, and even if you will be the only person who ever reads it, you must make a mini business plan. Don't start doing business without it. You need to have an idea of how many products you are planning to sell. You need to have an idea of how much profit you can make before you start your new venture. You might find that when you have done your forecasts, you are not going to make any money!

This is what your mini business plan should include:

- What do you plan to sell?
- Why are you doing it?
- Who will you sell to?
- Who is your competition and how can you beat them?
- What marketing will you implement to sell your products?
- Who will do all the work and why are they qualified to do the work?
- How many products do you think you will sell over the next year? What is your target?
- What are you going to do to make the target?
- How much profit are you planning to make?
- What is the average selling price of your product?

- What is the average shipping cost of your product?
- Are there any other taxes, e.g. duty, import taxes, etc.?
- What is the average packaging cost of your product?
- What are your monthly overheads? These are costs that you will have regardless of whether you are selling anything or nothing, e.g. if you plan to charge people's credit cards, you will need a merchant account and payment gateway, both of which usually have a monthly charge.
- Make a list of all the one-off set-up fees that will influence your profit.
- Your business plan will show all your expenses and estimates of your sales for one year, organised per month.
- Don't kid yourself, put down realistic figures!
- Make a spread sheet and add up all your expenses for the next year.

Add up the total sales you are projecting. Take your total sales figure and take off your total costs and see what profit you will make.

Less than one-third of all small businesses have taken the time to write a business plan. This factor alone may account for some business failures. Don't be among them! While having a business plan is no guarantee of success, it does provide a structure to build on. You can download free business plan templates (just search for it) from a variety of sources, so there is no excuse not to spend some time investing in your future.

k. What Are Your Gross and Net Profit?

You will need to know your gross profit and net profit to run a business and to make a business plan, as these are important financial concepts.

Calculate Your Gross Profit

Description	Amount
Total Sales, Excluding VAT	200,000
Cost of Goods Sold	120,000
Credit Card Fees	4,000
Gross Profit	76,000

Simply substract the cost of the goods from the total sales to determine your gross profit. Your gross profit in the above example is 76,000.

Calculate Your Gross Profit Margin

Description	Amount
Gross Profit	76,000
Total Sales	200,000
Gross Profit Margin	0.38
Gross Profit Margin Percentage	38%

Divide the gross profit by the total sales will give you your gross profit margin.
To calculate your gross profit margin percentage, simply multiply your gross profit x 100.

In order to get a better gross profit margin, you can either raise the price of your products or you can try to buy the products cheaper from your suppliers.

Your net profit is your gross profit minus all expenses deducted. That is your net profit before tax. You pay the tax on that amount and you are left with your net profit after tax.

Calculate Your Net Profit

Total Sales, Excluding VAT	200,000
Cost of Goods Sold	124,000
Gross Profit	**76,000**

Operating Expenses:

Salaries - Always Pay Yourself!!	40,000
Rent and Rates = None as you work from home	0
Office Expenses e.g. toners, printers, letterheads, etc..	1,000
Utilities: heat, light and power	1,200
Internet fees eg. merchant account, gateway, hosting	1,000
Motor expenses	1,000
Loans	3,000
Packaging expenses	2,000
Accountant	1,000
Bank Charges and Interest	200
Transport costs	3,000
Insurance	800
Bad Debts - customers that didn't pay you	200
Depreciation	2,000
Total Operating Expenses	**56,400**

Net Profit Before Tax	**19,600**
Tax at 20%	3,920
Net Profit After Tax	**15,680**

To calculate your Net Profit before tax, substract the Total Operating Expenses from your Gross Profit.

Some people use the term Operating Profit = Gross Profit - Operating Expenses

Note: I am not an accountant, but I believe the above spread sheets are correct.

Chapter 7. Launching Your Business

a. Forming Your Business

Having an idea for a business is great, but it's just one step towards starting that business. Before you even open your door for business, consider all the legal mumbo jumbo about how to set up the company. Select a name and a type of business entity. Starting a business without knowing how to structure it is like beginning to write a novel without a clue about the plot. Whichever entity you select for your business, you also need to make things legal by obtaining licenses and business numbers.

b. What's In A Name?

When you see the company name 'Poundland', you immediately know that everything will be sold at £1. This is what you need to aim for when thinking about your name; people should instantly know what the company is all about.

When you choose a name for your business, you want to achieve the same recognition for your activity. But there are some important things to keep in mind before you decide on a name for yourself.

The name has to be a legal name. You can't, for example, use a name of another company. You can easily find out whether a name is already in use in various ways. Go online or look in your local telephone directory to see if any businesses have already registered with the name you have chosen.

Select a name that can not only help to market your business by conveying what it is you do, but also will enable you to obtain an easy-to-remember website if you want one. If you're going to be doing wedding videos as a sideline business you run from home, don't call yourself Digital Weddings or Wedding Videos—the domain names (website names) for these businesses are already probably taken and it is always best to give your domain name the same name as your company name.

ALWAYS get a domain name with the keyword in that you want to target. This is VERY important for ranking purposes. Everybody likes their own name (almost everybody) or the name of their company but calling a website www.JohnSmith.com or www.SmithAssociates.com if your site is about window cleaning does not give Google any clues that your site is about window cleaning. Your domain name is one of the first things Google looks at to rank your site. It would be much better to buy the domain name www.WindowCleaningAssociates.com so it is immediately clear from your domain name what your business does.

c. Keeping It Simple or Making It Formal

If you incorporate your business, you must use Inc., Ltd., or Corp. after your name. If you form a limited liability company, LLC (Ltd in the UK) must follow your company name. It's the law and is designed to let anyone who does business with you know exactly who they're dealing with.

Business entities can be formal or informal, give you personal liability protection or not, make taxes simple or complex, and create a whole series of consequences you may never have dreamed about. Your decision on whether to take formal legal steps should be an informed one. Don't let the legal terminology or fear of cost deter you from making the best choice for your situation.

Your basic options:
- Sole proprietorship
- Limited Company (UK)
- Partnership
- Limited liability company LLC (USA)
- S corporation (USA)
- C corporation (USA)

There are some variations. As this is not a book about what type of company to choose, I suggest you contact a local accountant or business adviser or Google the subject. When you just start to earn money from home, there is no need to set up any company. Just see if you like the whole concept first and try and earn some money. When the money starts coming in, only then think about setting up a company. You might set up a company and never earn a penny, therefore there is no point in doing so from day one.

d. Flying Solo

If you're the sole owner and just start to do business, you've automatically formed your proprietorship. There's no legal action to take.
As a sole proprietor, you're also called a self-employed person because you're not an employee of your business.

As a sole proprietor, your business is your alter ego: you're virtually one and the same for both legal and tax purposes. Legally, you're responsible for any debts of the business. Say you sign a lease for a photocopier for your business so you can keep duplicates of invoices and make copies of your face when business is slack. After a few too many of those slack times, you can't keep up the lease payments. The leasing company can come after your savings and any other personal assets they want for paying off the remaining balance e.g. your car, TV, house, etc.

But just because your business organization is informal and your profits and losses are reported on your personal tax return, it doesn't mean you can be informal about how you run your business. You still need to keep things separate. You need separate records and a separate bank account for your business activities. A separate credit card is also a good idea. Keeping your personal life compartmentalized from your business life, even though it's under the same roof, is just plain good business practice.

Being self-employed also means you can't enjoy certain government protections that employees do. If you're injured on the job or you don't have work for a while, you can't turn to worker's compensation, unemployment insurance or state benefits. These benefits are restricted to employees and you're not in this category. However, when your business grows so that its income becomes vital in covering your living expenses, you can carry insurance to protect you from disability or certain business interruptions (such as those caused by a severe storm or illness).

When you go to register your business name, you'll find out whether another company is already using it. Do this before you print business cards so you won't have to throw them away and start over with a new name.

e. Teaming Up

You and your best friend have often talked about going into business to host children's parties. You each have a lot of experience in running these events and mothers who have attended your parties always comment on how great they are. Maybe you're about to take the plunge. When two or more people join together in a business with the intention of making a profit, they've formed a partnership. A husband and wife who own a business together not only are paired in marriage but maybe a business partnership as well. Owners of the partnership are called, aptly enough, partners. Partners are self-employed people; they're not employees of their partnership even though they work for it.

Legally, all partners are fully liable for partnership debts. The creditor can go after a single partner for everything he's owed, even though the partner only owns half of the business.

This is called joint and several liabilities, and here is how it works. Say you and your partner decide to video weddings as a business. The partnership signs a contract with the bride's father to provide video services at a wedding. On the day of the wedding, events conspire to keep you both from doing the job—you're sick and your partner's mother just died. Under the terms of the contract, the partnership owes a $5,000 (£3000) penalty, but there's only $1,000 (£617) in the partnership bank account. The father can sue you for the balance; he does not have to go after your partner.

Of course, the poor partner who shelled out his personal savings to pay off the partnership debt can seek (through a polite request or a legal action) some recovery from the other partners.

A word of advice if you have any co-owners: recognize that you're entering a marriage of sorts and write a prenuptial agreement to guide you through the relationship. Put in writing what happens when one partner wants to leave, when the other takes time off to have a baby, or when there is a disagreement about the direction of the business. The honeymoon may not last forever, and the written word put down when the relationship was solid can avoid costly legal wrangling and grief later on.

I have been in business for over 35 years and I have NEVER seen a partnership without problems so be very cautious! Friends that are your friends now very often won't be your friends when there are money problems.

Friends often don't stay friends when doing business together!

Chapter 8. Home Office Tips

In the early 1900s when cities began to spread into farmland and noxious factories encroached on neighbourhoods, a new type of law, called planning, began to evolve. Cities and towns wanted to control the type of development—commercial, residential, industrial—taking place within their borders. They wrote planning laws to say where people could do what.

Today, planning laws in most places have rules about what businesses can be run from home. The problem in some places is that these laws were written in the Dark Ages. This was before the computer age when home offices looked very different. Back then, planning laws were meant to prevent the introduction of industrial work (called piecework) into the homes. The city leaders wanted to limit the size of professional offices so traffic from patients or clients didn't disturb neighbourhoods.

Some places see the advent of home businesses as an opportunity to raise some revenue and charge licensing fees. Some places have modernized their rules or are in the process of doing so. Others haven't. If you want to run a business from home, find out the rules that apply to you and be sure you follow them.

a. Doing Business In A Residential Area

An angry neighbour or even a customer may turn you in and report you to the local planning authority. If someone files a complaint, your city or town will investigate. If they decide you've broken the law, you'll pay a lot. The good part is that with a little knowledge and planning you can avoid this kind of problem.

If you're told that there's no problem running your business from your home, ask which planning rule covers your situation and write it down. Get the name of the person who gave you the information and write it down. After all, you're putting a great deal of reliance on this civil servant's word. Do yourself a favour by e-mailing the detailed scenario to the official. When you get a reply, print it out for your records. If, later on, there is any doubt, you will have it all in writing.

If you apply to your local council to set up a business, they will usually send out a letter to all your neighbours to see if anyone objects to the type of business you are planning to set up. If too many neighbours object, you might not get permission to start your business.

Of course, if you are planning to start up a home-based business cleaning people's windows, you don't need to ask permission.

b. Do You Live In An Entrepreneur Zone?

How business-friendly is your town or city? Will it let you run a business from your home? If you don't know, you'd better ask somebody. You don't want to break the law and have to pay penalties and fines. But even if a reading of the rules makes you think you can't run the kind of business you plan to from home, you might be able to get permission if you go about it correctly.

To find out the planning rules in your area, check with your town or city. Once you've found the right person to ask, then be sure you ask the right questions. Ask hypothetically, "If I were to run a mail-order business from my home with one employee who doesn't live with me, would this violate a planning law?" Be sure to lay out all the variables that apply to you—the nature of your business, the number of outside employees, the frequency of visitors, parking issues, signs, noise, deliveries and anything else you can think of.

There are special rules for professional offices. For example, there may be a limit on the amount of parking for patients or clients, or on the number of employees who don't live in the home. The business can't have noise, odours, or hazards that go outside the walls of the home. There are also different rules about signs having the name of your business on them.

If you're told that you can't do what you planned because of planning rules, ask which planning rule covers your situation. What's the sticking point that would make your proposal violate the rules? Maybe it's just a limit on the number of outside employees e.g. you want two, but the rules say one employee who doesn't live with you. You might be able to modify your plans. Maybe one employee is all you'll need to get started from home. Or maybe you can contract out a portion of your work so you don't have any employees in your home. Maybe there are some legal steps you can take to get special permission to run your business from home.

The world of virtual employees or VA's (Virtual Assistant) has expanded. If your employees' job requires a computer, chances are you'll be able to let them work from their home instead of yours. Don't forget that you might find a very good employee on the other side of the world. So if your business needs additional bodies, don't assume that they have to all be in your home.

Once you've cut your way through all the rules and restrictions, you may find you don't have any planning concerns. As a practical matter, if your business is just you working in your home office and you don't bring in outsiders—employees, customers, or others—it is not a problem.

Be sure to find out whether you have to pay any fee for a permit or license to run a business from home. An increasing number of local authorities are more than happy to allow businesses to operate in homes—as long as those businesses pay for the privilege.

c. A Space In Your Place

Artist, plumber, mail order, children's clothing—all businesses are not created equal, and the space each needs is also different. The nature of your business dictates the kind of space you need. You may be fine at the kitchen table, or you may need to use a spare bedroom or the living room. Think about what you need to run your business—elbowroom, a good view, whatever you think it takes. Then pick the right part of your home to use for your business.

You'll be happy that you took the time to plan your physical setup. After all, you'll be spending a lot of time there. The more details you can work out in the planning stage, the more comfortable you'll be in your home office.

The cost of setting up your space is entirely up to you. If you already have what you need, your cost is zero. If you need to put up a partition in a room or buy a desk, carpeting and light fixtures, your costs will be substantially more.

Above all, have fun with your plans. Decorating an office can even add to the value of your home, if your budget allows you to go for it.

d. Desk Space

There's an old saying that clutter expands to fill the space you have: the larger the desk the more junk you can fit on it. To arrange your home office, you have to know two things: your available space and what furniture and other office equipment you need to put in it. What are your home office options? Do you have a spare bedroom? Do you have part of a family room or basement available for your business? Can an attic or garage be converted into office space? Look around and decide where you can fit your home office.
In selecting your office space, consider what you'll want to put in there. List the items that you must have in your office. These may include some or all of the following:

- Desk
- Desk chair
- Printer/Copying machine

- Bookcases or shelves
- Daybed for those "inspirational" naps
- Chairs and/or sofa for clients or customers
- Drafting table
- Computer
- Printer

Of course, you may not be an office type. Maybe you need an artist's studio for your design business. Or perhaps you grow orchids for sale. You can still accommodate these activities in your home and treat the space as your home office. Perhaps you can use an attic, converted garage, or greenhouse for your business. (Of course, you should check the planning regulations on these unique space arrangements). The key is to understand your business needs and choosing the space that will suit them.

e. Getting It On Paper

Once you've picked the right space in your home and have an idea of what you'll need to put there, it's time to lay out your floor space. You can do this best on graph paper. Think about where you're going to put all of your equipment. You can draw in your office furniture and equipment in pencil. Using pencil lets you "move" furniture around easily, trying out one arrangement and then another. Search for some general measurement guidelines for your office equipment so you know what space you will need.

If your space is limited, look into space-saving office furniture designed to fit a lot of equipment into a small space. Also check out multifunction devices that combine a printer, copier, scanner, and fax machine all in one. Instead of making room for an answering machine, get voicemail. Instead of planning for a TV and a computer monitor on the same desk, you can watch your TV on your computer screen. Don't think that everything has to go on your desk; you can put some equipment on a shelf or on the floor. There are even wireless multifunction devices that you can just plug in another room if you need the space. And don't forget where electrical sockets and telephone lines are when placing your desk in your room plans otherwise there will be extension leads all over the place!

Instead of pushing a pencil around graph paper to map out your home office, you can use a computer and software to do the same thing high-tech style. Half a dozen different software programs costing $35 to $70 (£21 to £42) allow you to fiddle with furniture placement, add lighting and even try out different wallpaper, carpeting, and paint. This helps you visualise what your office will look like after you remodel.

You may find that your space just isn't big enough for all your stuff. Your choices at this point can be difficult. If you own your own home you may be able to add on a room, convert a garage to office space, or extend an existing room. This alternative requires substantial investment, so consider it carefully. If you can't afford to remodel (or don't want to make the investment until your business is profitable enough to help pay off the costs), then you either have to give up the idea of working entirely from home or somehow scale back your office plans. Yes, these are tough decisions. But it's better that you make them now, not once you've left your day job and suddenly find you're too cramped to run your new business properly.

f. A Place For Everything And Everything In Its Place

If you're a consultant or provide a service, you don't have any stock that needs to be stored. Your storage needs are limited to your office supplies and client files. But if your business depends on stock, think hard about where you're going to put it. Depending on the product or products you sell, you may need a little or a lot of space.

Think outside the box when it comes to storage. Do you need daily access to all the storage? Could you rent a storage unit for some of your stock? Many businesses do. Could you hire someone else to do order fulfilment for your business? Some things you won't see on paper but you may want to plan for are good lighting and soundproofing. According to one study, less noise and better light improve productivity by 8 per cent. But even if you're not concerned with the numbers, you'll just feel better if you can see easily and you're less distracted by noises from other rooms in the house. Consider compact, fluorescent "natural, full colour spectrum" lights to brighten things up and the addition of acoustic tiles and plush carpeting.

Despite your planning, there may not be enough space to hold all your supplies or items for sale. Think beyond the walls of your home. Today, self-storage facilities are everywhere. Even in the most expensive communities, a heated/air-conditioned space can cost you less than $100 (£60) per month.

If you use a spare bedroom as an office, consider converting the wardrobe (closet) into storage space. Invest in file cabinets and shelves to deck out the wardrobe. You can buy organiser kits to customize your storage needs or you can have professional designers come into your house (the consultation is usually free) to create the perfect custom-made wardrobe for your business. Or if you're handy with a hammer, you can download lots of free wardrobe designs from the web.

Another option is to use your garden shed for storage but keep in mind that, depending on where you live, it gets very cold in winter months and very warm in summer months in these sheds so this is not suitable for certain products e.g. OK for glass but not OK for cardboard as that will get too damp in the winter months.

g. Paving The Way For The Public

If you're a freelance writer working alone, you can skip this part; you won't be having many guests in your home office. But if you have outsiders—clients, patients, customers, suppliers, or even an employee—coming into your home on a regular basis for business, what does it mean for you? Some businesses can't run without contact with the public. If your business is one of them, can your home handle it?

There are four main concerns about visitors to your home office: space, appearance, security and safety:

- Space. Where are you going to put everyone? You need to have a place for visitors to sit and transact business.
- Appearance. If you're the only person using your office, your paper clutter, your children's toys, and your pets may not be a big deal. But if you have business visitors, they may not appreciate pet hair on their clothes and dolls underfoot. You want your home office to look professional and business-like.
- Security. When someone rings your front door bell, make sure the person you open the door for isn't there to harm you or your property. Think personal safety. The cost of an intercom or other device to improve your control over public access may be well worthwhile. And you may also want to consider a security system to protect your office equipment or stock from theft when you're not at home.
- Safety. You may think your house is safe, but if you have regular business visitors, you have to make sure that your entrance and office space are hazard-free. You may need to install handrails by the steps into your home and you may want additional lighting in your driveway. You'll certainly want to remove any snow as quickly as possible and take any necessary nonslip measures. The last thing you need is a client breaking an arm by slipping on your front step and all the associated lawyers, insurance people, and general chaos that can ensue.

Make your office space not only safe for the public, but childproof as well. You don't want important papers marked with crayons or your child becoming entangled in your computer wires.

Chapter 9. Time Management Tips

How much time do you want to spend each day on your home-based business? This may seem like a simple question, but you may surprise yourself by not knowing the answer.

You may just say, "I'll spend as much time as I can." If you do, you'll find that there's no time; all of your time is eaten up by looking after your children, doing laundry, shopping, cleaning, or just talking to neighbours. On the other hand, many home businesspeople work 14 hours a day or more, 7 days a week without even realizing it.

You need structure. You need to be able to rise above the barking dogs and crying babies and get down to work. But you also need to know when to turn off the office desk light and stop working.

a. Set A Schedule To Get Work Done

One of the joys of working from home is that in theory you can do what you want, when you want to. But if you don't fix a schedule, in reality you may never find the time to do any work. Flexibility means taking responsibility for setting up a work schedule. This schedule doesn't have to be rigid. But you have to set priorities. When you need to return a client's call, you may have to put off starting dinner.

Make a tentative work schedule to get you going. In blocking out your time, set specific times for the personal things you have to do, like picking up your child from school or driving your spouse to the airport. In scheduling, you may need to adjust for the seasons. If your children are small and off school for the summer, you may not be able to put in as many hours as you'd like to for business during that time. Don't try to schedule work when you know you won't be able to get it done.

Also block out the time you think you'll have to spend on personal matters. If your children are young but in school, maybe you'll work only during their school hours and be with them once they get home. Or maybe you'll find you can squeeze in extra hours after they've gone to sleep.

b. When To Call It A Day

Those same souls who used to come home late from the office can now be seen in their home office late into the night. After all, they now live in their office. Work becomes the prime focus of their day and night.

When you work at home, there's no division between the office and home, so there's a tendency to work just about all the time. Home-based business workaholics have to learn when to quit.

Even if you're not a type-A personality who loves to work all the time, you may have a realistic belief that you can't afford to turn down any work that comes your way. You don't yet have the security of a well-established business to say no, even if it means working longer hours than you'd like to.

This pattern of working all the time isn't good. First of all, it's generally not healthy to work so many hours. Secondly, if you're working all the time, you're not taking care of your personal responsibilities. Thirdly, and most importantly, your family may resent all the attention you're giving to your business at their expense. They may be able to understand 9 to 5, Monday to Friday. But 7 to 7, seven days a week may be a little hard to swallow. Oddly enough, the answer to overworking is the same as the answer to procrastination, with a slight twist: set a schedule, and keep to it.

Don't forget: if you work on the computer all the time, go back to the beginning of this book where I warn you about the potential dangers to your health if you work in an office environment. I've learned the hard way!

If you have a tendency to go overboard in your working hours, having a fixed schedule will help you to set limits. Planning your personal activities—scheduling them in much the same way as you would your business tasks—will also help limit your work hours. Each week, make a list of the personal things you want to accomplish and then schedule them into your weekly appointment book or other planner. But don't just list them, actually schedule time for both your personal and business tasks. If you don't carve out the hours to make them happen, they won't.

Maybe you don't need someone to tell you how to spend your leisure time. But if you're like me, work is like a magnet drawing you in. You'll need to schedule time off.
As you begin to work at home, some of these planning tips may become second nature. After a while you won't formally have to set aside time for your personal life; it'll become automatic. But in the beginning, the exercise of planning for personal time may be important to have the confidence that you'll be able to fit everything in.
Don't forget to sleep (and include sleeping hours in your schedule). Some sleep foundations recommend eight hours of sleep for everyone each night, although Donald Trump boasts of getting by on just four hours a night and so did Margaret Thatcher. Think sleep isn't important? Studies have shown that daytime drowsiness can cause driving

accidents and, even if you're not behind the wheel but only behind your desk, you may not be at peak performance if you're too sleepy. Since you're at home, you may be able to add a catnap into your schedule!

c. Creating More Time

Whether you find it hard to get to work or hard to extinguish the midnight oil, you could probably do with more time. Yes, there are only 24 hours in a day. But you can use more of those hours for business if you need to and know how.

Hire help. The days of trying to be Superman or Superwoman are over. Accept it. You can't do it all yourself. You may need help—in your personal life or in your business. Hire someone to clean your house (a job you'd normally do) so that you can spend more time on your business. The same is true for help in your business. Consider hiring clerical help or farming out work to contractors to create more time for you. Even your childcare responsibility may have to be delegated. If your children are small and can't be left on their own, you may want to hire a babysitter or ask a willing relative for help.

Use machines and technology. One of the key benefits to technology is saving time. Machines can do the work faster than it takes to do it by hand. If you usually keep your books by hand, automate. Putting your financial information on the computer may save you hours and hours over the course of a year—time you can better use for something else. Most banks now have some form of online banking for no additional charge. (Actually, when you transact business with a bank online versus using a teller or an ATM, you are saving the bank a lot of money.) Online banking allows you to download transactions into popular small-business accounting software like Quickbooks or Microsoft Small Business Accounting. Many credit cards will also allow you to download transactions into this software as well. When tax time comes you'll be able to import all this data into your tax software and you'll have your taxes done in no time. (You may still have to pay the tax authority, but at least with all the time saved you can use that time to earn more money).

d. Keeping The Family And Business Separate

With your family and your business under the same roof, your family life can easily spill over into your business operations. How do you set boundaries—both psychological and physical? You don't have to build a brick wall between your office and your kitchen; there are less drastic measures you can take. Think about this and make some decisions.

e. Teach Your Family And Friends Restraint

If you live alone, there's no one at home to barge in on you. But if you have a spouse, a significant other, children, or a roommate, telling them not to interrupt you is difficult. Suddenly they're inventing reasons why they've just got to walk in on you. Don't be too hard on them; they probably just miss you. But once you've decided that you want to work between the hours of 1 and 5, you've got to stick to your guns. You have to train them to leave you alone for four hours.

Sounds simple? Well, it's not. It means telling them over and over again to hold their questions and solve their own problems while you're working. You'll probably find it's easier to get your kids to keep quiet than to get your spouse to leave you alone. After all, the kids are used to being disciplined, but your poor spouse thinks he/she has a say in what goes on under your roof. Ask your significant other to keep a running list of topics or questions he/she wants to discuss. Then schedule a time every day when you can give him/her the undivided attention he/she deserves.

Will a closed door stop people from bothering you? Probably not. Will a "Do Not Disturb" sign on the door keep your family out? Probably not. In short, it's up to you to adapt. You have to be the one to set the limits—but be ready to smile when your family crosses the line.

People in your home aren't your only problem. Friends who were used to having their morning coffee with you before you started your business also have to be taught about limits. Tell them that coffee is out and that they have to call after business hours to chat because you don't want to be interrupted during your work time. Of course, you'd probably like an occasional call to break up your business routine. Better that you're the one who sets out when it's convenient for you to talk.

f. Separate Business From Pleasure - Physically

Just as writers need their own space to write, in the best of all possible home-based business situations you will have a separate room with a door to work in. But that's not always possible. You may be forced to share space with your family. When you work on the kitchen table and your son wants to make a peanut butter sandwich there, it's hard to go on working. There's only so much space.

But space isn't your only problem. There are also the psychological intrusions on your concentration. Working in the kitchen, for example, may be a constant reminder of the fancy dinners you're no longer preparing.

It's a good idea to set aside a separate space for business if you can—one that won't be used by your family for other things. If you use part of a family room as your office, try to put your desk in a corner of the room that's away from toys and TV. Keep your supplies close at hand and separate from your family. You don't want your kids poking around your papers, looking for the pieces from their Monopoly board, for example.

g. Taking Time For Time Off

Remember those days when you got paid for a two-week vacation? It was certainly one of the perks of the job. Now you can take all the time off you want—or can you? One of the hardest things for many home-based business owners to do is to leave the office for vacation. There's no one telling you that you can't. But there's concern about what'll happen to the business while you're away. Still, even a home-based business owner needs time off once in a while—it's important to recharge your creative batteries, spend quality time with family and friends, and improve your health (a Boston University study showed that women who took a holiday twice a year lowered their risk of coronary heart disease by 50 per cent). Here are some ideas for fitting a vacation into your busy schedule:

- Schedule holidays for your slow season. As your business develops you'll be able to see what times of the year are busier than others.

- Take long weekends. If a week away would undermine your business, what about a three- or four-day weekend once in a while? Clients and customers are out of communication with you for no more than a day or two instead of a full week.

- Hire help to watch the office. While you're away, you can have someone else look after your business. You don't necessarily need someone to run your business as you would. You only need someone to answer calls, schedule appointments and handle simple problems that may come up with customers, clients, or suppliers.

Chapter 10. Working Alone

For most home-based business owners, working at home means working all alone. If you used to have a job, working alone at home is quite a change for you in many ways. Besides the nature of your work, your working social life has shrunk by about 100 per cent. There may be no one to talk to face to face. The only sound of a human voice you hear all day may be on the phone. You may actually begin to miss those meetings you always complained about.

But working alone doesn't have to be lonely. There are many ways to connect to the outside world. You may even come to love the solitude and increased productivity that working alone can give you.

a. When You're The Only One At The Water Cooler

If you're used to working at a job in an office or some other place outside your home, you may think back fondly on meeting other people at the water cooler and swapping company gossip or discussing the latest episode of the hottest TV show. You just can't do this when you work alone in your home.

Some people enjoy the peace and quiet in the home office when the rest of the family has left for the day. There are no human distractions to keep you from getting down to business. And there's more time because you're not wasting it socialising. You may be surprised at how much work you can get done every day. You can use these extra minutes for your business. Or you can use your extra time for errands, shopping or watching TV.

Some people don't like being isolated. They get cabin fever, feeling confined to the house day in, day out. They miss the social opportunities that working outside the home gave them.

You have to determine your own comfort level. If you like being alone and find it helps you do your work, then you don't have to find ways to get out and connect. But if you're the type who needs to meet people during the day, there are many ways you can do it while working from home.

Telephone Talk

Talking on the telephone is an important way to stay in touch. You can use your phone for business, but don't forget you can also use it for social contact throughout the day.

Nowadays this has changed to "sending messages" instead of talking on the phone.

Of course, it goes without saying, (but I'll say it anyway) that you need to balance your personal telephone time with your business needs. Tempting as it may be to talk to a good friend about their holiday for three hours, you need to set priorities so that your most productive time is not spent socialising. Make personal calls during breaks you schedule between the business tasks you need to get done. The break reminder software can help you with this. For example, if you normally spend the first hour of every day going through mail and e-mail and answering correspondence, slot in a personal call after you've finished your business letters.

Interact With The Internet

Today more and more people are socialising long-distance without ever speaking into a telephone. Instead of meeting face to face, they are talking through a computer. The Internet and commercial online services such as Skype, Facebook and LinkedIn allow you to meet people who may have interests similar to yours without ever leaving your home office.

Of course, you can stay in touch via e-mail. While it's a one-way conversation, it lets you get your thoughts across to another party without interrupting your work. What's more, if you want to, you can take the time to carefully compose what you want to say (and keep a written record of it for your files).

Get Out And About

Just because you work in a home office doesn't mean you have to stay there. Depending on the type of work you do and where you live, you may find that you spend a good deal of time out of the office on business. You may be visiting clients or customers, meeting with suppliers, visiting trade or other business shows and attending networking events.

But even if you don't have a business reason to get out of the office, you may find that you have the time to get out for personal reasons. Since you don't spend time commuting to work and since you don't spend time socialising at the office, you have more time for yourself. And you can spend this free time any way you want.

You can also schedule time away from the office. Once in a while, try to arrange personal or business lunches with your friends or business associates.

b. Connect Through Networking

Networking is word-of-mouth marketing in which contacts are made for the purpose of building trust in order to transact business together.

Networking has been around forever. The "old boy" network meant people who had been through education from pre-school to university together made and kept important contacts that they used in business for the rest of their lives. This "old boy" network is still around today, but it's not the only network in operation.

Formal networking groups started in the early 1980s, initially to give women the advantages the old boys had. These networking avenues soon expanded to include both men and women looking for business contacts. People who network make 23 per cent more than those who don't. So never eat alone. Networking is good for your mental health and may be great for your business.

Today networking is an important way for all types of business owners to interact with others of their breed. It allows you to swap stories and stay up to speed with your type of business and your business community.

But for a home-based business owner, networking is even more important than for business owners working outside of their homes. Networking is not only a vital marketing tool, it's also a way to break the cabin fever and socialize. Attending a meeting of an organisation gives you the chance to get out of your home and mingle with other businesspeople, some of which may also be home-based.

Be patient. Networking doesn't necessarily produce results overnight. One event does not create a list of new customers immediately. The more you put into it, the better your results will be. Attend events, join committees and distribute plenty of business cards! Search online for local networking groups e.g. breakfast networking.

Start Your Own Network

If there's no network organisation in your community (or if existing ones don't meet your needs), you may just want to start your own. This is the first idea in this book on how you could earn extra money: start your own network group in your area. Charge a small attendance fee for each meeting. Decide on your format—open or by invitation only. Fix the time and date of meetings (say, a breakfast meeting at 7 A.M. on the second Tuesday of each month).

It may take time and money to get a group started. Be prepared to give it several months before the group is firmly established. Also be prepared to pay the costs of getting it going (advertising, room rental in excess of money collected from attendees, etc.). After all your efforts, the group may never get off the ground and you may have to just walk away.

Let other businesspeople in your area know about your new organisation. If you don't have enough people to invite to your first meeting, place an ad in your local newspaper or get the word out to business owners you know in the area about your new network organisation. Put ads on local websites. Don't forget your local TV and radio station's community calendar on their website. A local restaurant, community centre, or even the public library might be the perfect spot for your new organization to meet.

Non-Networking For Connections

Perhaps the most effective way to network is to "non-network." Getting involved in your community without necessarily identifying your business can lead to positive network results for you and your business. People in your community get to know you and, it is hoped, trust and respect you. This trust and respect carries over to your business. People want to know what you do and, in an informal setting, hear about your business.

Non-networking can take the form of membership of your local political club, health club, university alumni association, PTA or Boy or Girl Scouts, or it can be through volunteering such as coaching sports. Herb, a sales trainer, joined the board of a local charity because he wanted to give back to his community. Along the way, he met another board member who in time became his biggest client.

c. Join A Trade Association

As a home-based business owner, you may feel like a small fish, isolated from the information and buying opportunities that large companies enjoy. You don't have to feel this way any longer. There are a number of trade associations geared specifically to home-based or small business owners. These trade associations let you act like you're a big shot when buying insurance, booking hotel rooms, lobbying for legislative change and more.

Trade association membership offers you:

- Business and personal insurance. Being a member allows you to buy your own insurance at group rates. The types of insurance include medical and dental coverage, special home office business insurance, life insurance, and even car insurance.

- Financial services. As a member you may be able to get merchant authorization so you can accept credit cards from your customers (something that's difficult to do as a home-based business owner). You may also be able to get legal and tax assistance with your business questions. You may even be able to take advantage of mutual funds and other investments.

- Communications. Membership may entitle you to special rates with some long-distance carriers. Each trade association also has its own newsletter, giving you regular news affecting home-based or small businesses.

- Products and services. You may enjoy special rates on travel, car rental and dining. You may get discounts on overnight delivery and copying services. You may be able to attend local educational seminars geared to small or home-based businesses.

Chapter 11. How To Promote Your Business

Many people use the terms marketing, advertising, promotion and sales almost interchangeably. Each of these terms, which you'll learn the meaning of in a moment, is distinct. Each plays a role in seeing that your product or service reaches the public so you can make money.

The term marketing really covers five separate elements: market research, distribution channels, pricing, advertising and promotion (the actual selling phase). Let's look at each of these elements, and a few others, so you can develop your own marketing strategy.

a. Market Research

Market research is really just a way of finding out if anyone is interested in paying for your product or service. Market research is the first stage in marketing. It's also the first stage in developing your business. Don't even think about starting a business until you find out if anyone wants what you're selling.

Some new business owners may think they don't have to do market research. After all, they say, they're small, don't have the time or expertise to conduct the research, and don't know what the research is for anyway. The answer to this attitude is simple: you can't sell anything to someone you don't know.

Market research is available from a variety of sources. The costs will vary according to whether you want results for a small location or subcategory, or very detailed national research of an entire category. You might be able to glean what you need by reading a company's press releases, but if you want to drill down into the data it might be worth the money to buy the full report.

Market research will help you identify the market you should sell to. Here's what your market research should tell you:

- Who are you going to sell to? You want to get a picture of the type of customer you're targeting. Is this customer male or female? What's the age group? Level of education? Household income? This will help you with your advertising.
- How big is your potential market? The potential market includes anyone who might be able to use your product or service. Put your potential market size into numbers. Are there 1,000 or 1 million people in your market? Maybe you'll see

that even if you could sell your product or service to everyone in your potential market, you wouldn't be able to make a living from it. Say you can sell your housesitting service to 10 per cent of the market. Well, if the potential market is only 1,000, a 10 per cent share is just 100 people—not enough to make it worthwhile.

- What are the geographic boundaries of your market? As a home-based business, you might think you're limited to your neighbourhood. Today, through e-commerce, it's possible to think big even if you're a small business. For example, you can have a national, or even international, market if you plan to sell on the Internet.
- How do you stack up against the competition?

Before you start any new business, you need to find out if people are searching for your keyword. You can use a keyword tool to find out how many people are searching per month for certain keywords. With Google Keyword Planner (KP), you can find out how many people are searching for a certain keyword per month.

Example: if you are planning to set up a business cleaning windows and KP tells you that 5 people per month are searching for the keyword "cleaning windows", that is NOT a good sign as not many people are searching for your service. You can set criteria in KP to search per area e.g. London, Washington, etc.

Obtaining a Google Adwords account is simple, totally free and can be done in five to ten minutes. Signing up is pretty self-explanatory.
Sign up here:
www.adwords.google.com
www.adwords.google.co.uk
Important to mention: you DON'T need to spend any money with Adwords, you just need an account.

b. Distribution Channels

As stated earlier, it is important to establish your distribution channels in order to figure out how you're going to get your products into the hands of the people who want to buy them. For more details see chapter 2, sub-heading 2): 'What Distribution Channel Do You Choose?'

Direct sales involve face-to-face selling instead of via a store or mail order. If you sell cosmetics door-to-door, you're using direct sales. The concept of network marketing is based on direct sales.

Internet sales represent the newest distribution channel, and may be one of the most effective ones.

As a home business, if you've got big plans for advertising and expect volume business, you may want to think about using a fulfilment company. A fulfilment company can take orders, store products for you, and ship them out for a fee.

c. Advertising And Promotion

Advertising means informing the public of the features and benefits of your product or service. Promotion is a way of stimulating an immediate sale, such as offering a discount coupon. Even Thomas Edison had to spread the word about his inventions to capture the public's interest. People weren't lined up at his door with the money for a new light bulb the first day it became available. You have to let people know that you have something to sell. This means advertising and promotion.

Advertising can take many different shapes. It can be direct advertising where you push your particular product or service—"buy my face cream" or "use my tax preparation service." Or, advertising can be indirect. Your entire business image is a form of indirect advertising, called branding. Try using a business logo or colour on everything that the public sees—your business cards, invoices, stationary, signs, even on a T-shirt. Eventually, you'll build up a business identity—your brand—that the public will come to recognize, and that translates into indirect marketing and sales.

Word-of-mouth from satisfied clients and customers is just about the best form of advertising you can get. It doesn't cost you anything and it's highly effective at bringing in new business. You can jump-start this process by asking satisfied customers for referrals.

Just advertising, telling the public about your product or service, may not be enough. Here's where promotion comes in. Sometimes you may need to add a little something extra to get the sale. Maybe you have to offer discounts. Maybe you want to offer bonuses. Think of the local bank that gives out a gift for opening a savings account. You're not a bank, but you too can offer a benefit. People sign up with www.CompareTheMarket.com just to get a cuddly Meerkat toy, for example.

If you provide a service, you may want to offer a free consultation. Be sure your offer is clear, such as "one hour free." Many people like to test a service before they buy. Just be prepared to give out a lot of free hours before you actually get some paid ones.

d. Sales

The last step in marketing is the most important step: the actual selling phase. This is the point at which someone pays you money for your product or service. It's sometimes called closing a sale. All of your previous efforts—market research, advertising, your logo on T-shirts—don't mean a thing if you can't close a sale. Read a few books about selling techniques if need be. There's a reason good salespeople are few and far between: selling is a skill. Some people are born salespeople, yet others have to learn how to sell. A lot of people are as frightened of selling as they are of major surgery. If you don't feel entirely comfortable selling, you just have to get over it and get on with it.

There are things you can do to become better at selling. Try writing a script for your sales pitch. Write down all the points you want to cover and how you'll present them. Here's a hint: don't talk about the features of your product or service; instead focus on showing how the customer will benefit from it. In short, you have to answer the customer's question "What's in it for me?" Practice the script with family or friends or in front of a mirror until you know it well. Then, as you work with your script in trying to make a sale, you'll be able to add to or delete from it to make it even better.

Benefits, benefits, benefits: When selling any products, you HAVE to concentrate on what the benefits are for the customer when purchasing the product. If you are selling a product online, exactly the same applies: benefits, benefits, benefits. Don't say: "This is a good quality chair". Instead, say: "Your back pain could disappear forever with this chair". Focus on what it does for your customer!

In devising your approach, keep in mind the different parts of your sales pitch:

- Identify your customer's needs. What's the situation and how can you make it better (how can you solve your customer's problem)? If you've already been asked to make a proposal, presumably the customer has already told you their needs.
- Make a proposal. Tell your customer what you're going to do and how much it's going to cost.
- Address objections. Be prepared for an initial 'no' but, as the saying goes, never take 'no' for an answer. Discover what objections your customer has and be ready to respond. If price is the only objection, then let's get to the next point.
- Negotiate. You may be able to make a sale if you're flexible. With this in mind, you need to put some leeway in your proposal to allow for negotiating.
- Close the sale. Get the customer to sign on the dotted line. If, at this final stage in the sale, you meet with just a 'maybe' or even a 'no', don't give up. Start the

process over again. Maybe you didn't properly identify the customer's needs, for example. You could ask "what if" questions e.g. What if I reduce the price to X amount, will you be happy to buy it?"

e. Marketing Plan

So, how are you going to get your business from zero sales to $50,000 (£30,800) to $100,000 (£61,000) to $1 million (£617,000)? If you don't know where you're going, you won't get there. Develop a game plan that you can use to bring your business along.

The important part of your game plan is not just drawing it up, although this is useful because it makes you focus on various points. The real key is putting it into action. Just sitting back and waiting for things to happen won't get you anywhere.

Action is the key to all success.

If you don't think you're able to create a good marketing plan and you have trouble setting goals on your own, try using a software program: you'll find several commercial software programs for writing marketing plans.

Set Marketing Goals

How will you measure your success unless you've got a yardstick to measure your progress against? Decide your short- and long-term marketing goals. A goal can be sales, customers, money…however you define it. How many sales do you want to make this year, or in the next three years? How many new customers do you want to find in the next month?

Dream Big **Set Goals** **Take Action**

In setting your goals, be specific and realistic. Set sales figures you think you can reach and mark the dates in red on the calendar when you expect to reach your targets. Create a chart of your goals (e.g. make calls, send information, schedule appointments, make sales etc.) When setting goals, you should have already performed your market research. You have to know your market size. You need to have strategically set your price.

When's the last time you opened the Yellow Pages (online or offline) and looked at the number of companies that do what you do? It goes without saying that for most businesses, the marketplace is very competitive. Find out about your competitors so you can stand out amongst them.

Know the "enemy." Who are your competitors? You can find out just by looking in the Yellow Pages or local ads or do an online search. You may find there are only one or two businesses in direct competition with you in your area. A direct competitor is one offering the same product or service. For example, if you're an interior decorator, your direct competitors are other interior decorators. Indirect competitors are those offering similar products or services. The local paint and wallpaper stores may offer some decorating assistance, so these stores would be indirect competitors. Also learn who your allies are so you can build a referral relationship with them.

You may find that you have dozens of direct competitors. For example, these days everyone's a web page designer. So what? If they're all working to capacity or you have a unique feel for design, then there may still be room for you in the market.

Try out the competition's product or service. Be a consumer and test what they're offering. Even if you can't afford to buy one of everything that's out there, at least let them send you their brochures and give you their sales talk so you know what they're pitching to your potential customers. Talk to your competitors' customers to find out if they're satisfied and will remain loyal. Talk to local merchants and bankers to find out about the reputation of your competitors. You can also learn about how your industry's doing in general by talking with these sources.

Understand Your Advertising Options
Advertising can take many forms. The ones you select will depend on what you're selling and the money you have to spend on advertising. Here are some ways to advertise:

- Billboards
- Catalogues
- Cooperative advertising
- Direct mail
- Display advertising
- Internet and other tech venues, such as "advert gaming" through video games and mobile advertising on cell phones
- Press releases
- Print ads (classifieds, magazines, newspaper ads)

- Promotional contests and prizes
- Radio
- Magazine/newspaper advertising
- Local papers
- Local community halls
- Online directories
- Local supermarkets

Some forms of advertising are free. Networking (making personal contacts that can translate into sales contacts) doesn't cost a thing. Networking is a continual and on-going process. Wherever you are and whomever you're with, there's an opportunity to network. Don't be shy. Talk about yourself and your business. The listener may do the same about her/his business. This type of simple conversation has often laid the groundwork for future contact.

Follow Up
Be sure to follow up on your marketing efforts. You've spent the money and succeeded in getting customer response. Now don't waste it. Maybe it's obvious what you have to do, but here are some reminders for customer follow-up:

- Return phone calls and respond to e-mails.
- Schedule appointments.
- Fulfil promises made in your ads.
- Ask about customer satisfaction.

Your follow-up is as important as the advertising itself.

Besides following up on your customers, you should also follow up on your advertising. You want to know whether your advertising efforts are responsible for the customers (or whether they're coming to you via another method). If you advertise in several different ways, find out which one reeled the customer in. You can find this out in several different ways. You can track ads directly by asking customers "How did you hear of us?" Or you can use an indirect approach. You make up a name, department, or box number and put it in your ad or on your brochures and promotional coupons. When customers respond and make references to this non-existent person or department, you'll know immediately that they came to you through your ad. If you find your methods aren't bringing in customers, you need to change them or review your entire marketing approach.

You can also mention a different coupon code in all the different advertising channels. That way you know which orders are coming in from which advertising channel, as people will mention the coupon code.

Understand that advertising, which is the process of informing the public about you, may not translate into immediate sales. People learn by repetition; you've got to repeat your ads until people remember your jingle, your motto, and your company name. It may be some time before you begin to see results. It's better to have several smaller ads run frequently than one large, expensive ad run once. Frequency, rather than size, is more effective in advertising. According to statistics people have to see an advertisement 7 times before they remember it.

f. Simple And Cheap Advertising Ideas

Even if you could afford to, you may not be able to use all types of advertising for your business. Planning restrictions may prohibit you from displaying a large sign or any sign at all at your place of business. The size of your advertising budget may price you out of the range of expensive forms of advertising, such as TV. For instance, infomercials, though highly effective, cost a lot to produce and more to run.

Radio, on the other hand, can be a surprisingly cost-effective strategy for certain markets. You may not be able to afford drive time ads on the top-rated station in your market, but there are a lot of stations and time slots on that dial. Contact all your local radio stations (not just the ones you listen to) to find out their rates and demographics. If the radio station has lots of talk shows, first suggest yourself to the producers of the shows as an expert in your field. Instead of paying for a 30-second spot, you may end up with a one-hour interview for free! But there are some types of advertising that just about any home-based business can use. You can't go wrong with having your satisfied customers spread the good word about you. You may want to look into what the Internet can do for your business (Facebook, for example). And of course, there are always classified ads and direct mail.

Samples
If you can afford to offer free samples, you must do so. Giving out free samples is an excellent way of getting new customers.

Word of Mouth
Your best advertising comes from a satisfied customer. You should spend some of your energy and money on keeping clients and customers happy. Use your common sense and

good manners. Thank clients and customers for their business. Follow up on problems, and don't let anyone go away unhappy with the results. You may want to send out cards or small gifts at holiday times as a thank-you.

Ask your good clients or customers for referrals. You can even think about offering incentives for referrals, such as $25 (£15) off their next order. Why spend money you don't have to? It costs 10 times more to bring in a new customer than to keep an existing one. So do everything you can to ensure continued customer satisfaction. A bonus to this is that satisfied customers will tell others about you, bringing in new customers without any added costs.

Advertising in Cyberspace
The Internet is a place for a home-based business owner to keep up with trends and sell a product or service. The information superhighway lets you compete in the marketplace with the big boys. You can get general information to help you run your business. You can also get marketing information that you can use for your business. For instance, you can find out about trade shows in your area of business.

Having a website may be essential to your business, for example selling Venetian blinds exclusively through the Internet. But even if you have a local lawn-care business or run an accounting practice from home, you can still use a website or Facebook page as a marketing tool to bring in new customers. You can let the public know you exist via the Internet. Your own web page can describe your business to thousands of potential customers. You can give information of general interest or specifics about your business.

Classified Ad
Perhaps the most familiar way to advertise what you have to sell is to place a classified ad. You can place the ad in newspapers, magazines, the Yellow Pages, or even on computer-classified services. Classifieds can be cheap, but highly effective.

The Yellow Pages (online or offline) may be a good place for you to advertise your business. You don't have to rely solely on your telephone listing to bring in business. You can have a featured ad in the section of the Yellow Pages for your type of business—under "cabinet makers," "calligraphers," "carpenters," etc. Check out the cost of running the ad as well as the cost of preparing it. It is surprisingly affordable to advertise in the online Yellow Pages. Usually the price will depend on how many and in which areas you want to advertise e.g. if you want to pay for "window cleaning in Maidstone", that would be cheaper than "window cleaning in London" (because Yellow Pages prices are based on the population of the place where you want to advertise). If you pay for this, that means when somebody searches for "window cleaning in London", your company will be shown on top of the list. I know several people who get 10 new customers per month from the online Yellow Pages by only paying $40 (£25) per month. So it is well worth checking out how much it will cost for your keywords to be number 1 on the list.

When producing the ad, be sure it's catchy. You might want to use a second colour (despite added cost) to increase responses. Showcase your specialty (quality, service, low price, guarantee). Be a problem-solver for customers (state how your product or service will be of help). Include your vital information (your hours, whether you accept credit cards, professional accreditation). Depending on the size of your advertising budget, you may want to work with professionals (graphic designers or even an ad agency) to design your ad. On www.fiverr.com you can get cheap ads done.

Direct Mail
Many small business owners use direct mail (send an ad right to the mailboxes of potential customers) and you can, too. Direct mail is relatively inexpensive. Your costs include the ad, the envelope and the postage. You can create the insert yourself (an ad that will go into the envelope) or use a self-mailer (a postcard which can be mailed as it is.)
Direct Mail has lost a lot of appeal due to the Internet but nevertheless can still be very effective and profitable - certainly if the older generations are your target audience.

Direct mail only works if three things are in place:

- You need the right list. You have to know who to mail your ad to. You can buy a mailing list. (It's called buying, but in reality you're only renting the list because you only buy the right to use it for a limited time).
- You need the right ad. As with any type of advertising, you have to get the attention of the consumer and make your point. You may want to try including a coupon for a discount off of your regular price for a limited time.
- You have to do your mailing at the right time. If, for example, you have a swimming pool maintenance service, you're probably wasting your money sending a mailing out in November. You would want to time your mailing to drop (be mailed) just before the pool season (say in the spring).

Keep your expectations about direct mail realistic. A typical good response is only about 2 per cent, often less. So if you're mailing to 10,000 households, that's only 200 responses. Every response is not a sale, though. From the 200 responses you get, maybe only 1 person will actually buy something. Direct mail is a numbers' game but still works.

Think that direct mail is too expensive? There's a cheaper way to get your message across—co-op your direct mail. It's called co-oping because your ad goes out with ads from other businesses in your area. There are many cooperative mailing companies that let you put an insert into their mailing envelopes, which are then sent to households and businesses in a particular location.

The cost of co-oping is very modest (about $400-$600 (£240 to £360)) for a two-colour ad that is sent to 10,000 households. This is far less than you'd have to pay for just the cost of the envelope and the postage were you to direct-mail on your own. And they can help you with your ad design. You probably already know who the cooperative advertising companies are in your area since you've no doubt received their envelopes from time to time advertising carpet cleaning, florists, accounting services, and the local Chinese food take-away.

Telephone marketing

You might have to call 100 people to get one sale but telephone marketing still works. We all need to start somewhere. I've started a few businesses this way. You'll have to toughen up though, as you will get hundreds of people who will slam down the phone. Just don't take it personally!

Brochures

Printing brochures these days is not expensive. You can print them on your own computer. They don't have to be flash! Put in a few sentences what you do, put a few pictures on it and make sure your contact details are on it! Distribute these everywhere you go.

g. Selling Tips

More direct than advertising or publicity, selling is at the heart of every business. As this is not a book about selling, it is not possible to go over everything that is important. I will cover some of the most important issues. Whatever kind of selling your business involves, from moving goods over a counter to negotiating complex contracts, you need to understand the whole selling process and be involved with every aspect of it.

Marketing involves the whole process of deciding what to sell, who to sell it to, and how. The theory is that a brilliant marketing strategy should all but eliminate the need for selling. After all, selling is mostly concerned with shoehorning customers into products that they don't really want, isn't it? Absolutely not! The more effort you put into targeting the right product or service to the right market, the less arduous the selling process is. However, you still have a selling job to do.

The primary job of the sales operation is to act as a bridge or conduit between the product and the customer. Across that gulf flow information as well as products and services.

You need to tell customers about your great new ideas and how your product or service performs better than anything they have seen to date.

Most businesses need selling and marketing activities in equal measure to get their message across effectively and get goods and services into their markets.

Selling Yourself

One of the most important operational issues to address is your personal selling style. If you've sold products or services before, you may have developed a successful selling style already. If not, you need to develop one that is appropriate for your customers and comfortable for you. Regardless of your experience, assessing your selling style helps define and reinforce your business goals.

> **Before you sell your product, you sell yourself first!**

We've all done it: asked a quote for something and received a price from person A and a cheaper price from person B. However you've ordered it from person A (the more expensive price) because "you couldn't stand person B".

Check that you always see things from the customer's point of view. Stand in your customer's shoes.

In assessing your selling style, consider the following:

- Always have a specific objective for any selling activity, together with a fallback position. For example, your aim may be to get an order, but you may settle for the chance to tender for their business.

- The right person to sell to is the one who makes the buying decision! You may have to start further down the chain, but you should always know whom you finally have to convince.

- Set up the situation so you can listen to the customer. You can best do this by asking open questions that require long answers as opposed to closed questions that solicit a 'yes' or 'no' response. When they have revealed what their needs really are, confirm these back to them and say you can fulfil all their needs.

- Explain your product or service in terms of the customer's needs and requirements.

- Deal with objections without hostility or irritation. Objections are a sign that the customer is interested enough in what you have to say to at least discuss your proposition. Once you have overcome their objections and established a broad body of agreement, you can try to close the deal.

- Your approach to closing can be one of a number of ways. The assumptive close means that as you and the customer are so much in agreement, an order is the next logical step. If the position is less clear, you can go for the balance sheet close, which involves going through the pros and cons, arriving at a larger number of pros.

- If you are unsuccessful, start the selling process again using your fallback objective as the goal.

Outsourcing Selling
Very few small start-up firms can afford to hire their own sales force at the outset, as it costs over $50,000 (£30,000) a year to keep a good salesperson on the road, including commission and expenses e.g. cars, mobile phones etc. Inevitably, you face a period where no sales are coming in yet you are paying out a salary and expenses. Plus, you run the very real risk of employing the wrong person.

A lower-cost and perhaps less risky sales route is via agents. Good agents should have existing contacts in your field, know buyers personally, and have detailed knowledge of your product's market. Unlike someone you recruit, a hired agent should be off to a flying start from day one. The big difference is that agents are paid purely on commission - if they don't sell they don't earn. The commission amount varies, but is rarely less than 7 per cent of the selling price and 25 per cent is not unheard of.

When interviewing a potential sales agent, you should find out:

- What products do they already sell? What other companies do they sell for? You want them to sell related but not competing products or services to yours.

- What is their knowledge of the trade and geographical area that you cover? Sound them out for specific knowledge of your target market.

- Who are their contacts?

- What is their proven selling record? Find out who their biggest customers are and talk to these directly.

- Do they appear honest, reliable and a suitable person to represent your business? Take up references and talk to their customers.

Finding professional representation is a challenge, so your product has to be first-class and your growth prospects good, with plenty of promotional material and back-up support. When you do find someone to represent your product, draw up an agreement to cover the main points, including geographical area, commission rates, when commission is payable, customers you want to continue dealing with yourself, training and support given, prohibiting competing agencies, and periods of notice required to terminate. Also build in an initial trial period, after which both parties can agree to part amicably.

Measuring Results

Sales results can take time to appear. In the meantime, you need to make sure you or your agent are doing things that eventually lead to successful sales. You should measure the following activities:

- Sales appointments made
- Sales calls made per day, per week, per month. Monitor trends, as last quarter's sales calls give you a good feel for this quarter's sales results.
- Quotations given
- Results
- New accounts opened
- Old accounts lost
- Average order size

The rule of 10

The rule of 10 is a business principle practiced by many businesses. It is also called the 10 per cent rule. In a sales environment, it means that if you have 100 potential sales leads, 10 of them will end up as potential buyers and 1 of them will buy (100 x 10% x 10%). So that is a 1% conversion rate (1 in 100 will buy).

Chapter 12. The 10 Most Important Things You Need To Succeed

In this chapter, I will tell you the things that I personally believe are extremely important in any business, whether you are working from home or not. I've personally practiced all of these during my business life.

Any idea can make money. It is as simple as that. You just have to think creative and be different. If other people are already doing what you are thinking about: just do it better. Find your USP and concentrate on that when selling your product.

1. What Is Your USP?

Your USP is your Unique Selling Point(s) or Proposition.
There might be hundreds of people selling the same product that you are selling. Why would customers buy from you? What is so special about your product or your service or about you? You need to be different from your competitors; you need to be Unique.

Your Unique Selling Point can be:
- Your price
- Your personal service
- Your customer service
- Your niche
- Your transport cost
- Extra detailed product description
- Exclusive products
- Your website
- YOU (as you sell yourself first)

Whatever you think your USP is, make sure you make this very clear to your potential customers. Your USP will make you STAND OUT, which is always a good thing. "Never follow the crowd" is what I strongly believe, whatever the business.

Don't follow the crowd.
There are a lot of whiners in every crowd!

Jump out to be different.

2. Do Your SWOT Analysis

Equally important is doing your SWOT Analysis. SWOT stands for Strengths, Weaknesses, Opportunities and Threats.

- Analyse what your strengths are — closely related to your USP.
- Analyse what your weaknesses are.
- Analyse your market opportunities.
- Analyse your threats — usually your competition.

Focus on your **strengths** when talking about your business.

Work out ways of improving on your **weaknesses:** do you need extra training, stock or equipment, for example?

Do your research on your market. Who are your existing and potential customers? What might their future needs be? Focus on making these needs into **opportunities** for your business by addressing these ahead of your competition.

Keep a regular eye on what others in your business sector are doing. Their new product ranges or pricing structure could become **threats** to your business.

Update your SWOT analysis regularly and remember to maximise your strengths and opportunities while minimising any weaknesses or threats.

3. Good Customer Service Is Crucial!

Good customer service is crucially important to succeed. Offer your products or services at a good price, get them done quickly and bend over backwards to offer very friendly customer service throughout the fulfilment process.

I once saw this sign:

> **Complaints department is on the 45th Floor.**
> **Elevator is out of order!**

Love it!

Here are a few customer service rules that I apply (when something has gone wrong) and suggest you to do the same:

-ALWAYS, ALWAYS apologise to your customer for what has happened. Even if you think the customer is wrong, they think they have a reason to complain, so you need to apologise.

- Listen to your customer; let them ramble on (they sometimes will), and when they have finished their story, tell them calmly that you are sorry for what has happened. Tell them you are not perfect, but you will put it right for them.

- Keep a list of your customer's complaints so you can learn from them and avoid the same thing happening to another customer.

- Under-promise and over-deliver.

- Respond IMMEDIATELY to a complaint.

- Don't EVER promise anything you can't do. Customers like it when they can say, "You promised me..." It puts them in a strong position to ask for extras from you.

- Respond IMMEDIATELY to a customer's email. Not in an hour, not later in the day—immediately! The customer will be VERY impressed by this, and you will have a better chance of keeping the customer happy and therefore ordering more from you.

- If a customer complains, that does not mean they will never order from you again. Providing you deal with the complaint promptly and solve the problem, the customer will be happy. Most customers experience awful customer service, so be different: be GOOD at customer service!

- All customers are humans who make mistakes, so you can make mistakes too. If you admit immediately that you made a mistake and that you will resolve it immediately, your customer will appreciate that.

- Keep your customer updated at all times. If you promised them an answer by email by 5 pm and you rely on other people, send the customer an email at 4 pm saying: "Sorry, I haven't got your answer yet, I will update you in the morning". Customers appreciate that.

- Don't keep a customer on hold for too long and if you do, play some hold music, otherwise customers don't know if they are still connected.

- Don't say, "Our terms and conditions say that...." Who reads them anyway? Customers don't like hearing this at all. They will immediately dislike you.

- Don't EVER shout and DON'T ever lose your temper.

- If you promised to call your customer, you MUST call them, even if you haven't got the solution yet. Tell them you are working on trying to get it resolved.

- Don't ever take it personally!

- Learn from your mistakes. We all make them!

- ALWAYS give your customer something as your way of saying sorry.

Your most unhappy customers are your greatest source of learning.
Bill Gates.

Give your customer something to "make up" for what happened. That will make them feel good; they will love it and they will appreciate it! Some examples are:

- A discount voucher for their next purchase.

- A gift card.

 - A flower.

- A discount voucher for a friend.

- Or even a box of Belgian Chocolates! Go the extra mile, buy a box of chocolates and ship it to your customer with a hand written sticky note saying "Sorry". People love it!

> **TOP TIP:** Identify your best customers. These are your most profitable ones, who come back to buy from you again and again. Work very hard to keep them happy. People are naturally proud to be special. Tell them they are a VIP customer and invite them to VIP-only sales/events.

Exceptions to the rule: very awkward customers, customers that you hope will never order from you again. That's indeed how awkward some customers can be, but you are still not ever allowed to lose your temper!

If you have staff: make sure they believe in all the above principles and apply them accordingly.

People will not remember what you sell, what price you are selling it for, but they **will** remember your attitude.

> **99% of what people remember about you is your attitude.**
> **Attitude is a little thing that makes a huge difference in your sales.**

4. Your Shoes

- ALWAYS, ALWAYS put yourself in your customer's shoes, whatever you do! This is THE most important business principle I think and one that so many people choose to totally ignore.

Yes, you do see a picture of shoes in a book about business ideas! Just so you remember to practice this principle, whatever you do in business: put yourself in your customer's shoes!

- Treat your customers the same way you want to be treated yourself.

- **Be** your customer, e.g. place an order on your site and see what your customer sees.

- Think like your customer.

- Empathy is extremely important in whatever business you are in. Empathy means to recognise your customer's emotions. Try to understand what your customer is feeling, why they complain, etc.

Let me give you one example of this: I went on a Cruise last year and when I entered into my cabin, I wanted to put my passport in the safe. The text with instructions on how to operate the safe was so small that I had to call my daughter (who was in another cabin) for help! Passengers on cruises are very often "older" people and their eyesight is not as good as a 20-year old. Now why did the person who designed the safe not make the text bigger so an older person (like me) can read it IMMEDIATELY? The answer is simple: the safe designer did NOT put himself in their customer's shoes; otherwise the text would have been bigger!
This might seem like a stupid example but if you pay attention to this, you will see for yourself that you will come across silly situations like this yourself.

If you don't care about your customers, someone else will!

5. Your Hats

You are going to need some hats! To be successful in business, you will have to wear several hats. The saying "wearing many hats" means you have different tasks or roles to perform. If you run your own business, here are the hats I think you will need to wear:

Thinking Hat: You will have to constantly think about new moneymaking opportunities.

Analytical Hat: You will have to analyse things e.g. will something make you money? How will you make it all work? Etc.

Commercial/Entrepreneur Hat: You'll have to look at everything with your commercial hat on. Look everywhere around you for business opportunities and new customers.

Patience Hat: Sometime things will go wrong, you are not earning the money you were hoping to earn or business is slow. You'll have to be patient, see what you need to do to change things around and get extra business.

Working Hat: Of course, you'll have to work and I mean work hard. In the beginning, that is. Once you've got your business going and you are earning some money, you can take on extra staff and perhaps take it easier.

Negotiating Hat: You need to be able to negotiate prices with your suppliers and with your customers. An example: if you offer a price to clean somebody's windows and your potential customer tells you the price is too high, you need to find out how much he/she is willing to pay and negotiate a price that is satisfying for your customer and yourself.

Focus Hat: You need to focus on your goals and don't stop until you've reached them. When you focus, you need to pretty much ignore everything else going on around you.

Focus On Your Focus!
Christine Clayfield

---

6. Cash Flow Is A Killer

I've already covered cash flow in the "Being An Entrepreneur" chapter, so please refer to that. Watching your cash flow really IS extremely important.

7. Pay Suppliers On Time

Your customers are most important but your suppliers are very important too. If you don't pay your suppliers on time, you won't get new stock, therefore you won't be able to sell new goods. This is a simple principle to always keep in mind.

If you start paying your suppliers too late, they might demand that you pay in advance for your next orders you place with them. This will affect your cash flow and as you already know...cash flow is a killer.

8. Buying Power

If you have to buy products for your business, make sure you negotiate the best buying prices possible. Buy some books on the subject if need be.
Don't forget the most important thing in buying is the same as in selling: you sell yourself FIRST to the buyer so he/she likes you. If the seller doesn't like you or your attitude, he/she won't give you good buying prices.

9. Don't Give Up

When times are hard and you are really trying to make some extra money: don't give up, keep going! Always remember Churchill's famous words:
Don't give up, don't ever, ever give up!

Winners are not people who never fail but people who never quit!

10. Your Mind

I kept the most important one for last: your mind! Whatever goes on in your mind is extremely important to what you will achieve.

The quality of most people's lives is a direct reflection of their expectations!

If you think you can't do it: you probably won't. You HAVE to always think positive and think that you CAN do it.

Get out there, do SOMETHING to earn some extra money. Forget all the soaps you are watching on the TV! Instead, plan how you are going to make some money! Read some interesting books about making money!

Remember: YOU have to make it happen. If you want to earn some extra money, YOU will have to work for it. Nobody is going to knock on your door and say: "I've got some money for you!". Well, it has never happened to me :).

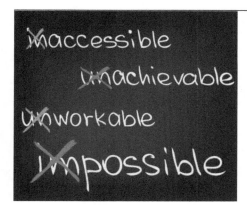

Get rid of the "un's" and "im's" in your mind but instead think as shown on the picture above.

Don't think life owes you something, because it doesn't! YOU have to make things happen. As an entrepreneur, you know that things don't just happen and that life is what you make it!

Say NO to these excuses:

- I can't do it

- I don't have any qualifications

- I haven't got the time

- I need to look after my children

- I haven't got the motivation

- My friends say I can't do it

- I am not confident enough

- I don't have any money

- It won't work

- I am OK and I don't need more money

Negative thinking will result in no action! Get out there and DO it! No more excuses: Excuses Are Your Limitations.

People who overcome their excuses are the ones who succeed!

Excuses Are Your Limitations!

And lastly: if you are too lazy to work, well, you could read a book with 1024 ideas but none of them will work if **you** are not going to put in the work. That's a fact!

None Of The Ideas In This Book Will Work **If YOU Don't!**

Chapter 13. Crazy Ideas Already Done

ANY idea is a good idea if it creates sales for you. Let's have a look first, before we start with the list of ideas, at some crazy ideas that are selling on the web.

 - Rent a cow: you can rent a cow for a period of time and the milk the cow produces during that time is made into cheese. All the cheese the cow produces is yours www.kuhleasing.ch (Swiss website).

- Buy a scrunched up piece of paper at www.origamiboulder.com

- Fake ATM receipts: you can buy fake ATM receipts showing a balance in excess of $400,000 (£238,000.) Ideal to impress your friends or potential girlfriend or in a restaurant, negotiating a house purchase, etc., by "accidently" dropping your receipt. Visit www.salesreceiptstore.com for more information. You can also buy fake hotel receipts.

- You don't like a certain person? Simply send some dog poo! www.dogdoo.com

- Buy sunglasses for dogs on www.doggles.com

- Buy a "willy brush" at www.willybrush.com

- Find your way in the dark with Glow strips www.jonnyglow.com

- Buy an eBook and make it into a printed book at www.homeboundbooks.com

- Send your message to the afterlife: www.afterlifetelegrams.com

- Pop bubbles on www.snapbubbles.com

- Want to have some fun with your friends/at a party? You can rent the Actroid DER2 Fembot (a female robot) for $3500 (£2100)! Just search for it.

- www.7billionworld.com 7,000,000,000 of us are displayed on this site!

- Find more silly sites on www.stupidness.com and www.totallystupid.com

Part 2) Make Money Offline

In this part are ideas to earn money for which you don't need a computer. However, these days, whatever business you are in, it is always a good idea to have a website saying what your business is all about as almost everybody searches online.

a. 35 Ways To Get Customers

Getting new customers for your home-based business doesn't need to cost a lot of money. Here are some ideas that you can apply for almost any of the moneymaking ideas in this book. Most of these points are based on *offline* activities. There are lots more ways to attract new customers when online. That could be a whole other book though, so I am not mentioning many of them here.

As already discussed, you can use other, affordable advertising techniques to attract new customers but here are some ideas that you can use for most methods mentioned later in this book.

1. Drop leaflets in people's post boxes. All you need is a computer, a printer and scissors. Design an A4 sheet with 2 or 4 small designs on what your business is about. One A4 sheet can contain 4 leaflets! You just need to cut them.

2. Tell everyone what you do and ask your friends to spread the word.

3. www.Vistaprint.com will print free business cards for you! Hand out your business cards everywhere you go.

4. Give out loyalty cards e.g. "£10% discount for your next purchase"

5. Put a sticker on your car and your friend's car advertising your business. A simple laser print out is OK as well; it doesn't have to be a sticker.

6. Advertise in the local shop, post office or super market. This can usually be done for very little money.

7. Place signs on community notice boards.

8. Place small advertisements in your local post office - usually a few pounds a month.

9. Attend local business meetings. These are usually free to attend and you can get a lot of new customers this way.

10. Join your local Chambers of Commerce. They usually have member directories.

11. ASK for testimonials. Don't wait until people give them to you. Great testimonials always work. You can show these to potential customers.

12. ASK for referrals. Don't wait until a customer gives you a potential name of a new customer. You've got to ask for it and you will be surprised how often people will just give you a new customer e.g. you've cleaned somebody's windows and your customer is very happy. Ask your customer: "Do you know anybody else that would appreciate my services?"

13. Door to door. I know this isn't much fun but hey, when you're first starting out, you've got to do everything possible to get new customers. Just don't go in your jeans and dirty T-shirt. You've got to make yourself look presentable.

14. Cold calling. You probably get, just like me, annoying phone calls from companies trying to sell you double glazing or a new phone, etc. These companies have been phoning people for over 20 years. Why? Because it works! You might have to make 100 calls to get one new customer but that might become a really good customer. Make sure you are always friendly and polite and don't be too pushy.

15. Look in the ad section of your local paper. There are often opportunities under the "Wanted" section.

16. Find out why potential customers didn't buy from you. You can learn a lot from this information to convince your next potential customer so they *will* buy from you.

17. Give away free samples in return of a testimonial.

18. School Newsletters Advertising. Every school has a newsletter and some schools allow advertising. Contact schools around you.

19. Go to trade shows and exhibitions, not as an exhibitor but to make contacts with the people who are exhibiting

20. Contact exhibition organisers. They often look for speakers during their events. Usually you can speak for free.

21. Give away coupons or discount vouchers.

22. Offer commission if customers refer you to new customers.

23. Send out a press release. Search for it online. Lots of press releases are distributed for free.

24. Create partnerships with other businesses.

25. Make sure you have a special introductory offer. Everybody likes good offers.

26. Radio Advertising on local radio stations is surprisingly affordable. Find out and run a few ads.

27. Put signs up in your front yard. Check regulations though.

28. Make sure you ask EVERY new customer where they've heard about your products or services. If 8 out of 10 people say they heard your ad on the radio, you know that your radio ad is a good investment.

29. Find out what your competition is NOT delivering and make sure you deliver that.

30. Look for speaking opportunities.

31. Reward your existing clients so they keep coming back.

32. Use the word "FREE" a lot. Everybody likes free stuff. The more you give away, the more you'll get back.

33. Always keep an eye on your competition and be better!

34. Always, always, always ASK for an order. So many sales people forget this!

35. Never forget that "Customer is King" and treat them accordingly. That way, they will keep coming back for more.

36. Contact local magazines and/or newspapers. They are always looking for stories from the local community. They might publish an editorial (usually free) on your new business.

37. Register online in relevant directories. A lot of these are free.

38. Social media is free: use it! Tell all your online friends about your new business.

39. Have a simple website explaining your services and make sure to put "Google Places" on your website.

40. Join online networking sites.

41. Start your own blog

42. Join social networks.

b. Counting The Pennies?

OK, now that you have a good idea of what is important in earning money/doing business it's time to look at all the ideas. It's up to you:

- Are you going to keep counting the pennies or do some extra work and have some money?

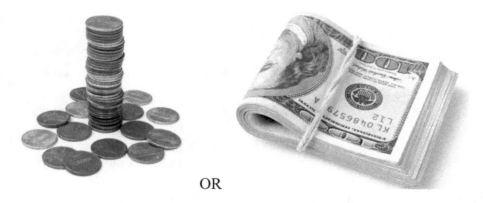

OR

- Are you going to be in debt forever or are you going to be free of debt?

Find some moneymaking methods that you like in this book and START working towards your goal! While you don't have to use a computer for any of the ideas listed in this part, some websites are mentioned as places where you might want to think about advertising your product or service if you decide to invest in a computer as your business expands.

c. Crowd funding

If you have a really good idea to start a business but you don't have the money, you can always try crowd funding or simply ask others for money. Crowd funding is where you explain your idea to people and people will invest in your business (giving you money) in return for something e.g. a share of the profit the business will make. The crowd funding industry is a billion dollar industry!

www.kickstarter.com
www.crowdfunding.com
www.crowdcube.com
www.indiegogo.com
www.venturefounders.co.uk
www.crowdfunder.co.uk

Chapter 14. Jobs With Animals

> **Important:** Ideas followed by "R" means that it is a repeat business. Once you have a customer, you will get repeat business from that customer, providing you do a good job. Let me give you an example. Let's say you have found work as a pet sitter. It is very likely that the person who pays you to pet-sit will want you back each time she/he needs your services. Another example: if are doing window cleaning and you find a few houses to do, the windows need cleaning every month/every six weeks so that is repeat business for you. It is always a good idea to start an "R business", as I call it.

Here we go. The long list of ideas begins here. I am an animal lover so I've decided to put jobs with animals first.

Do you like animals? There are numerous opportunities for those who enjoy being around dogs, cats, horses, fish and just about anything else that people keep as pets.

1. Pet Sitter - R

One thing about working with pets is that owners will pay to keep their pets safe, healthy, and yes, happy. This is a growing market, and people who provide these services can make as much as $40,000 (£24,000) a year. With this method, I am talking about you going to other people's houses. You can also do pet day care in your own house (see next method).

Of course pet sitting is more than just taking the family pet for a simple walk. Some of the duties of a professional pet sitter may include:

- Keeping the pet in your own home while the owner is away.
- Going to the owner's house and feeding the animal while the owner is away.
- Taking the dog/cat for a walk.
- Playing with the pet and providing stimulus and exercise.
- Taking the animal to the vet.

Generally most pet sitters charge anywhere from $15 to $25 (£10 to £15) per hour for these services. When keeping the pet overnight you can charge a higher rate, such as $35 to $40 (£20 to £25) per day. Think about this, if you average three pets per night, five nights a week, you could make $600 (over £350) a week!

116

If during the day, you also have numerous client requests for walks, then combined with your night boarding, it can become quite profitable and, more importantly, you are doing something you love and are getting paid for it.

Probably the most important factor needed to be successful in this industry is to just love animals and be willing to go the extra mile to provide outstanding care for them. Owners want someone they can trust and who will treat this member of their family just like they would their own. Pet owners are always asking other pet owners for someone who will take special care of their pet, so referrals are common. Provide great service and those referrals will keep coming.

So how do you start? Tell everyone you know that you are now a pet sitter. Volunteer at the local animal shelters or boarding kennels. You can get great experience working with animals and you will get to meet a lot of animal owners.

Leave your business cards or flyers at local pet groomers and vets. You may need to offer a referral fee in some cases. Perhaps for each customer they send you, you will pay a one-time finder's fee of $20 (£12). If your new customer continues to use you on a regular basis, the finder's fee will pay for itself in no time.

If you have a dog of your own, then walk it where other dog owners are walking theirs in your area. There are plenty of places; you just need to look for them. If you don't have a dog, then take your client's dog to those "fertile" places when you need to walk it. The point is that these are places where you will meet potential clients. When you see someone with a great looking dog, stop and tell them so. Start a conversation, exchange information, and when the opportunity arises, let them know about your services. This can be very effective.

You can register to be a pet sitter:
www.fetchpetcare.com
www.petsit.com
www.trustedhousesitters.com
UK:
www.animalangels.co.uk
www.findalocalpetsitter.co.uk
www.mydogbuddy.co.uk
www.petpals.com
www.petscastle.co.uk

2. Pet Day care - R

As a pet sitter, you could go to people's homes or look after the pets in your home. If you do pet day care, this usually means that the dog owner brings the dog to your home for you to look after for a whole day and maybe also a night. You could, of course, also arrange for you to collect the pet. With more and more working people owning pets, this can be a very profitable business. You could take 3 or 4 pets and get paid 4 times to do the same job.

When I take my dog to my pet day care, I pay $23 - £ 15 per day so if the day care centre has 10 pets (which they do in the case of my pet sitter), they will make $230 - £150 per day and $1,610 - £1,050 per week. Find out how much you can charge in your area.

Important: When I speak about pet day care I don't mean taking your dog to a kennel because the pets live in the house of the day care centre, not in a kennel.

This can give you repetitive income as once you've made a customer, they'll use your services on a regular basis.

3. Animal Kennels - R

I don't like to take my dogs to a kennel but there are plenty of owners who don't mind doing it. If you have a lot of space in your garden and you can put up some kennels, you could start an animal kennel business. The big difference with a day care centre is that when you take your animal to a kennel, they will be locked up most of the time but should come out to be taken for a walk at least once per day.

4. Dog Walker - R

If you don't have time to make the commitment that being a dog sitter involves, there are plenty of people who would pay someone to just take their dog for a walk while they're out at work.

On average you can make $15 to $25 (£10 to £15) per dog. You will need public liability insurance, just in case something happens to the dog or any members of the public whilst walking the dog.

5. Take Dogs To Training Classes - R

A lot of people own dogs but don't have the time to take them to training sessions. You can do it for them!

6. Pet Groomer - R

The advantage of this business is that it gives you a lot of flexibility. You can run this business from your home or you can provide an in-home service where you groom the pet at the owner's home. For this service you can charge a higher fee (see next method).

You'll need to be able to handle animals firmly but sensitively. It will help your credibility with the owners if you have a qualification in grooming, so it's worth contacting local colleges for details of courses, which vary in both length and cost.

Once you're qualified, put an advert in the local paper or pet shop and contact breeders or pet store owners to help promote you through word of mouth referral. This business often has repeat customers, so it is a good way to make money.

7. Mobile Pet Groomer - R

This means offering the same services as a pet groomer but you drive to people's houses. This is ideal if you don't have the room at home. An obvious disadvantage is that you have to drag all your tools around.

8. Animal Trainer

Have you had success training your own animals? If so, then you could offer your services to other owners. It would be worth considering getting a qualification to prove your ability. You can ask the owners to bring their pet to your home.

Then advertise in your local paper or at the local community centre. They often offer classes, and dog training and obedience is sometimes one of them. Also leave business cards or flyers with local vets, pet shops and boarding kennels.
I have not put this method as a repetitive income business as once the animal is trained, your services are no longer needed.

9. Mobile Animal Trainer

Offering the same services as an animal trainer but instead of doing it from your home, you go to people's houses.

10. Professional Pooper Scooper- R

How about being a Dog Waste Remover? Don't laugh, this is a job that a lot of dog owners do not want to do, and are willing to pay others for their service. The great thing about this is that it has repeat business. You are paid by the same clients every week or month for as long as they have dogs so there is tremendous financial security in a business like this.

You will generally have a contract that stipulates that you will go to their home a certain number of times a week. So let's say you have a client who you visit three times a week for $45 (over £25), and each visit only takes 30 minutes, including travelling time. If you were to fill your calendar and work a 40 hour week with clients like this, you could make over $60,000 (£37,000) a year!

You'll need to check out local regulations regarding waste removal, like how and where you'll dispose of what you've collected. Look in the phonebook or online for your town or city's Waste Management Service number.

www.pooper-scooper.com
www.apaws.org

11. Pet Parenting Lessons

Lots of parents have babies but don't know enough about educating babies in order for the babies to grown up into responsible and respectful adults. The same applies for pets: many people buy pets but don't really understand the pet world and how to best handle things so that the pet becomes a pleasant animal to be with. You can become a pet tutor and teach the pet owner important things to become a happy pet owner and to have a happy pet.
I believe there is a big gap in the market for pet parenting lessons.
You could teach things about feeding, what not to feed, when to feed and how often, behaviour issues, consistency is important, routine is important, tone of voice in commands is important, grooming, pet insurance, how much time should the owner spend with the pet for it not to become lonely, how often to walk, etc. Contact your local vets to get customers.

12. Animal Breeder

Or why not become an animal breeder? Many people still prefer a pet that is registered and has a traceable lineage. Breeding animals involves not just making money, but also responsibilities towards the animals you're breeding from, the animals they produce and potential new owners. For more information and advice consult The Kennel Club (in the UK), or its equivalent if you are outside the UK. You must contact your local government for rules and regulations.

13. Pet Relocation Service

People move house, people move country and moving a pet to another country is very often not easy to do because of the sea of regulations and legalities around pets. This is not always easy for pet owners to find out and is certainly time consuming. A pet relocation service will solve this problem for the pet owner. You will do all the administration, book the flight, deal with international permits and quarantine, etc.

www.ipata.org International Pet and Animal Transportation Association
www.airborneanimals.com
www.petaircarrier.com
www.happytailstravel.com

14. Pet Insurance Adviser - R

When pets become ill and need medical care, too often the pet owner does not have the money to treat the animal and therefore they either abandon the animal or take it to a shelter. This can often be prevented if the pet owner would have taken out pet insurance. There are too many pet owners who are not even aware that you can take pet insurance. Find out all the pet insurance policies available, analyse them and advise accordingly. Perhaps you can make a deal with a pet insurer so you get paid when you give them a new customer.
Some insurance companies will pay you a monthly fee for as long as the customer takes out the insurance - making this a recurring income method. Other companies will pay you a one-time fee each time you give them a new customer.

15. Dog Treat Baker - R

Can you cook? What about baking treats for dogs? Special dog treats are a booming business and many experts feel this could explode just like the speciality cupcake business has in the last few years. Some of the great things about this enterprise are that you get to be creative, you can do everything in your own home and your dog will love taste testing every biscuit experiment!

You can sell your product in local pet shops, vet surgeries, pet grooming stores, and even online. And when the business takes off and some large retailer contracts come in, the income potential is almost limitless.
Note: you will have to investigate the food labelling and food hygiene requirements if you deal with any food products, as there are very strict rules you will have to follow.

16. Gourmet Pet Food Specialist - R

Perhaps after you've mastered dog treat baking, you could move into becoming a Gourmet Pet Food Specialist.

Creating pet food that is organic, healthy and nourishing with the best ingredients is both gaining popularity and becoming increasingly profitable. Before you start, do some research and check out the nutritional requirements of different breeds of dogs or cats at different times in their lives. If you can target food towards, say, elderly dogs you could have a good niche market with lots of repeat business.

17. Home Made Dog Food - R

You don't need to be a Gourmet Food Specialist, you can just make dog food (or other animal food) and sell it to dog owners. People are busy these days and would like to give their animals alternatives to tinned food but haven't got the time to do it themselves. To start with, you can deliver the dog food locally in your car. If you grow big, you need to investigate packaging and labelling requirements.

There are some good books on Amazon on how to cook dog food and you can just buy these books and get started.

Instead of for dogs, you can also prepare homemade food for hamsters, guinea pigs, horses, goats and any other pets. You would be surprised how many pet owners don't like giving all the processed food there is available to their pets.

If you succeed in this type of business, you can build a very profitable business, as the animals have to eat every day!

18. Aquarium Maintenance - R

Maybe you prefer fish? Aquarium maintenance is a field that has some advantages. It does not have the inconveniences of dog walking or pet sitting. It does have the security of repeat business. People and businesses that need this service will hire you to come in on a regular basis for the long term.

A great-untapped market is servicing aquariums for businesses. There are many offices, restaurants, hotels and bars that have an aquarium on the premises. They often try to have the employees maintain it only to find out that they don't have the time or experience to do so. Fish die, everyone becomes upset, and a professional is hired and there you are: the aquarium maintenance professional!
You can get this sort of business by practicing "fear selling" e.g. you can say something along these lines: "if you don't clean your aquarium, your fish are very likely to die. Buying new fish will cost you a lot more than spending a little bit of money cleaning your aquarium". Knowing that some fish cost hundreds of dollars, this is an easy sale.

19. Pet Couture Designer/Seller

Are you creative and love animals? Like to sew? Maybe being a Pet Couture Designer/Seller is the way to go for you. This business enables you to design and/or produce your own brand of pet clothes, toys and accessories, or you can operate as a distributor of ready-made products.

20. Pond Maintenance and Design -R

People who love fish don't necessarily have the knowledge on how to design and make a pond or how to maintain a pond. You can create the pond and maintain it, meaning you will have to maintain it on a regular basis, resulting in recurring income for you.

21. Pet Minister

Losing a pet is like losing a member of the family for a lot of people. There are lots of pet owners who want to give their pet a "proper" memorial service. This is what a pet minister does: conduct pet funerals. The pet can be buried either on a pet cemetery or in people's gardens. You'll have to make sure you can cover both possibilities. Find out the legalities in your area, make contact with your local vets and distribute leaflets to get customers. You will need some money to set up to buy coffins, memorial plaques, a desk and a chair for your customer to sit in. You can sell basic funerals with a basic coffin and luxury funerals with a "state of the art coffin" and anything in between. You'll be surprised how much money people are willing to spend to say goodbye to their beloved pets.

22. Pet Grief Counsellor

The type of people who loved their pets so much that they can't cope with life any more after the pet died could speak to a pet grief counsellor. With millions of pets all around the world, there certainly are opportunities for this.
www.aplb.org is a non-profit organisation and stands for: The Association For Pet Loss And Bereavement.

23. Pet Memorial Plaques

If you think you can learn the art of engraving, you can design pet memorial plaques and signs. Just like people like to put a sign or plaque on graves, so do pet owners.

24. Pet Cemetery

Now I am not suggesting to start a pet cemetery in your backyard but if you own a piece of land (ideally in a remote location), you love pets and you don't mind the idea of running a pet cemetery, consider this one, which can be very profitable. Find out the legalities in your area.

Note: you could start all these up together as they are all very closely related:

- Pet Minister
- Pet Grief Counsellor
- Pet Memorial Plaques
- Pet Cemetery

Not a bad idea! I bet you can build a great business out of this if you put a lot of effort into it.

25. TV Or Magazine Advertising

Do you have a cute or clever pet? A dog or a cat or any other pet? Contact some advertising agencies as they are always looking for pets to use in magazine advertising or TV ads. You will get paid so they can use your pets in the advertisement.

26. Rent Your Land To Animals - R

If you own a large piece of land, you could rent it out for a play area for dogs. Charge $2 (£1.25) as an entrance fee. 20 dogs per day means $40 (£25) in your pocket! Dog owners are always looking for other dog owners so their dogs can play together. No need to say: only have friendly dogs that like other dogs!

You could also rent your land:

- For people who want to take their dogs for long walks e.g. if you own woodland
- For people who want to ride their horses
- For animal grazing e.g. sheep and goats as cattle can destroy your land.

I mention renting your land again later in the book but for methods that have nothing to do with animals.

27. Animal Parties

Children love parties and children love animals. Combine them both. If you have pets, set up a business taking your pets to children's parties to entertain the children. Instead of a clown, animals can entertain the children. Definitely worth considering if you have pets that can do cute tricks.

28. Host A Pet Party

Avon, Tupperware and 100's of other brands have built huge companies doing home parties. So why not host a pet party? You can buy things you will sell at wholesale prices and sell them with a profit at a pet party.

29. Open A Cat Cafe Or Dog Cafe

You've got a large room available in your house and some parking too? Why not start a cat or dog cafe? Animal owners like to hang out with other animal owners. You can make a great profit selling drinks, coffees, some cakes, etc. You could even rent a small space in your local area with parking to set up this business. Search for "calico cat cafe in Tokyo" to see a cat cafe, well...in Tokyo.

30. Animal Restaurant

Another idea that has done well for one person is a pet restaurant: search for "doggy style deli" on Google or YouTube and you will see what I mean. Brilliant idea! Animal owners are always looking for things to do with their dogs. The owners can meet up with other animal owners and the animals can meet up with their friends: works both ways! And each animal gets a birthday cake, well...on their birthday that is!

31. Animal Hotel

Why not go one step further and instead of a cafe or restaurant, open an animal hotel! We all like to spend time in a luxury hotel, and so do animals. They will be pampered! You can let the owner choose options like you do in a normal hotel:
- Single room
- Double room
- Family room (lots of dogs in one room)
- Room service
- TV in the room (yes, some animals like watching TV)
- etc.

32. Pet Photography

Maybe you love animals and are good at photography? Become a specialist in pet photography. Lots of pet owners like to have professional pictures done of their animals.

33. Pet Artist

Rather than photos, you can become a specialist in drawing pets or pets and their family members.

34. Sell Handmade Pet Accessories

Perhaps you love animals and are good at knitting or making things? This is the perfect business for you. You could sell clothes, bow ties, dog jewellery (yes, why not!), dog neck warmers, toys, etc. Visit the websites listed below and search for "dog accessories" to get some ideas. You can sell your created products at fairs, car boot sales, markets and also online.

www.etsy.com
www.folksy.com
www.artfire.com

35. Pet Food Home Delivery - R

We all know that if you buy items in bulk, they become cheaper. The downside: carrying around bulk items is a burden and most people don't like doing this. You can do it for them! Buying dog food is expensive but carrying around a 50 pound (25kg) bag of dog food is something none of us like doing. This is a relatively easy business to start and all you need to have is:
- A bit of money to buy stock
- A car
- Some space in your house to stock the products
- A wholesaler that will sell you bulk animal food

You can turn this business into a subscription service: e.g. each month you supply the same bag of food to the same customers.

36. Pet Massage

Pets, just like humans, get arthritis or any other conditions that are painful. Lots of people get pain relief through massages and so do lots of animals. So if you love animals, and you have a dog massage diploma, you've got a business!

37. Dog Bathing - R

Most owners give their dogs a bath now and again but are not always looking forward to this. Why not solve their problems and bathe the dogs for the owner? Again, you can get regular business out of this as, if you do a good job, the owners will come back to you on a regular basis.
You could bathe the dogs in your own home or in the owner's home.

38. Worm Farming

If you have some space in your garden, why not consider starting a worm farm. Worms are sold to sporting goods stores and gas stations for fishing bait. Worms are also sold for use in compost bins and gardens. Even worm poop is being sold!

39. Cricket Farming

Lots of animals (lizards, salamanders, etc.) eat crickets for their daily food and owners of these pets usually buy their crickets somewhere instead of farming them. You can farm crickets and sell them to pet stores, sell them to individuals or sell them online. This is relatively cheap to start as a business. Search online for more details on how to start. These companies have done it:

www.millbrookcrickets.com

www.ghann.com

40. Maggot Farming

Maggots are sold as fishing bait and there are millions of fishermen all around the world. There is a farm in the USA that sells four million maggots every single week so this can be a profitable business.

41. Pet Taxi

Pet owners often don't have the time to drive their pet around e.g. to the vet, to the kennel, to the pet sitter. You can do it for them and advertise your services at a local pet shop.

42. Pet Writer

If you have a lot of knowledge about a certain pet, share it with the world. It has never been easier to publish a book these days. Your book can be on Amazon in no time if you sign up with www.Createspace.com, which is Amazon's book publishing business.

43. Build Doghouses

Sure, you need to be creative for this one but if you are good at building things, I believe there is a big market for personalised doghouses. You can start by just selling them by putting them in your front yard or on eBay.

44. Sell Printed Pet Products

A mug with the owner's dog on? A mouse mat with a picture of a cat? A pen with a fish picture? A pin badge with "I Love My Labrador" on it? It is all easy to do these days. All you need is a computer, a scanner, transfer paper and a heat press. You can make one-off mugs, caps, T-shirts, etc. and sell them at fairs, flea markets and more.

You could design key rings, mugs, caps, T-shirts, bumper stickers, button badges, balloons, mouse mats, etc. Use your imagination. Search for "heat press machine" to find out what you need.

45. Be A Taxidermist

Lots of people like to see their animals forever and pay a taxidermist to "stuff the animal". Taxidermy is removing the skin from an animal and use that to make an exact replica of the animal. People are prepared to pay a lot of money for this because they love their pets so much. Perhaps your local vet will let you put business cards on their counter.

46. Sell Seasonal Pet Products

You don't like working all year but don't mind working a few months per year? Selling seasonal pet products is something to consider. Everybody seems to be in a spending-spirit around Christmas and pet owners don't just buy presents for the family but also for their pets. Visit www.jacquelinesoriginals.com or www.bonniedogs.co.uk for some ideas or search for "seasonal pet products". You can buy the products wholesale and sell them with a profit. You can sell your products at fairs, flea markets and maybe even at your local vet.

47. Keep Some Livestock

Keeping animals in your garden can be great fun and relaxing as well. If you have the land available – or even just a small backyard – keep some chickens, ducks or goats and sell eggs and milk to the public. If you only keep a small number of birds or animals, you can simply put a sign up on your gate or advertise in the local paper. Make sure to check out your local regulations.

48. Run A Mini Zoo

If you have some land and some animals and you also love kids, a mini zoo might be your thing. Kids love animals. Ideal animals to keep are: mini goats or goats, chickens, a dog, a cat, a duck or two and perhaps even some pigs. Mums are always looking for things to do with the kids in the weekends. Charge an entrance fee and sell food as well to make even more money. If you have a pony, you could also charge for a ride on the pony.

49. Sell Honey From Your Bees

You can keep bees these days with very low start up costs and there are lots of books available on how to keep bees. Honey is healthy and most people are prepared to pay for nice, fresh honey.

50. Horse Riding Lessons

You have a pony or a horse and some land and you know how to ride a horse? Give riding lessons, charge a cheaper rate than your competition and you're likely to get some business.

51. Become A Vet Assistant

A vet assistant helps the vet but is not allowed to prescribe medications, do operations, etc. To become a vet assistant, you don't need years of studying, as it is easier to do.

52. Help In An Animal Shelter

Most animal shelters are very busy and have difficulty keeping up the work needed to care for the animals. You can help out. You won't earn bundles of money but still some shelters do pay for their helpers.

53. Assess Suitability For A Guide Dog

My regular dog sitter gets new puppies in all the time as she assesses if the puppies will be suitable to be trained for guide dogs. After approx. 9 months to a year, the dogs leave her house and either new owners are found for them or the dogs that are suitable are going to be trained for a guide dog. You will need some training. Contact the guide dog association to find out if there are vacancies in your area.
Be aware that you will need to be strong, as you will have to let go of the dogs after you've built a bond with them.

54. Show Your Animals

If you fancy showing dogs and you are good at training dogs, this might be suitable for you. Find out where the dog shows are and go and show your dog. If you have other animals, there are lots of different types of animal shows e.g. birds, chickens, goats, etc. You must realise first though that only the winners get paid and not all the participants.

55. Foster Animals

Sometimes animal welfare organisations get dogs or other animals who need to be socialised and cannot be alone for a long time. In this case, those animals go to foster homes until a new owner has been found. You can give a home to a foster animal but be aware that you will have to give the animal back so make sure you're not getting too loved-up, otherwise it will be too painful to give the animal back. Contact your local animals shelters.

56. Pet Franchisee

The pet trade and everything to do with pets means huge business! Not surprisingly, there are a lot of pet franchises available, and you could become a franchisee (own a franchise). If you have the money to invest, perhaps being a pet franchisee is right up your street. I have listed a few but if you search for "pet franchise", you will find a lot more.

USA:

www.preppypet.com
www.petbutler.com
www.dogdaycare.com
www.happytailsdogspa.net
www.barkbusters.com
www.petlodgeusa.com
www.petsareinn.com
www.doodycalls.com
www.petsuppliesplus.com

UK:

www.animalsathome.co.uk
www.husse.co.uk
www.joggydoggy.co.uk
www.oscars.co.uk
www.petpals.com
www.petshomesandgardens.co.uk
www.petstay.net
www.scampsandchamps.co.uk
www.waggingtailsfranchise.co.uk
www.walkmydog.co.uk

And ... you can also apply for a part-time job with any of the franchisees as they will need staff members.

57. Inventor

I have put this one last in the methods to earn money with animals because inventing something and getting it to a successful business is time consuming and expensive. If you have a great idea for inventing something pet-related, there is an enormous market open for you. You could invent a cat toy, a dog toy, a special drinking bowl, a bird toy, a bird feeder, an aquarium ornament, animal clothes, a pet collar, a pet house, a pet bed, etc. Use your imagination!

Chapter 15. Make Money From Your Car

58. Driving - R

If you hold a driver's license and have a reasonably new, clean and well-maintained car, you can make money out of using it. You can offer your services to drive people to the airport, pick up and drop off children at school (this would be recurring as you'll have to drive the children to school every school day), take the elderly to different locations etc.

You'll need to inform your insurance company and check with the local authority regarding any licenses you may need for this type of work. Advertise in your local paper, day care centres etc. You can expect increased trade through repeat business and word of mouth recommendations.

59. Become A Courier - R

If you own a car and have insurance, there are numerous ways to turn it into a profit machine. In spite of all the modern communication technology, there is still a need for Couriers. A Courier is basically someone who personally drives something from one location to another. For instance, when a car repair shop needs parts, an auto parts courier picks up the parts at the suppliers and delivers them to the repair shop.
Lots of blue chip companies with offices in large cities use motorbike couriers all the time e.g. they want to pick up a prototype and need to get it from one site of the city to the other within an hour. Can't be done by car but can be done by motorbike. As a motorbike courier you can earn good money: one of my employee's friends does this and he gets paid $100(£62) per trip. Sometimes he does 5 trips per day, that's $500 (£312) per day!
Big downside though: inhaling the car exhausts being on your motorbike most of the day.

You'll need to let your insurance company know about your new business and check with the local authority regarding any licenses you may need.

60. Removals

If you have a truck or van, you can offer removal services. There are always people ready to pay for these types of services and if you've ever had to do this type of work, you know there are opportunities to make money here.

61. Restaurant Delivery Driver - R

Drivers will often contract with take away restaurants, such as pizza houses, to deliver orders that have been phoned in. While in some cases the couriers are employees, others may be free lancers.

It is not always easy to commit an employee to courier services, and a business may prefer to contract someone like you to perform these services, or pay you per courier job.

People who make money as couriers have told me that the best way to enter this field is to do a lot of calling and visiting businesses that need this type of service. Many will turn you down because they already have someone. But eventually there will be opportunities if you are persistent.

62. Hire Out Your Car

If you are not using your car on a day-to-day basis, you can easily hire it out to other users.
https://carclub.easycar.com (in the UK)
www.relayrides.com (in the US) allow you to either rent or lend your car to others, and get paid in the process.

www.starcarhire.co.uk They source special cars for all types of events.

63. Take Children To School - R

A school run in the morning can make you some extra money. You can get 4 kids in the car and perhaps to two or three different runs - depending how long traffic will take you to get to school. Of course, you can often pick up the kids again when school is finished.

64. Advertise On Your Car - R

There are companies that will pay you a monthly fee to advertise their services on your car. From $50 (£30) per month you can have a small sticker displayed on your window to up to $900 (£575) per month if you advertise all over your car. That is SUPER easy income! Visit:
 http://www.supercarads.co.uk
www.car-wraps-advertising.com
www.freecarmedia.com
www.autowrapped.com
www.comm-motion.com
www.myfreecar.com
www.mycaradvert.com
www.carquids.com

65. Car Sharing - R

Start car sharing with a trusted friend or colleague: take it in turns to drive, with the non-driver paying part of the petrol costs. There are a number of websites dedicated to this including
www.liftshare.com/uk/
www.zipcar.co.uk
 www.carpoolworld.com/ in the US
www.gocarshare.com
www.shareacar.com
www.blablacar.com

66. Become A Driving Instructor

You will probably find lots of competition with this but nevertheless it is easy to get started: teach people how to drive to get their driving license. Find out legalities in your area.

67. Start A Repossession Service

In lots of parts of the world, economy is not going all that well and where there is a recession, there are people who can't pay their debts. You can work for loan companies and banks and pick up cars from people who can no longer afford to pay their bills. You will usually get paid per collection you do.
You will, of course, need a tow truck for this as well as storage space for your truck. Check out legalities in your area.

68. Become A Driver

Uber is a company that finds drivers for people who want to get from A to B without using a traditional taxi service. Uber's services are now available in over 53 countries and rapidly growing. Their services are cheaper than a taxi. Apply to become a driver at www.uber.com

Lyft is a similar company. You can apply to become a driver:
www.lyft.com (USA only)

You have a large car e.g. for six or seven passengers? Definitely worth applying, as I've read online they have a shortage for these vehicles and high demand.

In both cases (Lyft and Uber) you can download their App.

69. Become A Licensed Taxi Driver

As a taxi driver you can set your own hours and if you are in a busy city, you only have to work a few hours a day to earn some extra money. Found out in your area what is needed to become a licensed taxi driver.

70. Provide An Airport Shuttle Service

Without a doubt, there will be lots of people going on holiday within a 10 or 30 miles radius from where you live. You could become specialised in taking people to the airport and picking them up after their holiday. Provide a cheaper service than your competition. Distribute leaflets and spread the word. Try and do a deal with a local travel agency.

71. Rent Out Your Trailer

If you have a trailer just sitting on your land, you can rent it out. Charge a lot less compared to the bigger companies that rent out trailers.

Chapter 16. Make Money From What's In Your Home

72. Rent Your Couch Or Rent A Room - R

Couch surfing is becoming more and more popular. You can rent a couch or a room, as some people are happy just with a couch for a few days. If you have a spare room in your home e.g. a loft, basement etc., you can significantly boost your income by renting a spare room. You can also turn this spare room into a temporary place to stay if you live in a town or city, for example by letting commuters stay for a night or so during the working week. If you own your own home you can do what you like with it but it would be advisable to let both your mortgage and insurance companies know if you decide to go down this route. If you are renting your home, you'll need to check with your landlord first.

www.airbnb.co.uk: you can list your property and the site will take a percentage of what your renting price is.

www.roomorama.com

You can register your room free on www.easyroommate.com and www.spareroom.com

73. Host A Foreign Student - R

You can also rent your room to foreign students who need a place to stay. Search online to find companies specialising in finding rooms for foreign students. You will also have to provide meals to the students but you will get paid for your expenses. This can earn you hundreds of dollars/pounds per month and of course, you will get paid every month as long as the student lives with you. Take two students if you have the room!

www.homestaynetwork.com

www.into-education.co.uk

74. Offer Storage Space - R

If you have one or two rooms you never use, why not clear it out and sell it as storage space. This is a growing business in many parts of the world. The Big Yellow Company is doing very well simply from renting storage space. Offer storage cheaper than the well-known companies and you might be surprised how quickly you will get customers.

You can advertise your services on websites such as www.gumtree.com

www.elance.com

www.craigslist.org

Etc.

It must be mentioned that one's homeowner insurance will not cover the value of merchandise stored that they do not own.

75. Rent Out Your Driveway - R

If you have an extra car parking space available, why not rent it out. There are thousands of people commuting who pay lots of money for the car park spaces of the train stations. Offer your space a lot cheaper and you will likely rent it. This is all year round income. Start by just putting a sign on your driveway saying people can rent it. The harder it is to find on-street parking in your area, the more money you can charge for parking.

Rent out your drive or car parking space at:
- www.parkatmyhouse.com
- www.parkonmydrive.com
- www.usemyspace.co.uk
- www.yourparkingspace.co.uk
- www.yourparkingspace.co.uk
- www.justpark.com

76. Rent Your Pool

Should you be so lucky to have a pool, why not make some extra cash by renting it out. If you have an indoor pool, this can be extra money all year round. Contact some local youth organisations to make a deal with them: they might come every week with 10 kids or so. Of course, you'll have to be prepared to clean up afterwards. You've got to pay for your chemicals to keep the pool clean all year so why not get some money back!

77. Run A Bed & Breakfast

You could also turn your home into a bed and breakfast (B&B). You can start advertising your home in your local paper, register with the local tourist board or online sites such as www.tripadvisor.com. Make sure to check your local rules and regulations.

78. Make Your Home A Movie Star

It is not just Britain's stately homes or landmark buildings that are in demand by directors of films or TV shows. Many of these use ordinary homes or flats, and you could earn money by offering your home as a space to film in. You can contact an independent agency such as www.lavishlocations.com or www.filmlondon.org.uk.

79. Hold A Garage Sale Or Yard Sale

Get everything out of your house that you never use or don't really need and sell it. Distribute some leaflets in your local area and put a sign outside your house, near the road, announcing the date and time of the sale. You would be surprised at what people will buy!

80. Rent Your Land - R

If you have a large piece of land, you can rent it e.g.
- For caravans to park on
- Campers
- For hunters (if you own woodlands). It is legal to hunt for certain animals. Check out the regulations in your area.
- For parking space
www.airbnb.co.uk is a site where you can list your back garden for rent.

81. Rent Out Garden Allotments - R

Lots of people like growing their own fruit, vegetable or flowers but don't have the space. If you have a large garden, you can divide it into allotments and rent them out. You will get repetitive income from this, as you will collect either monthly or yearly rent. Of course, you will need to be a sociable person as you will always have people on your property but on a positive note you will get to know a lot of people in your area and perhaps make some new friends. Make sure you also have parking spaces available.

82. Rent Your Stuff

You can make extra cash by renting your stuff: your power tools, your trailer, your leaf blower, your horse, your pregnancy clothes, your bike, your video games, clothing, books, musical instruments, trailers, snow equipment, office equipment, sports gear, workshops, parking, garden equipment, baby equipment, tools, gadgets, handbags, books, camping gear, etc.
www.loanables.com
www.rentmyitems.com
www.rentnotbuy.co.uk
www.rentything.com
www.zilok.com
www.rentmyitems.com
www.bagborrowsteal.com
www.spinlister.com (specialised in bikes, surfing and snow equipment)

83. Advertise On Your Fence - R

If you have a large fence and don't mind it being cluttered (in return for money), you can contact local businesses to see if they are prepared to pay you to advertise on your fence. The companies will make the sign, give it to you and all you do is hang the sign up and take the money. It doesn't get much easier than this. Check out legalities though.

84. Photo Shoots In Your Home

Magazine and film companies are always looking for places for photo shoots. Visit www.locationworks.com for more information and prices

85. House Swapping

This will in a way earn you money, as you won't have to pay for a hotel or villa when you go on holiday yourself.

You can swap your home with another family whilst you go to their home, so you are swapping houses for the duration of your holiday.

www.intervac.com
www.homeforexchange.com
www.lovehomeswap.com
www.easyhouseexchange.com

86. Chop And Sell Wood

Do you have trees on your property? Why not create an income from them by chopping the wood and selling it as firewood. Get a chainsaw and some big bags and you're good to get started. Start by spreading the word and put a sign up in your front yard. If you don't have trees in your garden, contact people in your area and split the profit. Lots of people do have trees but are too lazy to chop the wood.
Make sure to check out the legalities in your area as, in some areas, it is illegal to chop a certain type of trees.

87. Host A Quiz Night Or Poker Night

Get some people together and charge a small fee to attend to host a fun evening. You'll be surprised how many people will turn up and they are all willing to pay a small fee to you for organising the event. Have some fun and get to know some people, why not!

88. Rent A Dark Room

If you have a spare room, you can turn it into a dark room and rent it out to photographers who don't have a dark room in their own house.

89. Rent A Tanning Bed - R

If you have a tanning bed, why not rent it out. Even if you don't have a tanning bed but you have a spare room, you can buy a tanning bed and rent it out. Make sure your customers do know about the dangers of tanning too much and too often. Protect yourself from possible lawsuits by hanging up signs warning customers of the dangers. Millions of people still use tanning beds, even after they know the potential dangers.

90. Turn Your Home Into A Children's Playhouse

If you love children and you've got a spare room, why not turn it into an area ideal for children to play in. Parents are always looking for places to go with their children and are prepared to pay a small fee for attending.

91. Foster A Child - R

Adoption agencies are sometimes looking for temporary accommodation for children. Why not get in contact with them if you have a spare room? You will get paid for it and help a child at the same time. Visit www.adopting.org. You will need to qualify as a suitable candidate and therefore undergo some tests and a police-check.

92. Sell Soil

If you have some extra land, sell the soil! There are always gardeners looking for some soil. How simple is this? All you need to get started are some big bags and a sign outside your house.

93. Rent Your DVD's

You've got a stack of DVD's hanging around? Instead of selling them, why not rent them over and over again. The word will soon spread and before you know it you are renting 20 DVD's per week!

94. Sell Your DVD's, Games And CD's

Lots of people sell stuff on eBay but you can avoid the eBay listing fees by selling on other sites:
www.spun.com
www.musicmagpie.com
www.decluttr.com
Or sign up for an Amazon Reseller Account.

95. Sell Your Books

An Amazon Reseller account is the best way to sell your unwanted books. All you need to do is type in the barcode number of the item and Amazon does the rest for you: taking the payment and sending you the order. Amazon will take a commission on the sale and pay your earnings in your bank account. All you need to do is post the book to the buyer. You can also sell them on eBay or:

www.webuybooks.co.uk
www.zapper.co.uk
www.ziffit.com
www.bookscouter.com
www.mybookbuyer.com

96. Sell Your Old Jewellery

If you have old gold or silver jewellery, you may be able to sell it for a good price to a gold dealer. You can also sell scrap gold, if you have any. You can visit a local dealer or send your jewellery by post.

97. Sell Everything You Never Use

Go through every cupboard in your house and put everything you've never used in the last 10 years on a pile. Chances are you won't use it in the next 10 years either so just create some income and sell it. There are lots of auction sites and selling sites other than eBay, a few being:

www.amazon.co.uk
www.amazon.com
www.bidstart.com
www.bidz.com
www.bonanza.com
www.cardcash.com
www.cqout.com
www.ealtbay.com
www.ebid.net
www.gazelle.com
www.gumtree.com
www.half.com (half.ebay.com)
www.ioffer.com
www.madbid.com
www.onlineauction.com
www.oodle.com
www.preloved.co.uk
www.rubylane.com
www.sell.com
www.swoggi.co.uk

www.the-saleroom.com
www.tias.com
www.totalbids.co.uk
www.vivastreet.com
www.webidz.com
www.webuy.com

For arts & crafts:
www.folksy.com
www.etsy.com
www.folksy.com
www.artfire.com
www.artpal.com
www.zazzle.com

Chapter 17. Home, Garden And Outdoor Jobs

98. House Sitter - R

You can earn money by looking after people's houses while they are away on holiday/business trip/weekend. Picking up the mail, looking after plants, switch lights on or off and making sure the house is secured are some of the duties that you can negotiate with your clients. It would be a good idea to have these duties confirmed in writing. You'll need to arrange insurance to cover you against any losses, damage or breakages that happen while you're in the client's home.

To start with, advertise yourself as a house sitter in your local newspaper. You can choose how often you want to 'sit' and which areas you'll cover. You'll get the chance to live in a wide range of properties and areas with a good possibility of repeat business and personal recommendations from satisfied clients.

99. Cleaning - R

There is always a demand for reliable house cleaners. You only need a few basic tools and cleaning products and, to begin with, you could use your clients' equipment. Tell your friends that you're now available for house cleaning and advertise in local shops and your local paper or respond to ads from people looking for cleaners. There are usually a lot of ads in the papers for cleaners.

100. Natural Cleaning - R

Out of respect for the environment, many people now don't like to use chemical products to clean their house. If you become specialised in cleaning but only with natural cleaning products, you might get lots of customers and the beauty is that you will get repeat business as once cleaned, everything just gets dirty again...

101. Window Cleaning - R

You don't need any diplomas or certificates for this one; all you need to do is be able to clean windows. Now anybody can do this! People are busy these days juggling work, kids and household jobs. I've never met anybody who likes cleaning their windows. So there is a massive market for this.
I met a guy four years ago who started a business cleaning windows, he charges $3 (£2) per window with a minimum spend of $20 (£13) per house.

He now has 5 people working for him and is living a reasonably luxury lifestyle. Most of his new customers come from word of mouth.

I have a window cleaner myself and I probably always will!

102. Caravan Cleaning - R

Is there a caravan site close to you? All those caravans need cleaning on a regular basis to impress the customers who stay in the caravans during their breaks or holidays. Of course, the inside of the caravans will be cleaned by the site's cleaning staff but they also need cleaning on the outside. That's the job I am talking about here. All you need is some safe ladders, a bucket and sponge and you are good to go. The beauty of this job is: if you can clean one caravan, you can usually clean all of them. The best part: they need cleaning on a regular basis so it is repeat business therefore repeat income.

103. Carpet Cleaning Specialist

If you become a specialist in carpet cleaning, you can earn good money relatively easy. All you need is a car and a professional carpet-cleaning machine. You can charge per room or per house. You can easily charge $45 (£30) to clean a small room, which will take maximum one hour with your professional machine. You can do 5 rooms per day and earn $225 (£150) per day! Your only investment is a bit of petrol for your car and some cleaning products, all the rest is pure profit! It is much cheaper for the owner to have a carpet cleaned compared to having to buy new carpet so this business is easy to sell to potential new customers.

104. Curtains And Blinds Specialist

Homes, restaurants and businesses: they all need their curtains cleaned now and again. If you specialise in this, you might not have a lot of competition in your area.

105. Car Cleaning - R

Car cleaning is always in demand. You can do this from home if you live in a town or city, but otherwise you can stand at a busy road and offer your services.

Contact local companies and see if you can do a deal by washing the cars on the employee's car park. You can also wash the cars of people in your area. Millions of car owners prefer their cars washed by hand rather than machines. All you need is a bucket, shampoo, water, a sponge and some cloths. How easy is this?

106. Car Detailing

For some people just a car wash is not enough, as they want their car to properly shine like a mirror. You can make these people happy by waxing and polishing their car inside and give your customer a car that is super duper clean inside and out. Every single space, however small, will have to be cleaned. Hard work but if this is your thing: enjoy. Companies' cars need to look "top-notch" for the services they provide e.g. funeral business, companies who hire wedding cars, etc. These are great potential customers for you.

107. Boat Cleaning - R

I know several people who own boats and they all say the same thing: they don't like cleaning their boat. I am pretty sure if they would find a leaflet on their boat one morning with cleaning services, they would take up the offer.
The good thing is that, because of the sea salt, the boats will need cleaning on a regular basis to keep them looking nice so this is repetitive income. Some resorts and harbours have boat-parking areas, where the boats are stored away out of season. This is an ideal place to offer your cleaning services by distributing leaflets.

108. Event Clean-up

Organising events can be fun and attending an event more fun but who likes to do the cleaning up after the event? Nobody! This is where you come in; you can advertise your services to clean up events such as weddings, corporate parties, birthday parties, charity events, etc. This, again, is easy to earn money with as no investment other than a car and some cleaning material is needed.

109. Ironing/Laundry Services - R

There is always demand for busy families to have their ironing/laundry done. You can do this from your own home and advertise your services locally or respond to people who have placed ads looking for people to do their ironing.

110. Become A Housekeeper - R

In most marriages, both wife and husband work so juggling the kids, food, housework, etc. is not always easy. People who have good incomes can afford a part or full time housekeeper and that could be you. Your duties could be cooking, doing the laundry and the ironing, making food, doing the washing up, cleaning, etc. Literally everything that a housewife would do in the house. It's not only mansions and castles that have housekeepers. Ordinary people do as well: one of my friends has had a housekeeper for over 10 years and she will have one as long as she can afford it, so she says.

111. Become A Local Handyman

There is always demand for a handyman for plumbing, decorating, carpentry, garden work etc. Collect together a basic toolkit and start by advertising your services in the local paper/free local paper or online directories.

Think of all the opportunities available. Some require hard work, and some minor skills, but they are there. If you live in a cold climate, you can be a Snow and Ice Remover, or Gutter Cleaner.

If you have a little more skill or experience around the house, you may want to offer your home services as a Roof Repairer, House Painter, Pool Cleaner, Maintenance Technician, Fence Installer, Deck Maintenance and Repairman, Solar Energy Consultant or Pest Control Specialist.

The great thing about all these opportunities is that they can be started with little to no money, especially if you are willing to knock on doors or simply drop leaflets in people's post boxes. If you are working with the homeowner on one of these services, you can offer others as well. So let's say you have a gardening service, you can offer to perform pool cleaning on the same days that you do the gardening. In the winter you can offer snow-removing services, and in the autumn, gutter cleaning. So you have a year round income.

Building a network of other home service professionals who you can refer, and who can refer you, can create many unexpected income opportunities.

112. Gardening - R

Many homes have their own gardening equipment, even if they also use a gardener. By using their equipment, you are able to start generating income immediately with only the cost of business cards. Gardening is a very popular service and, if you get just one job and give a good service, you'll pick up recommendations in the neighbourhood. As you save a little money, you can watch out for small ads for a good quality used mower and use this. The great thing: you don't need any diploma or certificate to do some gardening and it's healthy being in the fresh air! A lot of people with large gardens have the money to pay for a gardener.

113. Lawn Care Specialist - R

Let's look at lawn care first. This is one of the simplest businesses to start. If you are willing to print up business cards and walk door-to-door you can build such a business. Of course, going door-to-door is not for everyone. But if you can do it, you can be successful in just about any of the businesses described in this chapter. You may not have the tools in the beginning and they might require a small investment. If this is a problem, then you can try offering a discount rate to homeowners if they let you use their own lawn equipment. So how does it work financially? The rates you can charge will depend on your area and the services you provide. Typically, you would charge your client a monthly rate. That might include a weekly or fortnightly visit. As well as mowing, it might include other services like trimming shrubs and trees, leaf and debris clean-up, providing nutrients to the lawn and plants and other general or specialised needs of the homeowner.

What you can charge depends on your area, your competition and your clients. Not to mention that if you offer exceptionally great service, clients are often willing to pay more than the going rate.

If becoming a Lawn Care Specialist sounds interesting to you, you can eventually turn it into a speciality such as an Organic Lawn Care Provider, Landscape Artist or Composting Specialist. There are also opportunities to become a Commercial Landscape Specialist - think about all the hotels, restaurants and office buildings you have seen that have flowers, grass, or plants on the premises. Perhaps the best thing about being a Lawn Care Specialist is that as long as you take good care of your customers, they will be loyal and you will have a dependable long-term income.

114. Floristry

If you have the garden, and weather for it, you can grow your own flowers and sell them as a florist. Or you can cash in on selling artificial flowers to local retail outlets, restaurants etc.

115. Vegetables & Fruit Growing - R

If your garden space is suitable, you can plant and grow vegetables and fruit to sell to local shops, farmer's markets or to residents. Start with a sign outside your door.

116. Herb Farming - R

Herbs are extremely popular these days. I am not just talking about herbs that you eat, I am talking about all kinds of herbs: herbal tea, herbal baths, herbal candles, medicinal herbs and not to forget aromatherapy. If you like gardening, why not consider a herb farm. You can sell your herbs to retail or even wholesale. You can start this very small and grow it to a large business if you are successful.
Your customers can be wholesale distributors, restaurants, grocery shops, health product manufacturers, etc.

117. Grow Plants And Sell Them

If you've got some space and love working with plants, why not grow them and sell them at local fairs.

118. Start A Hydroponics Business

Hydroponics is a way of growing plants without soil but using mineral nutrient solutions and water. You can sell what you've grown.

119. Become A Task Rabbit

Go to www.taskrabbit.com / www.taskrabbit.co.uk and sign up to be a 'Tasker'. This will allow people who are visiting this website in need of help with tasks to find you and your services. Taskrabbit is a site where people outsource errands that they don't want to do, including gardening, packing to move house, and being a handyman. All you have to do is advertise the tasks you can do, and people will contact you if they need your services. Taskrabbit takes a small service fee of 20%, but your pay is negotiated with the person setting your task.

120. Making Corsages

If you have a lovely flower garden, instead of wasting beautiful flowers when giving your garden a touch up, you can make corsages out of them. Weddings and proms would give you a huge market in the local area, but you can also sell them online at specialized arts and crafts stores like www.Etsy.com, www.folksy.com or general sales websites such as www.ebay.com or www.ebay.co.uk

121. Rent Bouncy Castles

Kids parties, we've all been to a few! You must have noticed that lots of children's parties have a bouncy castle. You only need to invest once in an inflatable bouncy castle and you can rent it out over and over again! A very good business model! Word of mouth will get you a lot of business, as all mums know other mums.

122. Do Chores For Cash

There are lots of small tasks you have to do but you don't like doing. Well, there are people who have money who don't like doing the tasks either. You can do it for them and get paid for it. Spread the word that you will do "all sorts of chores" for cash and you might get yourself some regular customers. Example tasks: ironing, folding laundry, painting a fence, sorting out cupboards, cleaning a garage, chopping firewood, grocery shopping, spring cleaning, polishing silver, etc.

123. Care For Plants - R

If you know a lot about plants and how to care for them, you can offer these services to people in your area or to companies. Lots of companies like to have plants in their premises but nobody knows how to take care of them. You can build this to a substantial business and have lots of repeat business because, if you do a good job, you can take care of the plants for years to come and companies will pay you a regular income to do this.

124. Repair, Paint Or Install Fences

The good thing - for you as a fence installer - is that fences don't last a lifetime. They constantly need to be repaired and painted. No set up costs for this as the homeowner will pay for all the materials. Start by putting leaflets through doors or just drive around and you will guaranteed see some fences that need repairing.

125. Re-glaze Bathtubs

Bathtubs don't last a lifetime but most people don't have the money to install a new bathroom when the bathtub starts to look ugly. You can make the bathtub look new again. Low start up as the homeowner will pay for the materials.

126. Become A Gutter Cleaner - R

This is a very easy business to start, as all you need is a ladder and some cleaning tools. Most people hate this job and there will be plenty of people who have the money to pay you to do it for them. Once a gutter is cleaned, it will just get filled again so if you do a good job, you can clean it again.

127. Become A Locksmith

Another business with very low start up costs: putting new locks in people's doors. Millions of people lose their keys every year and need a new lock. If you are prepared to work on the weekends, you have a good chance of making this a success.

128. Pool Maintenance - R

People who have pools very often have the money to pay somebody to do the maintenance. Very low set up costs, as the homeowners will pay for all the tools you'll need.

129. Festival Staff

Lots of festivals recruit staff and usually the entrance to the festival is free. Visit some festival websites and find the "recruiting" page or visit www.festaff.co.uk. I don't know the equivalent for the USA but a simple search will give you the answer.

130. Sweep Chimneys

Sweeping chimneys is not what it used to be. I had a chimneysweeper in my own house a few weeks ago and he wasn't even dirty when he finished the job as he used the modern tools for the job. Visit www.ncsg.org, the National Chimney Sweep Guild.

131. Do Appliance Repairs

One of my friends has set up a business doing this and it is now his full time job. After 8 months of having his first customer, he said goodbye to his boss and he now has 3 employees. You will have to invest in spare-parts, that's the down side of this business.

132. Clean Out Fireplaces - R

Somebody has got to do it and usually the owner doesn't like cleaning out the fireplace and is happy to pay to have it done. If you do a good job, you can clean the fireplace on a regular basis, so it will be recurring income.

133. Tidy Cables

Some spaces in lots of houses are just a mess with cables going from A to B, B to C, C to A, etc. With all the electronic gadgets we all use nowadays, lots of cables are needed. You can become a specialist in tidying all the mess and putting the cables nice and tidy around the house. Lots of equipment and tools are available to make a messy corner a neat and tidy corner.

134. Become A Pedicab Driver

You love the outside and love cycling? Why not make money from it and become a pedicab driver? It is also great to stay in shape! You can find pedicabs in city centres all around the world: a bike in front of a hooded cab that can carry 2 to 3 people. It is also called a bug or rickshaw.
You can visit www.bugbugs.com to become a driver in London or simply get your own bike and apply with your local government to become a licensed driver.

135. Become A Charity Fundraiser

You can become a chugger (or charity fundraiser). Charities are always looking for people to stand on the street to try and raise money from people walking in the streets. Most charities pay an hourly fee for this. Contact your local charity to find out if they need people.

136. Do A Street Survey

Several marketing research companies pay you to interview people in the streets. Search online for "apply for a street survey job" and get your application in.

137. Clean Ovens

We all have an oven and we all hate cleaning it. You can offer this service. This is very easy to set up and low cost. You can buy oven cleaning kits online or in local stores. You can easily charge $150 - £100 to clean one oven and it only takes one hour or so per oven so you can easily do 4 ovens per day.

138. Become A Solar Energy Consultant

Solar energy is big business. You can become a consultant and recommend solar energy companies. Contact some companies and tell them you want to be a consultant and get commission from customers you will refer to them. Most companies will be willing to give you the knowledge and training you need. The company has nothing to lose and you have the possibility to earn money, so this works both ways. Of course, you will have to portray a professional image to the homes you will visit.

139. Become A Green Consultant

Consumers as well as companies are often willing to pay the extra for green products. You can consult people on how to do things more environmentally friendly e.g. cut energy use and waste. Companies are put under pressure to become more eco-friendly but a lot of small companies don't have the money to employ large consulting companies.

140. Upholstering

There are plenty of videos and books available to find out how to upholster. All you need is some tools...and some customers.

Chapter 18. Make Money With Your Body

141. Ugly Modelling

If you think you're ugly or you are covered in tattoos, have weird earrings or something unique or special, you can register with The Ugly Model Agency www.ugly.org and get paid to model.

142. Donate Sperm

Become a sperm donor and help give the gift of life, if you are aged between 18 and 41. Just look on the Internet for your local sperm bank, or ask your doctor about the process. Make sure you read and comply with all of the terms and conditions before considering sperm donation. You can start off with a one-off donation to see how you like it, and can then become a long-term member. You'll be paid for each donation.
To become a suitable sperm donor you will have to go through months of testing first.

143. Donate Your Eggs

Whilst the male can sell their sperm, females can donate their eggs. You can potentially earn $10,000 (£6300) to donate your eggs. The screening process is long and complicated.

144. Medical Trials

First things first, make sure you understand all of the terms and conditions before you enter into a medical trial, as these do not come without risks. Medical trials usually involve you trying out new drugs before they have been approved for widespread public use. You will either be given a placebo drug or the real drug to see if it works. You can earn thousands of pounds from these trials, and the risks are not usually high, however there are obviously always risks. There is a huge range of different types of research into health and disease. A lot of research is carried out in the NHS (National Health Services in the UK), but some take place in universities and research institutes, in social care services or in the private sector.

You can look for research studies yourself by asking your doctor or a patient organisation or by looking on the Internet (search for Clinical trials). Alternatively, you may be approached to take part in research. Be cautious and don't be afraid to ask questions.
Find more information on Just Another Lab Rat : www.jalr.org
For clinical trials:
www.centerwatch.com

www.clinicalconnection.com

145. Become A Research Subject

If being a guinea pig for the betterment of humanity doesn't appeal to you because you're scared of, say, needles or you've always preferred homeopathic remedies to conventional medication, there's a kind of study or research you can participate in and still earn money. In this case, we're talking about psychological studies. Participating in this kind of research can be fun and interesting for you, on top of making money out of it.

Being involved in research studies is pretty much the same as being a clinical trial subject in terms of monetary compensation. Another benefit is of course the findings you get for free from the psychological or psychiatric research, which otherwise will be very expensive. Another way is to join focus groups in your city. There are online focus groups that are used for product marketing and sales, so you might want to look around for that in Craigslist or other advertising websites.

146. Life Modelling

If the idea of making money just sitting down appeals to you, this is for you. You can do life modelling and get paid between $12 and $15 (£8 to £10) per hour for clothed modelling and more for unclothed modelling.
To start this business, simply contact local colleges, art schools, evening schools, etc.
www.modelreg.co.uk
www.live-models.co.uk
Just search for "life modelling" in your area.

147. Become A Model

You don't need to be stunningly beautiful or extremely slim to become a model. Lots of companies now hire "bigger and bolder" models. When you do your research, make sure to read the agreement and the small letters in it. This can be a nice little earner as you can get paid anything between $150 - £ 95 and $1,000 - £640 per modelling job you get offered.

148. Become A Foot or Hand Model

Perhaps you don't like the idea of being a model and you are scared of the catwalk. Don't worry, you can just model your feet or hands. Shoe companies need foot models and jewellery companies need hand models. Find out if there are such companies near you and get your application in.

149. Sell Your Hair

Hair extensions are becoming more and more popular, especially as some celebrities have admitted that they have hair extensions.

If you have lovely long hair, you can now earn money with your hair.
www.buyandsellhair.com
www.thehairtrader.org
www.onlinehairaffair.com
www.hairwork.com

Visit www.gumtree.com and www.craigslist.org and you will find lots of ads from people who want to pay you cash for your hair. You could also become a "hair-dealer" and contact lots of hairdressers to pick up long hair and then sell it on.

150. Donating Plasma

In the USA, you can legally trade plasma for cash. In most large cities in the USA there are clinics that will pay money for your plasma. You can donate once or twice per week. You need to be healthy and drug free to become a donor.
On www.donatingplasma.org you can find a Plasma Centre and answers to all your questions.
Visit www.blood.co.uk for information on giving blood in the UK.

151. Lap Dancing

I saw an article in the newspaper 2 weeks ago reporting that a lot of students take up lap dancing and get paid $470 - £300 per evening! Student or not: this could be for you if you like lap dancing. Make sure it doesn't cause any arguments with your partner though! Lap dancers are also different to prostitutes, as it is not common practice to have sex with the customers; it is just dancing. If this is not for you, that's fine!

152. Become A Dating Escort

May business people are so busy that they don't have time for a partner, wife or for romance in general. However, they still want to attend company events, meals, balls and business events. That's when they go to a dating escort agency and hire a partner for the evening. Make sure that, when you research dating agencies, you check that ONLY a date is required and nothing else. You can earn up to $100 - £63 per hour so it can be a nice little earner and as a bonus: you will get free meals and drinks. There are lots of professional agencies to choose from.

Chapter 19. Organiser Jobs

Do you like working with people and making them happy? Are you outgoing, people oriented and easy-going? There are a lot of businesses that can use your special talents.

153. Wedding Planner

For instance, do you love weddings? Would you like to make people smile on their special day? How about being a Wedding Planner? There are numerous lucrative opportunities in this area.

In many ways this job combines the roles of ultimate organiser, coordinator and therapist and top-notch wedding consultants can earn over $100,000 (£60,000) a year. You can work all year round, you can set your own fees (and if you are good they can be high), you can choose whom you want to work with (no bridezillas!), and you help make people fulfil their dreams.

However, this job is not for everyone; it can be stressful and time consuming. Some brides can be very demanding but most will be eternally grateful to you for taking on the most important day of their lives. They will recommend you to their friends and next brides-to-be.

If you have no event planning experience, you may need to offer your services for free initially. This will allow you time to make the necessary connections, understand the different venues, and build your knowledge on the job so that you can give great advice to the couple.

If you can't find any brides to hire you, then offer your time and services to a reputable Wedding Planner in your area. Many would love to have an extra person on their staff for free.

154. Event Planner

Once you gain some experience in wedding planning, you can then offer your services as an Event Planner, Corporate Party Planner, or Show Organiser.

After you have done your first wedding, then most other events will seem easy in comparison. So bar mitzvahs, large birthday parties, anniversaries, and other events will all be possible. In fact, many people who stage large conventions and other major events began their career just this way.

But what if you want to be a part of weddings and other events, but don't want to have the responsibilities for everything? The Wedding/Event Planner works with many individuals and there is no reason why you can't be one of them.

155. Become A Professional Organiser

You can help companies get organised to be more efficient or you can help people who need help on this level e.g. to organise their cupboards or their houses. You will have to get specialised in maximising the use of small spaces and get up to date on what organising tools are available.

There is even a National Association of Professional Organisers: www.napo.net. People who need help register on this site. As a professional organiser you can earn $30,000 - £ 19,000 per year.

Chapter 20. Jobs With Food

Do you enjoy baking or cooking? Then there are many ways to use your talents working from home. If you're going into this as a business, though, you should check with your local authority first regarding the latest regulations on food safety standards and you may also need to take a course in food hygiene.

156. Homemade Baked Goods Maker - R

There are countless stories about people who started a small business in their home kitchen, selling to their family and friends, and turning it into a profitable enterprise.

Ten years ago you couldn't give a cupcake away. Today there are gourmet cupcake shops selling a single cupcake for as much as $10 (£6) each. If you don't like baking cakes, make sweets or chocolates instead. There's a ready market for individual and personalised confectionery, selling to both individuals and companies for their corporate functions.

The key to success here is to have such a quality product that retail businesses will want to sell it and the public will want to buy it. One way of achieving that is by giving it away for free initially. Perhaps at a church function, making it a part of a charity auction or delivering it to local clubs. But eventually people will start asking if they can order them for their private events such as weddings, anniversaries and birthdays. If you get to the point where large retailers will carry your product, then you are on your way to making some serious money.

157. Cake Decorator

Do you enjoy decorating cakes as much as, or more than, baking them? Why not become a cake decorator. You'll be in demand for birthday, anniversary, bar mitzvah and wedding cakes. You can work all year round and set your own prices: the average cost of a wedding cake is over $500 (£300).

Take some photos of your completed cakes and make a portfolio to show potential clients. Leave business cards or flyers with local wedding venues and planners and advertise in your local paper and bridal magazines.

158. Food Adviser/Chef- R

Another avenue is to be a Food Adviser or Personal Chef. Some people love home cooked meals but don't want to cook for themselves. Some have poor eating habits and need help managing their weight. Others need a very strict diet for health reasons and require food to be prepared in a special way. All these people are willing to pay a good cook to help them.

One of the advantages of being a personal chef is repeat business. You can often contract with the client to provide a certain number of meals a month so you always have a regular planned income.

Successful chefs tend to start out as experts in a particular type of cooking, such as vegetarian, vegan, or gluten free. Branding yourself as an expert in a particular niche will separate you from all the competition and customers will actually seek you out once your skill becomes known. This is the type of business that can really grow with a little networking. Meet and/or leave your business cards with gym trainers and offer your services to their clients trying to get in shape and needing a special protein or cardio diet.

Meet and/or leave your business cards at doctors' surgeries and let them know about meals you offer that are good for patients with diabetes or heart problems. You could also meet with personal weight consultants and discuss how your specially designed meals can help their customers lose weight. Again, leave your business cards here too. A good way to build this type of business is to give discounts or free meals to clients who offer referrals to you. Those referrals will turn into paying customers.

159. Personal Cook - R

Why not become a personal cook for a family? Lots of people have busy lives, earn good money and have disposable income. They get home late and don't have much time for cooking. Personally, I hate cooking and I have a cook. She comes every day between 4 and 6 and cooks my family a meal. Every day she knocks on my office door and says: "Your meal is ready". She is not a chef, she is just someone who loves cooking. She doesn't prepare very posh meals for me, just everyday food. So, if you can cook, why not give this a go.

160. Caterer

Thinking bigger? A caterer can make thousands of dollars or pounds in one evening. This is a lot more ambitious than being a personal chef, and requires a lot more planning. Some of the things you will need to consider:
- Stock

- Food spoilage
- Food safety regulations
- Health & Safety regulations
- Getting a hygiene certificate to produce food for sale from your home kitchen
- Possibly leasing a commercial kitchen or kitchen equipment
- Learning how to scale each job

While more difficult, it can be done. Martha Stewart got her start with a catering business run out of her basement and today is worth over $600 million dollars (over £354 million).

161. Company Cook - R

Although cooks like cooking, they often don't like the hours they have to work, like evenings and weekends. If you are a cook but would prefer to work only during the day, then being a company cook is for you. More and more small to medium companies have an in house cook to prepare lunch and dinners for their staff. You can prepare the meals at home and deliver them to the companies. Contact all the companies around you for opportunities.

162. School Cook - R

Another brilliant opportunity if you like cooking but prefer to work during the day: apply to your local schools to become a cook.

163. Make And Sell Home Made Wine

Buy a few books on how to make wine, go buy some grapes and start making wine. Sell your wine to people you know to start with.

164. Make And Sell Home Made Cheese

Cheese making is not all that complicated. Lots of people love homemade cheese and will keep buying more and more.
Go one step further: get some goats and make goat's cheese.
Look online for cheese making recipes.

165. Make And Sell Home Made Jam

Another idea for which you don't need a huge investment: you need a cooking pot, some fruit and other ingredients and you're ready to start selling.

166. Make And Sell Your Delicious Recipes

Your guests or your family tell you constantly that your sauce or your cake taste outstanding? Well, that is a sign that you can make money with your recipes: prepare your secret sauce, cake, or whatever it is and sell it.

167. Sell Sandwiches And Snacks To Local Companies - R

I know a guy who started this from his home, delivering pre-ordered sandwiches to local companies. He now has 15 vans, in 15 different cities and earns good money. The companies phone in their orders for a whole week, he prepares them and delivers them to the companies. Very simple idea that can make a lot of money, as employees are always happy to buy snacks, drinks and sandwiches.

168. Sell Home Grown Fruit And Vegetables

If you have fruit trees in your garden or a vegetable bed, don't just eat it all yourself but sell some of it at the local market or put a sign up in your front garden.

You can also buy fruit and vegetables wholesale and sell them directly to the public e.g. at fairs, markets, etc.

169. Food Photography

You can specialise in food photography. Contact local restaurants, fast food chains, bars, garden centre restaurants, food wholesalers, etc. They all have flyers or special offers done on a regular basis.

Chapter 21. Creative/Crafting Jobs

What if you are creative but not talented in the kitchen? How about being a Crafter or Designer of handmade goods?

170. Gift Basket Designer

Gift baskets are very common these days and are popular as presents, especially for birthdays or as thank you gifts. The creative possibilities are endless.

Sports themed birthday baskets for young boys, education themed baskets for students leaving home for college or university, a "night on the town" basket as an anniversary present with theatre tickets and vouchers for dinner for two, a "Hello Kitty" basket for a little birthday girl and so on.

Today, baskets come in all varieties as well. Flower baskets (maybe the start of a Floral Design business?), fruit baskets, wine baskets, bread and cheese baskets and more.

171. Design Diaper Cakes

From a distance, a diaper cake looks the same as a multi-layered wedding cake. Diaper cakes are a brilliant gift at baby showers. If you are a crafty person, this might be just the thing for you.

172. Soap/Candle Maker

You can also use the same methods if you are a Soap Maker or a Candle Maker. Yes, even a candle maker. At the age of 17, Michael Kittredge started his candle making business in his parent's garage and turned it into the Yankee Candle Company, the largest scented candle company in the country. A few years ago he sold the company and its 500 retail stores for $500 million dollars (over £295 million)!

There are numerous books detailing how to make soap and candles at home. You could theme your soaps and/or candles for different times of year e.g. Christmas. Advertise your products through your local paper or take a stall at a local market. You'll soon find people recommending you to their friends who are looking for individual handmade gifts.

173. Jewellery Designer

Are you creative and enjoy fashion? Then how about designing jewellery?

The purists tell you that to be a jewellery designer you need to study design, metallurgy, metal fabrication, soldering, casting, and more. These skills are helpful to get to the next level, and they would put you in the category of professionals, but you really don't need to know any of that to get started.

In fact, jewellery designers have numerous ways to create and sell their creations without any special skills, tools or a lot of money. It can be as simple as purchasing a plain bracelet or ankle chain and adding charms to it. Voila…you are a Jewellery Designer. Of course, you will need to practice, experiment, and ask everyone you know for their opinions of your designs. They will also give you new ideas to add to your existing product range.

Once you have samples that you are satisfied with, you can try to get them in local jewellery or gift stores by selling them directly to the owners for re-sale. If they are hesitant to do so, then offer them your creations on a sale or return basis. With this method there is no risk to the store and you get the advantage of having your designs on show in a store.

In addition, once you get your work in one store, it is much easier to get it into many others. Many famous designers got their start just this way, one store at a time. You could also try selling through any regular local markets, one off craft sales and in gift shops at tourist attractions.

174. Fashion Designer

Maybe you like crafts and being creative but prefer working with clothes rather than jewellery? If people are always admiring your clothes and style and you have good drawing and sewing skills, how about working as a Fashion Designer, Costume Designer, or even a Fashion Consultant?

Not ready for those? Then volunteer your services as a Seamstress for a Fashion Designer or Costume Designer and learn the trade.

These types of businesses allow you to be very creative and to put your mark on your work.

175. Sewing And Alterations

If you have sewing skills, you can provide these skills as a service. You can make clothes, bags, quilts etc. or do alterations. Tell your friends you're now providing this service and advertise in your local paper.

It is relatively easy to build a simple website aiming for keywords like: "alterations in Birmingham", "made to measure clothes in London". etc.

176. Face Painting

If you are good at face painting, get a small stall at a local fair or market to earn some extra money. Or advertise in the local paper and offer face painting for children's parties. Be sure to use good quality, non-toxic, hypoallergenic face paints.

You can also do face painting at carnivals, zoos, company parties, craft fairs, etc.

177. Photography

You can sell your photography skills by becoming a pet photographer, baby photographer, wedding photographer etc.

178. Aerial Photography

If you have a friend with a helicopter, ask him to fly it around whilst you take photos of people's houses. Develop the photos, put them in a nice frame and go knock on people's doors to sell them.

If you don't like door-to-door selling, just develop some sample prints with an order form and your contact details and go and put them through mailboxes.

You can pay your friend per hour or split the profits of your sales with him.

You can also easily hire a helicopter pilot on an hourly basis.

179. Caricatures/ Portraits

If you have a knack for drawing or art, you can always sell your work. You can sell it on websites such as:

www.folksy.com
www.etsy.com
www.folksy.com
www.artfire.com
www.artpal.com
www.zazzle.com

Or even start your own website selling them.

180. Make Trees Of Steel

Are you really creative and good at art? Why not make steel trees and make them look like real trees? Very good money can be made doing this. Have a look at www.naturemaker.com and see how spectacular a tree of steel can look. You could just start with making some plants of steel instead.

181. Repairing Damaged Objects.

You could repair dolls, paintings, sculptures, etc. Some objects are very valuable to their owners and they would pay good money to have their possessions repaired. You could also buy damaged mannequins e.g. from superstores, repair them and sell them as used mannequins.

182. Paint House Numbers Or Names

People are constantly moving house and every owner likes different things and lots of owners like their house to be unique. One thing a lot of people are looking for is to have a unique looking house number or house name. With a little bit of money, you are good to start this business. Paint house numbers on a suitable house plaque in all different shapes and sizes.

183. Create Post boxes

Just like people like to have their own unique looking house plaque, they also like their own unique looking post box. You can create post boxes e.g. hanging ones, standing ones, round ones, square ones, metal ones, plastic, etc. and sell them. As the ones you make will be totally unique, you can charge more compared to a standard looking post box.

184. Furniture Upsell

Buy old furniture at flea markets or buy online and give them a coat of paint, repair them, make them look nicer and sell them for a lot more money.

185. Create And Sell Balloon Models

On www.balloonmodels.com you can find out how to make fancy balloons. Create some and sell them at your local flea market. Parents walking around with their children will be happy to see you so the children can be quiet (well for two minutes or so) when they've got a balloon in their hands.
Watch videos on www.youtube.com for some more ideas.

186. Decorate Homes For Parties

People love parties, but people either don't have the time or are not creative enough to decorate a room for a cosy atmosphere. You can become a party decorator: buy some party accessories and before you know it you have a lot of stock and can make money over and over again with the same party stock. You can also charge extra to do the cleaning up afterwards.

187. Sell Your Knitting or Crochet Works

Good at knitting? Knit or crochet some sweaters, socks, dog clothes, gloves, cushion covers, baby clothes, blankets, etc. and start selling either at flea markets, local shops or online. There is a huge market for handmade products.

188. Blow Glass

Perhaps you can make beautiful glass products? Start now and start selling!

189. Make And Sell Greeting Cards

Birthdays, Christmas, Easter, Valentine's day, Mother's day, Father's day, getting a driver's license, births, get well soon, moving house, pet's birthday, etc. People are sending cards by the millions all over the world.

Millions of people like to send a really beautiful, unique or unusual card so if you are good at creating cards, there is money to be made.

You can sell them at local fairs or sell them online on

www.folksy.com
www.etsy.com
www.folksy.com
www.artfire.com
www.artpal.com
www.zazzle.com
Or eBay

190. Become An Interior Designer

Help homeowners with decorating their room. You can set this up with none or very low expenses, as the homeowner will pay for all the materials you need.

191. Become A Muralist

A mural is artwork painted directly onto a large surface, wall or ceiling. You can list on www.findamuralist.com (USA only).

192. Do Embroidery

If you are handy, you can start an embroidery business. You only need a few things to start up: an embroidery machine and a computer. You can embroider all sorts of garments, towels, golf towels, uniforms, etc.

193. Make Casts

There are plenty of mums who have a cast done of their belly whilst being pregnant. You can make the cast and paint them with flowers, trees, birth date, etc. whatever the parents fancy. This is easy to start up, as all you need is one room and plaster. No need to mention you will have to build a professional image, as you will need to see/touch the mum's stomach.

You can also do casts of new-born babies' feet, hands or any object. If you make a cast of an object. e.g. a camera, you can paint and decorate it and sell it at craft fairs or flea markets.

194. Car Art

Perhaps you've seen cars that are beautifully decorated with pictures, twirls, lines, landscapes, etc. These cars have all been under the hands of a cart art person. You will need a big room, best away from your home because of the paint smell, some paint, a paint spray gun and some imagination.

195. Tattoo Art

Personally, I am not into tattoos but I only have to look around when I am out and about to conclude that millions of people do like tattoos and are covered in them. As an artistic person, you can do tattoos from a spare room in your home.
Make sure to follow the necessary training, take out an insurance policy and let people sign a disclaimer form to avoid lawsuits. Make sure your customer's health, safety and care are a priority for you.
You might need a license, make sure to check this out.
No huge expenses to set this up: a tattoo gun, needles, transfers, ink and some furniture.

196. Mobile Tattoo Art

Instead of doing tattoos in your home, go mobile and drive to people's houses. Same applies here as already mentioned under the previous point "Tattoo Art".

Chapter 22. Beauty Therapy Jobs

Beauty therapy jobs are, if you please the customer, repetitive income. Once your customers have had a foot massage, they will want another one...and another one.

197. Beautician - R

You can offer your services as a beautician for minimum start-up costs. You can offer manicures, pedicures, hair, waxing, make-up, nails etc. from your own home. Start by advertising locally, or in the newspaper. This is a business that you can set up with very few expenses.
Of course, you can also go to people's house with your massage table.
Tip: Sell beauty products to your customers to earn more money.

198. Aromatherapy - R

This is a popular way of using essential oils to relax and to heal. You can take a course or read up about the various oils and their uses. Then set up a room in your own home and offer this treatment.

199. Become A Masseuse / Masseur - R

Why not specialize in giving people massages? Your customers will probably come back for more! Very likely there are some affordable evening courses to get your massage-diploma. . All you need is a room, a massage table, a few candles and some relaxing music.

200. Become An Alternative Healer - R

You can make money as a hypnotherapist or a Reiki therapist. Accredited training would be an advantage and there are many courses available through colleges and online.

201. Become A Nail Technician - R

Nail technicians are very much in demand. A nail technician is a specialist for the grooming and appearance of people's fingernails and toenails. You've probably seen women with stunning long nails; often these are acrylic nails, very likely done by a nail technician. The great thing: woman who have their nails done with acrylic nails have to go back for a "touch up" regularly, so this is recurring income.

202. Put In Hair Extensions

Hair extensions are a massive "in" thing since some celebrities have admitted that they have hair extensions. Look up where you can follow a course and you're ready to make people's hair more beautiful. You will need some start up cash but you will soon get your money back as you can charge a lot of money for one person's extensions.

203. Hairdresser - R

It's not difficult at all to do people's hair from your home and if you do a good job, people will come back all the time.

204. Mobile Hairdresser - R

To get even more business: become a mobile hairdresser. It's very cheap to set up, as all you need is a brush, scissors, some clips and a hair dryer. What could be easier? I have a hairdresser that comes to my home each time I need her to. There will always be women who like the comfort of their own home and who have the money to pay for your services.

205. Mobile Beautician - R

Rather than providing services from your home, you can become a mobile beautician and go to people's homes to do their nails, do their make-up, give them a mask, etc.

206. After Hours Beauty Therapy Jobs - R

The majority of beauty therapy salons only operate between 9 and 5. Problem is that most people are at work during those hours. Consider starting up a beauty therapy business - mobile or in your own house - and work late evenings and weekends. I am convinced you will get lots of business on a Sunday. I know I would have my feet done every two weeks or so if I would find a leaflet in my post box offering these services.

207. Do Makeovers

Thousands of people, probably only in your area, would like a makeover but when they search for it online, they can't afford it. You work from home so you don't have overheads therefore you can charge a lot less for a mini make over. You would do people's hair, their make up and put some fancy clothes on. Take a few pictures with a professional camera and a backdrop screen and you can start earning money.

208. Offer Spray Tan Services - R

Tanning beds are still popular but not as it used to be many years ago. Some people are aware of the link between using tanning beds and skin cancer and no longer want to use them. Luckily for these people and for you, people can now get a tan with a spray. Turn a spare room into a spray tanning service. This is relatively easy to set up as you need a spray gun, a tan tent, gloves and the tan itself.

The tan doesn't last forever so people will come back for more, making this a business with repetitive income.

Make sure you take out an insurance policy and put up signs to protect yourself from a possible lawsuit. Make the customer sign a contract before you start spraying.

You can get complete spray tan kits on Amazon for little money, just search for "spray tan kit".

Many manufacturers selling spray tan kits also offer training as spray tanning can look horrible when not done right but beautiful if you know what you are doing so make sure to follow some training.

209. Mobile Spray Tanning - R

This is instead of doing spray tans in your house.

Make sure you take out an insurance policy and show people signs to protect yourself from a possible lawsuit. Make the customer sign a contract before you start spraying.

Many manufacturers selling spray tan kits also offer training as spray tanning can look horrible when not done right but beautiful if you know what you are doing, so make sure to follow some training.

You can get complete spray tan kits on Amazon for little money, just search for "spray tan kit".

Chapter 23. Tutoring / Coaching Jobs

You can sell your skills or knowledge by teaching classes. For example, if you're an exercise guru, you can sell exercise classes from your own home. People are willing to pay to learn all kinds of things, including playing an instrument, dancing, yoga, learning languages and many more. Start by advertising in your local paper and contact your local schools, councils and colleges. Once you've built up a reputation, you should find yourself getting repeat business and word-of-mouth recommendations.

If you enjoy working with children or young adults you may be interested in being a tutor or a coach. If you have strong knowledge in any particular subject or skill, you may be able to get paid for passing on your talents, for example in English, maths or science. Some people may need help with athletics or the fundamentals of sports like football, swimming or gymnastics. Are you a good golfer? Many adults will pay a Golf Coach to give them tips and help improve their swing. In fact, there is quite a lucrative niche market for left-handed golf instructors.

Do you have any other hobbies or interests? How about running, tennis, chess, scrapbooking, collecting, Tai-chi or yoga? The point is if you have something to offer that you are good at or are knowledgeable about, there are people willing to pay you for that knowledge. A great place to try it out is as an instructor at a community or leisure centre. You should check whether you will need to take out separate insurance to cover your classes or whether you'll be covered by the venue's policy.

210. Teach A Foreign Language - R

You can use your native language to teach foreign students from home. You can get in touch with your local language schools to help advertise your services.

211. Music Teacher - R

Can you read music and play an instrument? Then maybe you can help someone else learn the basics of playing that instrument. You'll need to be patient and encouraging and able to communicate your love of music. Though you could become a music teacher without qualifications, you might have more chance of finding work if you've studied for a recognised qualification.

212. Give Singing Lessons - R

Love signing? Teach others how to sing!

213. Teach Computing - R

There are still many people who are not accustomed to using computers. If you are, you can pass on your skills and make money. You can advertise locally and use word of mouth to find customers. You could also develop this business by becoming a computer repairer/ trouble-shooter.

214. Organise Dance Classes - R

Not many expenses needed: if you have a big room in your house, use that room. If not, hire a hall in your area. The only other thing you need is music and a device to play the music. You can even make some new friends! Specialise in a certain niche: e.g. dancing for the over 60's or dancing for teenagers, etc.

215. Teach Anything You're Good At

If you are good at something, there is a good chance somebody else wants to be good at it as well. Why not teach them what you know?

216. Become A Substitute Teacher

All schools have teachers call in sick very often and the schools will then hire a substitute teacher. Contact all schools around you and let them know you are available. You will need to undergo some tests but you will be paid for being a substitute teacher.

217. Become A Saturday/Sunday Teacher

Students work hard to get their diploma but lots of them need extra lessons e.g. in the weekends. Why not educate them with your knowledge?

218. Run Activities In A Retirement Home

Old people love activities. Search online for retirement homes in your area or visit www.retirementhomes.com Example activities: a puzzle afternoon, a quiz morning, sing-a-long hour, go for a walk, board games, cooking, perhaps even a karaoke, etc.

219. Become A Public Speaker

Do you have a lot of knowledge in something? Why not speak about it and become a public speaker? If you have something to sell when your speech is finished, you can earn even more.

Chapter 24. Jobs With Children

220. Child Minder - R

If you love children, another opportunity is working as a home-based childcare provider. Parents leave their children with you for the day while they work and pick them up in the evening. This can be perfect for stay at home mums. Start by advertising locally or on www.care.com (covering the UK, US and Canada), or www.sittercity.com in the US. There will be governmental control on child minding in your area so, like all the ideas in this book, you must look into what the legal restrictions and regulations are if you are interested in this.

221. Out of Hours Child Minder - R

Many people are prepared to be a child minder during the day but less people want to do evenings and weekends. If you specialise in this, you can charge more and there will be less competition, so it is worth investigating.

222. Nanny - R

If you prefer to work closely with only one or two children at a time, you can be a nanny working in a private home caring for your employers' children. You would work out with the parents exactly what the hours and duties would be and these would vary according to the ages of the children being cared for. You could be caring for new-borns up to pre-schoolers and be washing, dressing, feeding and changing nappies. You would also be involved in helping teach social skills and keeping the children entertained, so you'll need to be patient and tolerant, with a good sense of humour.

While you can work without any qualifications, most potential employers would expect you to have one. In the right circumstances, working as a nanny can be very rewarding and often the nanny becomes a part of the family.

223. Childproofing Expert

If you have raised your own children, you probably have learned many things that would be useful to new parents. One occupation might be a Childproofing Expert. You would examine the home of expecting parents and look for potential dangers to the baby. Are electrical outlets exposed? Any sharp corners or edges on the furniture? Doors that can be opened too easily? Low sited breakable items such as glass lamps? If you can spot potentially dangerous things like these, then this may be a natural business for you.

224. Run After School Activities - R

Millions of people juggle work and home and very often don't get home from work by the time school is finished so they send their kids to after school activities. You can run one of these activities. Just to give some examples: have a picnic, find shells on the beach, alphabet games, dance lessons, musical instrument lessons, playing with dough, sports, painting, etc. You see, for a lot of these activities you don't need diplomas that are hard to get.

Chapter 25. Helping Jobs

Like to help people? Does it sound rewarding to combine that with actually making a living out of helping people? Well, there are many opportunities to do just that.

225. Caring For The Elderly/Disabled - R

If you are still healthy and mobile yourself, this is an option for you. There are many carers who need to take a break, and you can earn some money by taking over the care part-time. This will require basics such as errand running and giving regular company to people as well as hygiene care and nursing. It would be useful if you could show you've had some experience and training in this field and your local college will probably offer courses you can take while you're gaining experience.

226. Companion - R

One rewarding way to make money is to be a hired companion. There are many senior citizens who need a little help or have no transportation. These are not necessarily people who need medical attention, but they do not have the ability to do some of the things they would like to do, and they may not have family in the area to help. So that is where you come in. Maybe they need to be taken to a grocery store or maybe to a park for some fresh air, even to the cinema or for lunch at a local restaurant. Maybe they just need help organising their wardrobe. If they own a house, there are a lot of other things you could help them with, such as paying their bills, or arranging for a repairman to visit. Often their children are willing to pay someone to look in on their parents frequently, to make sure they are OK and to see if they need anything.

One way to start a business like this is to visit the local centres for the elderly and retirement homes – leave business cards and get to know the administrators who can recommend you. There are a lot of people living in retirement homes who don't have dementia, so they are allowed to leave the premises but don't have anybody to go with them. In some areas there are large retirement communities. These are all great places to get your name and services out there. You can also meet potential customers by volunteering at these same places.

227. Personal Shopper - R

Some people who have started as a carer or companion have been able to expand enough to become a personal shopper, since not just the elderly need help. People who have illnesses or injuries such as back problems, arthritis or issues with maintaining balance, and anyone else with physical impairments may use your services. Even young, healthy people may be too busy to get everything they need done. So you might be running all their errands such as arranging for dinner, grocery shopping, gift buying, picking up the laundry at the cleaners and numerous other things they may need.

228. Doula

A doula is a nonmedical companion of a woman in labour. You would be a birthing partner and friend throughout the pregnancy. Some doulas offer postnatal support as well. Bear in mind that as babies can be born at any time, working hours may sometimes be antisocial. You could advertise your services through the local paper, at antenatal classes and any groups for mothers and babies. Word-of-mouth recommendation would be a good source of on-going business. Be aware though that this can be a stressful job and certainly one that comes with lots of responsibility.
www.dona.org
www.britishdoulas.co.uk

229. Exam Proctor

As an exam proctor, you supervise the administration of an examination or a test. You don't need to have any knowledge of the test that is being taken. You just need to make sure that all students doing the test are following the test guidelines.
Of course, you will have to do some tests to be accepted.
For more information:
- www.procturu.com
- www.servsafeinternational.com
- www.certiport.com
- www.prometric.com

230. Event Staffing

Companies organising events are always looking for staff. You could be serving dinners, cleaning up, serving drinks, opening doors, etc. Contact your local events companies to offer your services.

Chapter 26. Writing And Reading Jobs

Can you write? The answer is yes! If you can send an email, you can write. The great news is that there are numerous ways to build an income by stringing together a few sentences. Of course, the better writer you are, the more opportunities there are to make money. If you have moderate writing skills, you may be able to offer services in areas where writing can be formulaic, meaning that when given a guide or template, you can create the necessary content.

Advertise in your local paper or distribute business cards around local businesses or business parks. If you produce good work and always meet deadlines, you should pick up repeat business and recommendations to new clients. As you become more successful you might want to consider having your own website to showcase your talents.

231. Ghostwriter

If you enjoy writing or feel you have a natural talent for it, you can make money by becoming a ghostwriter: writing books or articles for other people. Start by advertising in your local paper and letting your friends and family know that you're now a ghostwriter. You can find lots of opportunities for ghostwriting on outsourcing websites, www.elance.com being of them. I realise that this part of the book is for jobs where you don't need a computer but you can find the jobs with a computer and then you can write the book on your typewriter! Having said that, the person you are writing the book for will want the book delivered in an MS Word file, so this one might be a bit tricky. I am mentioning this opportunity here anyway as my uncle *does* write books as a ghostwriter and he *does* use his old fashioned typewriter to write the books. His daughter then types in the book on a computer and my uncle delivers it to his client as an MS Word file. So the client my uncle works for *thinks* he is writing it in MS Word. Whatever floats your boat I guess!

232. Calligrapher

You can learn calligraphic writing and sell your services. It is a popular option to have marriage invitations handwritten with calligraphy.

233. Proofreader

If you prefer reading to writing, why not become a proofreader? Often content creators will want someone to review their work looking for mistakes. Using products such as MS

Word makes this much easier, however, there are still many instances where MS Word misses what seem to be obvious mistakes to the human eye.

Some examples are confusing words like "knew" with "new," or "sale" and "sell" or "there" and "their," or "affect" and "effect," or "then" and "than." Depending on the sentence structure, MS Word may not catch it, but you will.

Proofreaders are used in every industry and often work from home. Advertise your services in the local paper or contact local writers' groups and publishers. Colleges and universities are another source of work: academic papers and dissertations need to be fault free. Perfect proofreaders are very hard to find, however much money you pay them. I speak from experience as all my books are proofread before publishing but people still point out mistakes to me.

234. Will Writer

If you would put leaflets through people's door about professional will writing, I am pretty sure you would get some business. There are millions of people who don't have a will and really should have. Check out in your area what legalities are required to be a will writer. Often all you need to do is follow an affordable course and you can be a professional will writer.

235. Grant Writer

Governments and large institutions need grant writers and very often this is given to people who work from home. You will put together proposals after having researched everything. Search for "how to become a grant writer" for more details. I have known companies who give commissions to the grant writer, should the company get the order, so this can be very profitable.

236. Write Jokes

You've seen magazines and newspapers with jokes in. Did you know that you will get paid if you send jokes to various publications? Only if they print the jokes. Usually the publications will have the contact details in or look it up on their websites and find out where to send the jokes to. Make sure not to forget to put your contact details on the jokes you will send them so they can contact you to pay you. Often you will get paid around $25 - £15 per joke. Send 10 jokes that will be published and you've earned $250 - £150. Easy! Send the same jokes to different publications and get paid more than once.

Chapter 27. Miscellaneous Ideas

237. House Parties And Multi Level Marketing

You've probably heard of some big names in direct marketing: Tupperware, Avon, Kleeneze, The Pampered Chef, etc.

A lot of people know this as MLM = Multi Level Marketing. In a nutshell: you are person A selling to people. You point out person B and he/she can sell to people as well. If person B sells something, you get commission from his sales. You can find people up to Z and earn commission from all of them.

A lot of people organise house parties selling all sorts of stuff. You need to be a very social person to enjoy this though as it is all about convincing other people to sell for you. Here are a few well-known and established companies:

www.amway.com
www.kleeneze.com
www.tupperware.com
www.marykay.com
www.steepedtea.com
www.avon.com
www.herbalife.com
www.jamberrynails.net
www.thirtyonegifts.com
www.wildtree.com
www.beachbody.com

Jewellery:
www.azuliskye.com
www.origamiowl.com
www.stelladot.co.uk
www.origamiowl.com

Fashion:
www.avagraydirect.com

You can find a list of Multi Level Marketing companies here:
http://en.wikipedia.org/wiki/List_of_multi-level_marketing_companies

238. Turn Videos Into DVD's

Thousands of people have videos hanging around and would like them converted to DVD's or put on a memory stick. There are, of course, companies doing this but most people don't like sending their videos with the post or a courier company, just in case they get lost. If you pick up the videos and deliver them back to your customer, they will be much happier with that, assuming you earn their trust.

There is, I believe, still a lot of money to be made with this and all you need is a video to DVD converter, which you can get for a few hundred dollars or pounds.

239. Make Digital Pictures From Old Photographs.

This is another great and easy moneymaking opportunity. The same applies here as for the videos: people don't like sending their photographs in the post or with a courier company, just in case they get lost. If you pick up the photographs and deliver them back to your customer, they will be much happier with that, assuming you earn their trust.
You need a good scanner, a computer and a little bit of knowledge about digital photographs, that's all.

240. Make A "You've Been Framed Video"

You can earn $390 - £250 for every video clip that you post to You've Been Framed. If your clip is shown, you'll get paid. It's as simple as that. I am not sure what the alternative is in the USA but if you are from the USA, there's good chance you'll know and I assume you also get paid in the US.
Some people actually record video clips especially to send so the clips that you see on TV are not all "real accidents".

241. Become An Extra

Film agencies are always looking for extras. In case you don't know what an extra is, these are the people you see on a movie who don't play a major role at all e.g. the people eating in a restaurant or walking around in a railway station whilst a scene is being filmed. Have some professional photos done and register with a few companies or just call them.
- www.filmextras.co.uk
- www.extras.com Pay starts at $135 (£85) per day plus travel expenses.
- www.universalextras.co.uk

242. Run A Few Errands

You can run errands for local people just by looking on www.taskrabbit.com. You can search listings of errands posted by others and earn money by doing them.

243. Win Prizes With Radio Contests

Lots of radio stations run contests where you can win prizes. Call them over and over again until you'll win something. You can sell what you've won.

244. Make Money From Waste - R

If you have land available and you own farm animals such as horses, ducks, sheep or cows, you can sell their manure to be used as fertiliser. You can put a sign up in your front garden and advertise in the local paper.

245. Grease Hunting

Cooking grease is used to produce bio-diesel fuel (a renewable fuel). Don't throw away the fat from your fryer but sell it! Contact the restaurants around you saying you'll pick up their grease. Even thieves are stealing grease to make money! Search for "selling cooking grease" or "selling gutter oil" for more information.

246. Become A Truck Driver - R

I will always remember my astonishment when my brother's friend Mike bought a house. Now this sounds pretty ordinary because millions of people buy house. The reason I was so surprised is because my dad always told my brother: "he is *only* a truck driver" so he will never be rich. I now know my dad was wrong as Mike and his wife were both truck drivers, mainly during the nights and weekends but you should have seen the house they bought with the money they both earned "just working as a truck driver" for 15 years: a massive house, 6 bedrooms, golden taps in the bathroom, impressive gardens, etc.
You *can* make a lot of money being a truck driver, especially if you are prepared to work evenings and weekends.
All you need is a truck-driver's license and to apply for jobs with transport companies. Often you can set your own hours.

247. Sell Weather Clothes

It's raining and there's an open-air event near you? Sell umbrellas or ponchos on the street.
It's freezing cold and there's an open-air event near you? Sell gloves and hats!
It's extra warm for the time of the year when there is an open-air even near you? Sell sunglasses.
All you need is some money to buy some wholesale stock and sell your goods with a

profit.

248. Sell Food And Drinks At Events

When I was a child, my parents would take me to events e.g. exhibitions, open-air concerts, outdoor sporting events, etc. I always used to enjoy counting the people who buy food and counting the money the food stall takes e.g. if a hamburger costs $2 *(let's say that equals £2 for ease of calculation)* and the stall would sell 100 hamburgers per hour (they had 4 staff and long queues), he took $200 - £200 per hour. If he sells for 8 hours, he took $1,600 - £1,600. If he does that 20 days per month, at different events, he takes $32,000 - £32,000 per month! Not bad for selling hamburgers.

I guess you must have worked it out: I wasn't a small kid because I was already thinking about making money.

If you are prepared to work hard and you have the money to buy a hamburger cart, this really is a good moneymaking opportunity with BIG profit margins.

249. Rent Maternity Clothes

Pregnancy is a special time for any woman and family; however, it is also a time when women are faced with a lot of fashion challenges, and also a lot of expenses regarding their attire. When you need an outfit to attend a wedding, formal occasion, special occasion etc., and you are 30 weeks pregnant, you don't really want to buy an outfit that you probably won't wear again. So, renting out your old maternity clothes is a great idea, as you make money instead of throwing out your clothes. You can advertise your services on websites such as www.gumtree.com, www.rentnottobuy.com or even set up your own website.

Buy some cheap maternity clothes on eBay/markets/charity shops, have them dry-cleaned and rent them out. You'll be surprised how many customers you can get.

250. Become A Waiter - R

Restaurants, bars and fast food chains are always looking for waiters. You don't need to have any special knowledge for this. Visit some local places and you might be able to earn some extra money working very close to your home.

251. Work In A Store - R

Stores near you are constantly looking for sales assistants, people to put stock away, people to sit at the tills, etc. Walk in the stores and apply for a part-time job.

252. Work In A Fast Food Chain - R

McDonalds, Pizza Hut and all the other large food chains need people to serve the customers, to work in the kitchen or to clean up. Apply at your local chains.

253. Design Family Trees

Lots of people are interested in their family tree but don't know where to start or simply haven't got the time to do the research. You could do all the research and if you are artistic you can turn the result into a very nice family tree design.

254. Metal Detecting

Now this really is easy to get started: get yourself a metal detector and start looking for metal on beaches, in the dunes, in wood, etc. You can sell what you can find and so create an income.

Now and again somebody is in the news having detected stuff that is very valuable. As the finder, you will get paid a large part when the products are being sold. People have found ancient coins in the past for a value of hundreds and thousands of dollars!

255. Recover Golf Balls

If there are a lot of golf clubs around you this might be for you. There are always golf balls to be found outside of the golf clubs. You can either sell the recovered golf balls to the golf club owner or sell them on www.ebay.com if the owners allow you to do so.

If you are good at scuba diving, contact the golf club owner and tell him/her that you will look in all their ponds for lost golf balls. You can clean the balls and the golf club owner will probably buy them from you. Usually pay is per golf ball recovered.

256. Salvaging Scrap Metal

Stephen Greer wrote a book called "Starting from Scrap: Entrepreneurial Success Story" in which he explains his story. He stumbled into the scrap metal business without intention and built a $250 million (£159 million) scrap metal business!
You can start this business simply by telling everybody you know that you are picking up metal if they have any. You can sell what you've picked up to scrap dealers. The metals currently recycled are copper, aluminium, brass, silver, platinum e.g. aluminium car wheels, empty drink cans, etc.
I know a guy who took his old car to a scrap metal salvage yard and got enough money for it so he could buy a better car with that money.
50 empty drink cans can give you $3 (£1.90) income. Of course, this is not a lot but you

can probably find thousands of cans if you look everywhere e.g. streets, bins, parks, woods, etc.

Check out the legalities in your area.

257. Copper Hunting

Scrap copper prices have risen a lot in the last few years. That's why I am giving this a separate header as you can make some money getting together Copper. You can find copper in printed circuit boards, plumbing pipes, air conditioning units, copper wire, coins, etc.

www.recycleinme.com
www.greengatemetals.co.uk
www.londonscrapcopper.co.uk
www.londonscrapmetalrecycling.co.uk

258. Trade In Empty Ink Cartridges

Millions of empty ink cartridges are thrown away each year whilst you can make money with them. You can start with collecting cartridges in your local area and either collect them totally free - some people will just give them to you - or pay a very small fee for them. Suppose you pay them $2 (£1.28) per cartridge and sell the cartridge for $4.50 (£2.88), that is 200 per cent profit!

These websites all pay for cartridges:
www.cashfortoner.co.uk
www.tonertrader.co.uk
www.cashforcartridges.com
www.therecyclingfactory.com
www.recoupnow.com

Search online for more companies that will pay you money for empty cartridges.

259. Become A Hangover Helper

On www.helpinghangovers.com you can get paid to serve people with hangovers a "good-for-hangover-meal" and to clean up the room where the party happened.

260. Busking

You play an instrument or know some other tricks worth seeing e.g. juggling. You can always try busking. If you are lucky, you can indeed earn some good money with this. Several famous singers started out with busking. This is illegal in some areas so make sure to check out the law.

261. Become A DJ

If you are a music lover, becoming a DJ can be your thing. More and more people hire a DJ instead of a live band because a DJ is cheaper. You can earn $700 (£450) in a weekend if you have several bookings per weekend. The best part...most of the week you will be free and you will work almost all the time on weekends.

262. Buy And Sell Lost Luggage

Thousands of suitcases get lost everywhere around the world. Often, these are sold at auctions. The Unclaimed Baggage Centre in the USA is in Alabama and receives 800,000 visitors per year! In the UK, there are also auctions for lost baggage. One of them is Greasbys in London. Luggage from British Airways is sold here.
You never know what you will get in the suitcase you are buying but it sure sounds like a lot of fun!
You can sell all the items in your suitcase on eBay or other auction sites.
If you find new books or DVD's in your suitcase you can also sell them as an Amazon re-seller.
For more information on auction houses for lost luggage:
www.baggageauctions.co.uk
www.greasbys.co.uk
www.wellersauctions.com
www.hertsauctions.com
www.unclaimedbaggage.com

263. Buy Liquidation Products

You can make a lot of money if you buy liquidation products and sell them. The people you are selling to won't know you've bought the products from liquidations so you can make good profits. Search for "buy liquidation stock" to find deals in your area or read the local newspapers, as often these sales are advertised.
On www.quibids.com you can buy overstock, liquidation stocks, close out stock, etc.

264. Distributing Newspapers - R

Are you an early bird and enjoy walking? Delivering newspapers might be just the thing for you. Contact your local post office or local newspapers to see if they need someone.

265. Distributing Leaflets - R

Restaurants, cafes, local shops and local companies often want leaflets and menus delivered, so contact them to see if they need your services.

Make sure to check out the legalities in your area e.g. in some areas you will need a permit to put leaflets on people's cars.

If you find two local companies that want distribution in the same area, you get paid twice but only need to do the round once!

266. Crime Scene Clean Up - R

There are always jobs that most people don't want to do and this is one of them. There is huge earning potential if you are prepared to do this. You will need to clean up blood etc. but somebody has to clean up the scene once bodies have been removed and all the necessary authorities have done their job.
Contact your local police or search online for more information.
There are crimes everywhere so if you do a good job you will definitely be asked back, which will give you recurring income.

267. Sell Used Course Books

It is generally known that students don't have a lot of money, therefore if they can save on buying course books, they certainly will. You can buy student's course books at the end of the year and sell them at the beginning of the next academic year when students are buying books.
You can sell the books on eBay or as an Amazon Reseller.

268. Remove Graffiti - R

Another job that not many people want to do: remove graffiti. For most councils this is a growing problem. Lots of companies also have their building targeted these days. You can see graffiti everywhere you travel so it won't be difficult to find jobs and this is potentially a good earner but hard work as well! Once you've cleaned one wall, another wall appears so you will always have work with this. Make some contacts with your local authorities and tell them to contact you every time new graffiti appears - you might have work every single day and earn some money.

269. Scan Your Groceries

You can earn rewards and points by scanning your purchases with the National Consumer

Panel (NCP) www.ncponline.com

How does it work?
- You apply to be a participant.
- If accepted, you will receive a scanner and you need to scan the barcode of every purchase you make in stores.
- You send your data to NCP and brands will make changes to their range based on feedback from all the NCP participants.
- You earn rewards and points that are redeemable for household items, gifts, toys, etc.
- You can sell the items that you will receive and so make money.

All members will be entered into sweepstakes that include nice prices such as cars, money and vacations.

270. Earn Money Whilst Shopping

There is a lot of competition and therefore companies try different things other than traditional advertising. This is great for people who want to earn some extra money. You can get paid for what you are doing already: shopping.

www.receipthog.com Download the App and earn money. Scan your receipts and you will be awarded virtual coins that can be turned into cash with PayPal or an Amazon Gift Card.
www.shopkick.com Download the App and start earning kicks. They have over 6 million users.
www.ebates.com You can get cash back from 1,700 stores. There are no fees or points to redeem. Their members have earned over $250 million to date. You can get between 2 and 16% cash back on what you've bought. You can also earn money by referring friends and if you refer 400 people, you can make $7,000 - £4,400!
www.ibotta.com (only in US) Scan your receipts and get cash back.
www.topcashback.co.uk They have over 3.5 million members!
www.quidco.com has over 4,200 retailers

271. Health Care Jobs - R

There is an explosion of work-from-home health care jobs. Some of these jobs pay very high salaries and according to www.forbes.com, some people are earning six-figure salaries.
Jobs can include: radiologists, outpatient management and financial resources.
You can be hired by:
www.carenetjobs.com

www.fonemed.com
www.imagingoncall.com
www.mckesson.com
www.medicaljobsonline.com
www.medzilla.com
www.sironahealth.com
www.unitedhealthgroup.com
www.staffnurse.com - UK
www.jobserve.com - UK

272. Prepare A Placenta

I think with this method your competition won't be huge, although the demand is rising. Consumption of the placenta by mothers who believe in the health benefits of eating the placenta is growing. Not only the mums but also the dads eat the placenta.

There are several ways to eat a placenta but the two most common ways are:
- Prepare the placenta e.g. cooking it and adding ingredients to make it into a meat-looking dish.
- You can do Placenta Encapsulation. This means preparing the placenta in such a way that the end result can be taken in capsule form.

Informative: placentophagy is the act of mammals eating the placenta of their young. Search online how to prepare a placenta and contact all hospitals near you that have a baby delivery unit. The mums will likely ask the midwives about eating their placenta so the midwife can refer the mum to you. If you are lucky, you never have to do a thing to get new customers as babies are born all the time, everywhere!

273. Rent Or Sell Plus Size Wedding Dresses

One of my friends was getting married but couldn't find a nice dress in her neighbourhood. She is a plus size and a rather large lady. I believe there is a shortage for suppliers of plus size wedding dresses. I have never understood this really: a lot of women anywhere you go are plus size and need plus size dresses. Why is there not more supply for these women? You could tap into this market and source some dresses and rent or sell them. If you are reading this and you are in the USA, I guess the market there is totally different and there will be plenty of suppliers for plus size wedding dresses. I think in the UK there is space for more suppliers.

274. Party Entertainment

Maybe you are a good clown or magician? Or you play the violin or another instrument? You can juggle or are a good comedian? You could offer your services for party organisers. Get in touch with party organisers and tell them what you can do. You can easily earn $300 - £250 for a few hours work, whilst you have some fun.

275. Run A Home-Based Franchise

Take advantage of the power of being a franchisee: the franchise company has done most of the work for you and some of them are very well established, making it easier for you to make money. Note: you will need a lot of money to start up. Just search for "home-based franchise" and you will find 100's if not 1000's of opportunities e.g. cleaning, pets, children, gardening, online, cars, cruise planning, finances, home helpers, home care, decorating, home tutoring, vending, dating, golf, pest control, business, sport, blinds, dance classes, etc.
Whatever you are good at or whatever you fancy, there's probably a franchise opportunity for you to investigate.
Search online for "dog +franchise" or whatever niche you are thinking of.

276. Become An Importer And Distributor

Have you ever travelled somewhere and thought: "That is a good product, it's a shame I can't buy it in my own country?" Well, if you've thought so, other people probably thought the same. You can find out where the manufacturer is (usually on the packaging), contact them and find out if they have a distributor in the country where you live.

That's how easy it can be to become an importer. Once you've imported the goods, you can sell them to retailers. Once you are selling a lot of goods, you will need space for storage but you can easily rent some space near you.

277. Deliver Alcohol Late At Night

If you are prepared to work evenings and weekends, this might be a good opportunity for you. Very often people having any kind of party run out of alcohol and are too drunk to get in the car and get more. You can deliver the much-needed alcohol for them. Not only students will welcome your service but people of all ages.
You will need a license to sell alcohol: find out from your local council what you need to do to get one.

278. Become A Business Babysitter

Millions of small business owners do have the money to go on holiday but can't leave the business running on its own, so they need a business babysitter. You would answer calls, answer emails, fulfil orders, etc. whilst the business owner goes on holiday. All that is needed is a call forwarding service and some secretarial knowledge.

279. Become A Match Maker

Debra M. Cohen from New York has set up a multi-million-dollar business and all she does is match people e.g. a home owner is looking for a plumber and she will find a reliable plumber in return for a finder fee or a percentage of the job price that the plumber will ask for.

Visit www.hrnbiz.com to read her story. She teaches how you can duplicate her business model for a one-time charge.

This model is a Homeowner Referral Network (HRN) and it is booming and you can take a slice of the income pie.

280. Party Rentals

If you are prepared to work evenings and weekends, you can earn money by renting items for parties. Anything from games, slides, decoration, plates and cutlery, artificial plants, furniture, inflatables, etc. You will need a van, some storage space and capital to buy stock. The great thing about your stock is that it will make money over and over again so this can be a very profitable business. Make sure you get insurance though.

281. Make Homes Sell Faster

Lots of homes are for sale on the market for years but are simply not selling. Often the reason for this is that the homes are not nicely presented to a potential buyer. You can become a specialist in changing this and increase the chances for the home to be sold quicker. Contact local real estate agencies to offer your services.

Chapter 28. Seasonal Jobs

282. Pick Fruit Or Vegetables

If you are looking to earn some money only a few months per year consider fruit picking. It certainly is not the best-paid job around but it does get you in the fresh air. Search online for "fruit picking" or "vegetable picking" and see where you can work in your area.

Do you enjoy holiday times like Christmas and Halloween? Has anyone ever complimented you for coming up with great or unusual ideas? If so, you are probably creative, and there are many business opportunities for those who can think outside the box.

283. Christmas Tree Retailer

At Christmas time, many entrepreneurs make enough money to live on for the entire year by selling Christmas trees in November and December.

As a Christmas Tree Retailer, you provide live trees to the community. You need to have a wholesaler who will supply the trees to you and a location at which to sell them. You can do this with very little money.

Typically, you have to lease a site for two months and you want to negotiate to pay the full lease amount at the end of the first month with nothing upfront. This, in effect, is paying the first and last month at the same time, and allows you to pay the lease after you have earned income for a full month first. Property owners are often flexible because it allows them to receive income on property that is otherwise stagnant.

If they won't work with you, you can always try your front garden if permissible, and if you don't have a garden or yard, pay a small amount to someone you know who does. There are other issues you may need to look into, such as insurance and licenses from your local authority.

As for the trees, try to get them on 'sale or return' so you only pay the wholesaler for trees that you actually sell. They will prefer that you pay for the trees upfront and they may buy back unsold ones. However, if you are a good negotiator, you may be able to get your entire stock at the beginning with a delayed payment.

It is important in this business to have a solid business plan and understand how many trees you will need to sell in order to return a profit. While this business sometimes looks easy, it does have risks, and without proper planning you could expose yourself to losses.

284. Pumpkin Patch Retailer

If this type of business appeals to you, and you are successful your first year, you may want to lease the property for a longer period your second year, and become a Pumpkin Patch Retailer.

The business model is the same as the Christmas Tree Retailer and allows you to leverage your lease costs across a longer period and perhaps for less money. And, of course, you can start this process in reverse by first starting the pumpkin business and then moving into the tree business.

People are often very loyal to these businesses year after year so the opportunity to create a lifelong business that generates recurring income is very possible.

285. Holiday Decorator

For years, families and businesses have taken on the responsibility of decorating for the holidays. For businesses, especially retail, their customers expect the stores to be festively decorated. Holidays are good for sales.

For families, holiday decorations are a tradition but as people get older they may not really want do it anymore. In business, employees don't have the time to decorate and keep up with their regular job responsibilities too. Decorations are accumulated every year and eventually they become too much of a burden. And the biggest reason for not bothering with decorations is that no one wants to clean up afterwards!

This is where the Holiday Decorator comes in. Sometimes it is as simple a job as putting up (and taking down) Christmas lights or a Christmas tree. But a good Holiday Decorator can build the business to extend year round.

Think about it: New Years Day, Super Bowl Sunday, Valentine's Day, St Patrick's Day, Easter, Fourth of July, barbeques on Memorial and Labour Days, Thanksgiving, March Madness, graduation time, and of course the two big paydays of Halloween and Christmas.
There is an abundance of opportunities.

Retail stores change their seasonal themes year round. Starting with a few clients will keep you busy and tie you over until October, November and December, the busiest months when you will probably make 80% of your income.

So what does a Holiday Decorator do? At Christmas time, you provide holiday decorations to many of the businesses in your area. Often businesses will have their employees set up and take down the tree and place a few decorations, randomly, around the office. You can offer to do that, with better taste, enthusiasm and flair, for a minimal fee.

If you can show that your service will benefit the employer by eliminating employee downtime and inefficient use of employee time, and maximising employees' productivity, as then it will make sense from a financial perspective. At the same time, it may help employee morale since they often don't even need to do the decorating.

At first, you will not have much stock of your own so you can offer to use the client's decorations. Tell them that will help keep their costs down, as you will charge less. They will appreciate that and it will allow you time to build up your own inventory. The next time you work for them you can charge a rental fee for your items.

Private homes can also be lucrative. Many people just don't want to put those lights up and will eagerly pay others to do it for them.

The one caveat here is electricity. There have been unfortunate situations where the homeowner wanted excessive lighting and their electrical system could not handle it. Make sure you put in your contract with the homeowners that they take all responsibility should they request more than your recommendation. You don't want them calling you every night saying their circuit breaker has shut down!

286. Hauntrepreneur

Halloween has numerous opportunities both for a Holiday Decorator and for an entrepreneur, or in this case, a Hauntrepreneur. A Hauntrepreneur creates haunted house attractions. It is usually a dark maze that paying customers walk through for the purpose of being scared by actors dressed up as ghouls and goblins. There are Hauntrepreneurs all over the country, making a very good living by working one month a year in October.

So how does it work? Haunted Houses can be set up almost anywhere: in closed retail shop locations (you only have to rent a unit for one month), in fields and unused warehouses. It can be created as an extra attraction for a current business, and even for a convention.

Once you have the location, you build the maze, hire the actors (friends or family) to scare the customers and open for business. You can charge anywhere from $10 to $20 (£6 to £12) per hour. This sounds simple but it is a fair amount of work and requires a lot of planning and some money.

The good news is that many, if not most, of these Hauntrepreneurs started their business by building a maze in their garage or yard. They take pictures and build up a picture portfolio that way. They let everyone in for free the first year and if it was a success they were ready to take what they learned to a bigger stage the following Halloween. If you have not done this before, then this may be the best and less risky route.

Start small and build up your experience, knowledge and fans. Some very successful Hauntrepreneurs make as much as $400,000 (almost a quarter of a million pounds) a year! You won't be able to do the work all on your own in this case, but you will have plenty of money to hire help.

287. Haunted House Consultants

With the success of haunted houses, there are new opportunities in the industry, for example, Haunted House Consultants, who teach the Hauntrepreneurs how to build the maze and market the event.

Haunted House Suppliers, who build the sets, are becoming more common too and are a great way to enter the business risk free. If you are not a fan of Halloween, fear not. There are many more opportunities surrounding the holidays.

288. Fireworks Retailer

If you have a good location, and a good deal on the lease, you will be able to do this year round: as a Fireworks Retailer for the Fourth of July (in the US), for Bonfire Night (in the UK), Christmas and New Year and selling other products such as gift baskets and seasonal items for the rest of the year.

However, there is an increasing amount of regulations around selling fireworks so you should check the latest safety and license requirements with your local authority/city/state.

289. Christmas Overstock Reseller

Retail stores often sell their Christmas overstock after the holiday. They often have a lot of unsold stock and nowhere to put it. Most stores have a very small warehouse and don't want to fill it up for the next twelve months with last season's Christmas paper.

Instead, they will typically mark it down at 50% off initially. Then a week or so later it will be 75% off. Sometimes even more. A successful Christmas Overstock Reseller would buy as much as he/she could at 75% off (or more) and store it in his garage for the next year. The following holiday season, he/she would take it to swap meets, small stores, holiday fairs, and sell it for twice the price he/she paid.

For example, if a roll of Christmas paper was originally priced at $3.99, (£2) and the store sold it at 75% off, then the price that he/she paid was $1.00. (£0.75) The following season, he/she would sell it for $2.00 (£1.50), which was a 100% mark up, but still 50% of the original price for the customer. Multiply that by thousands of rolls of Christmas paper and you can see the potential of this business.

It is not uncommon for business people to start with one small idea similar to these and eventually turn it into a very successful moneymaking enterprise.

290. Seasonal Ornaments

If you are arty and creative, you can make Christmas ornaments or decorations to sell to hang around the house or on the tree. You can also make Halloween, Easter, Mother's day etc. ornaments and sell them for a profit. Sell them at local Christmas fairs, markets, etc.

Part 3) Make Money Online - NO Website Needed

With all the methods in this part of the book, you can earn money simply with a computer and an Internet connection. You don't need your own website. You will never have to leave your home - or your comfy chair. However, please be aware that these days, people search for everything on the web so it is always good to have a website to sell your services. That way you will find new customers, as most people now search online for whatever it is they are looking for. Even if it is just a one page website with your contact details on and a brief explanation of what you do. It doesn't have to be a website with all the bells and whistles.

Everybody hangs around online. Everybody buys stuff online. We all know that a lot of the high streets look like this:

People are still buying and spending but they are spending it online, so you can earn a lot of money online. The different ways of making money online listed in this part of the book are not all tried and tested by myself (I am a full-time Internet marketer but I haven't tried *everything*). It is purely a list of moneymaking opportunities.

Chapter 29. Introduction To Making Money Online And Internet Marketing Terminology

Do you have any idea what the single biggest obstacle to making money online is? It is not bad luck, lack of money or even lack of information. It is information overload.
As strange as it may sound at first, it's this very thing that is largely responsible for hindering so many people in their attempt to become successful online.

Making money online has huge advantages:
- Minimal start up costs
- Decide your own hours
- Open 24/7/365
- Your target market is the whole world
- Automatic order processing
- Automatic payments
- Product is delivered instantly if you sell eBooks or downloadable products
- No rent
- No staff
- No stock (unless you sell physical goods)
- No outstanding debts as customer pays online immediately with purchase
- You can create automated income on autopilot
- You can create passive income
- You can make money whilst you sleep

I hope you'll enjoy reading this part of the book and please remember to keep an open mind - you only need to apply one method successfully to turn your life around.

Earning money online *does* require that you have some basic knowledge of Internet marketing terminology. My book "From Newbie To Millionaire" explains Internet marketing very well and if you are a newbie to Internet marketing, I suggest you get yourself a copy. I am not saying this to sell you my Newbie book because, at first, I did actually copy parts of that book in this book, resulting in this book being over 400 pages! I have decided to take that part out and refer to my Newbie book for those who are reading this book and don't yet know Internet marketing terminology.
I will, however, explain a few things in this book as I refer to these terms on a regular basis: what is affiliate marketing, what is ClickBank, what is an auto responder, what is outsourcing? Etc.

- What Is Affiliate Marketing?

If you are from the "older generation", remember the days when the man from the insurance company would come and sit in your kitchen and try to sell you insurance? When he sold you some, his boss – the insurance company – would pay the salesman say, 10% commission. That is affiliate marketing the old fashioned way. I guess you could also call it commission marketing because that's what it is: somebody gets paid commission for selling somebody else's product. The insurance company is the affiliate merchant, or vendor, and the salesman is the affiliate as he gets commission from a sale.

Now imagine this scenario on the Internet: the insurance company has a website that sells insurance. The salesman has a website that tells you the pros and cons of insurance and here and there on his website he puts a link that, when you click on it, gives you the chance to buy insurance. If you buy via that link, the insurance company will pay the salesman commission.

So in this case you are the salesman who will be selling for other companies, and every time you sell something, the company will pay you commission. You are the affiliate (the one who receives the commission) and the insurance company that will pay you is called the merchant or the vendor. All you need to do is put the same affiliate links on your website that refer to the insurance company's website, and you get paid when somebody buys via that link.

Everything else is automated. Commission ranges from 1% to 75%. Physical products usually pay between 2% and 25% commission but www.ClickBank.com, which sells mostly digital products, can pay up to 80% commission or even more. I explain ClickBank in more detail later.

A merchant is an online retailer with a website where you can buy products or services.

An affiliate or online publisher is the person who drives visitors to the merchant's website and gets paid commission when customers buy something by clicking on the link that is on the affiliate's website. An affiliate drives buyers to the merchant's sites and gets paid for it. The merchant pays the affiliate commission only when a sale is made. The affiliate will sell your product or services for a commission. Affiliates are other Internet marketers or other website owners.

Affiliate networks are automated websites on which merchants can put their name to say they are looking for affiliates to drive traffic to their websites. You, as an affiliate, go to the affiliate network to grab an affiliate link to put on your website. The affiliate network pays you your commission. All you need to do is stick a link on your site and drive traffic; all the rest is done automatically for you.

Affiliate marketing is the whole automated set up to do with affiliates, merchants and affiliate networks.

Once you are into affiliate marketing you will never look at a website the same way again. You will constantly look for links on the top of your browser. You will constantly look for new ideas. A lot of people search for "top 10 digital cameras" or " best flat TV" or "review video software". Years ago I used to believe the reviews on websites. Unfortunately, reality has taught me that some websites don't publish honest, impartial reviews. They will award top prizes to the company with the affiliate link that pays them the most money.

All the "buy" buttons will be an affiliate link. The first "buy" button might take you to the Amazon store; the second "buy" button might take you to a computer store. So if the website owner earns a lot more from the Amazon link, he might put that first even if it doesn't merit the win.

Some review websites do give honest opinions. But be cautious with what you buy and what you believe on the web.

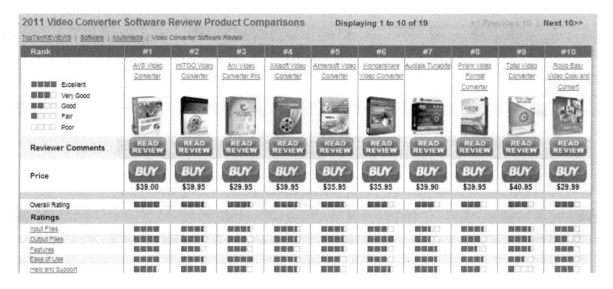

Here's an example of an affiliate link that you might see in the browser when you click one of the Buy Buttons:

https://www.regnow.com/softsell/nph-softsell.cgi?linkid=ti5508644&item=9641-126&affiliate=22430

If you come across any website – once you are an Internet marketer – you will probably pay a lot of attention to what is in the browser bar on the top of your screen. Anything that says something like ID6487541 or Affiliate = 789p or IDlink 1290 tells you that somebody is earning money from affiliate marketing.

So the website owner (in this case the one with the website showing all the buy buttons) is the insurance guy, or affiliate, sitting at your table who earns commission. The website that you navigate to (in this example regnow.com) when you click the 'buy' button is the merchant who pays the commission to the affiliate.

As an Internet marketer you can become an affiliate and sell other people's products BUT it is even better to have your own product and let other people sell it for you. All you need to do is become a merchant (by asking people to sell your products).

Here are a few screenshots from the browser bar where it is very obvious that it is an affiliate link. The give away can be: ID, Partner, TID, Link 1234, Affilatecode…, AFFIL1234, Cookie, etc.

There is one big problem with affiliate marketing and the clue is in the name: marketing. The affiliate network does not help you with that. Getting a site stacked with affiliate links is easy but getting visitors to your site is a lot more difficult. It's the marketing of your site that is going to be the hardest.

- What Is ClickBank?

Well, in their words:
ClickBank Is The Web's Most Trusted Digital Marketplace. Founded in 1998, ClickBank is a secure online retail outlet for more than 70,000 digital product vendors and 110,000 active affiliate marketers. **ClickBank makes a sale somewhere in the world every three seconds,** *safely processing more than 27,000 digital transactions a day. They serve more than 200 countries, and are consistently ranked as one of the most high-traffic sites on the web.*
Source: www.ClickBank.com.

ClickBank mostly sells digital products: eBooks, software, videos. The products range from 'how to stop your dog barking' to 'how to make money on the Internet' and everything else in between. Because all products are digital and the delivery cost is zero, the commission rates are very high: between 50% to 75% and even more.

ClickBank is a database where affiliates can find products to sell or where vendors can find affiliates to sell their products.

ClickBank is the Internet marketer's dream come true. The big advantage of ClickBank is that it has its own payment processor, so you can sell products and charge peoples' credit cards – ClickBank does all this for you automatically. Before ClickBank was online, you would have to get your own merchant account from your bank and as a new business that would be almost impossible. With ClickBank, you can sell stuff online without ever having sold anything before - ClickBank will charge your customer. ClickBank collects the money from the buyer, pays the affiliate the commission and pays the vendor the rest.

Signing up as an affiliate with ClickBank is free. If you have written an eBook on "piano repair" but you are not very good at selling or building websites, you can become a vendor on ClickBank and put your eBook there for anybody to sell. In return you give the seller part of the selling price. As an example, you keep 40% and the affiliate gets 60% when a book is sold.
On the other hand, if you know nothing about piano repair but you think that there is a gap on the Internet to sell books on piano repairs, you would sign up as an affiliate on ClickBank and find a piano repair book to sell on your website. You would get 60% (or whatever the commission rate is) of the selling price because you have put in most of the

effort in the sale of the eBook.

Being an affiliate has the following advantages:

- No license fees needed

- No need to create your own products as you will sell other people's products

- There is no contract to sign with anybody

- You can log onto your work anywhere in the world

- You can make money while you sleep (after you have put in some hard work)

- You can sell in any country, worldwide

- You can sell in any niche

- You never have to process orders

- You never ever have to ship orders

- You never ever need to worry about stock taking, over stocking or surplus stock

- You never need a Customer Service email or telephone number

- You never need large start-up capital to begin trading

- You never need a Payment Processing Gateway (a bank that charges your customer's card)

- You don't need employees

- You don't need sales experience

- You don't need to know anything about a niche

- You have no production costs to worry about

- You never have to leave your house

- You never have to speak to anybody if you don't want to

- You can choose the hours you work

- You can be your own boss

- Very easy to get started

- You can start up a business that can grow 200% or more each year, which is almost impossible to achieve in a business outside the web

- You never have to go to the bank to pay in cheques, as it's all is done electronically

- You never have to chase late payments as everything is paid in advance

- There are no cash flow problems (if you manage your money correctly) as you receive your money immediately

- No refund worries as ClickBank does this for you – everything is automated

- Easy to scale up

Important: ClickBank changes the rules sometimes so make sure you know the rules before you start working with them as a vendor or as an affiliate.

- What Is An Auto Responder?

An auto responder is a software program that automatically sends out emails on a pre-scheduled basis to all the opted-in people on your list.

Once you have built a list, the idea is that you send them some freebies or send them a newsletter or an affiliate link etc. You can't possibly do all this manually each time you receive a new opt-in. An auto responder does this automatically for you. Let's say you want to create a five-part email course. You set the intervals for the emails, say once a day. All you need to do is type in the emails once in your auto responder software and your list will get an email once a day. Anyone joining your list will automatically be sent those emails for the next five days.

So the owner of the list uses auto responder software to set up a sequence of emails that go out at regular intervals. You must have an auto responder when you have an opt-in box on your website.
You will have seen these messages at the bottom of your emails:
To unsubscribe or change subscriber options visit:
www.aweber.com

When you click on that link you can unsubscribe. By law you need to put an unsubscribe button at the bottom of each email you send. If people no longer want to receive your emails and click unsubscribe, your auto responder will remove that person automatically from your list and your next pre-scheduled email will no longer be received by the person who has unsubscribed.

Which auto responder is best?

The best email auto-responder on the market is, in my opinion, www.aweber.com, but a good, free alternative is www.mailchimp.com (if using a limited list). Other automated email responders include: www.getresponse.com and www.autocontactor.com.

You have to make sure that you use a professional auto responder service because that way you are more protected from spam complaints. There are more free auto responders in my book Design Free Websites.

- What Is Outsourcing?

Outsourcing is simply giving a task to somebody and paying them to do it. Outsourcing on the Internet is done on outsourcing websites. Almost anything can be outsourced on the Internet. The general principle on these sites is the opposite of eBay. As eBay is an auction site, the product goes to whoever pays the highest price. On outsourcing websites the freelancer bids low on a job in order to win the work. For example, freelancer A might quote $200 (£120) to design a five-page website but freelancer B might undercut A with a quote of $180 (£107). www.elance.com is my favourite outsourcing site. Thousands of jobs are posted on this site each day.

You can get an outsourcer to write a 120-page book on any subject for $500 (just over £300). As writing a book with unique content (not just PLR products - Private Label Products- copied and pasted) will take several weeks, you might wonder why somebody would do this for $500. The reason is that a lot of people who are registered on Elance are based in sub continental countries. The cost of living in such countries is much lower than in other countries, like the USA or the UK.

So it's a win-win situation: the outsourced freelancer gets a lot of money and the person giving him/her the job gets a good price. Make sure to check the feedback from the person you are thinking of hiring because you will need to select somebody who can write perfect English, without spelling mistakes. There are a lot of native English speakers on the outsourcing sites, but in my experience they often quote higher for the jobs.

- Can Outsourcing Sites Be trusted?

Thousands of businesses use outsourcing sites everyday to hire and manage online, so yes they can be trusted. If you trust eBay and Amazon, you can trust the well-known outsourcing sites as the principle is more or less the same: 99% of people who do business on those sites can be trusted but unfortunately there are dishonest people everywhere on the web. The outsourcing sites listed below are very well known in the Internet business.

Here are some reliable outsourcing websites where thousands of freelancers bid for all sorts of jobs: writing, translating, web design, slideshows, marketing, admin, multimedia, design, engineering, finance, legal, manufacturing... the list goes on.

www.elance.com (the one I use all the time)
www.fiverr.com There is a huge amount of services here for $5 (£3): backlinks, more Twitter followers, installing your website for you, consulting... you can even pay a woman to dress up in a cat-suit and jump around shouting whatever you like (although that will probably not help you earn money from your site).
www.agentsofvalue.com
www.clickchores.com
www.domystuff.com
www.fieldagents.net
www.freelance.com
www.guru.com
www.ifreelance.com
www.microworkers.com
www.mturk.com
www.odesk.com
www.peopleperhour.com
www.shorttask.com
www.staff.com
www.virtualbee.com

Chapter 30. Make Money Using Internet Marketing Techniques

291. Become An Affiliate Marketer

I have already explained what affiliate marketing is. In short, it is promoting and selling other peoples' products and services in exchange for a commission. It's a very lucrative model of online marketing because it's designed to benefit both parties.

An Ideal Affiliate Marketing Model:

- Choose a few affiliate products in the same niche that you want to promote/sell
- Find or create an eBook to give away
- Make a squeeze page where you offer the free eBook
- Use an auto responder to capture the email address of the person who requested the free eBook on your squeeze page. These people will now be added to your list.
- Create a few emails with your auto responder to send to your list to build a relationship with the people you now have on your list.
- Now and again send the people on your list an email in which you recommend a product (that will solve a problem for the people on your list) and put an affiliate link in that email.
- Each time a person on your list will click on your affiliate link and buy a product, you've earned some money.
- Keep sending traffic to your squeeze page to build your list.

There are a lot of different platforms that offer affiliates the chance to sign up, enter their preferred payment method and they're ready to start promoting products the very same day! One of the most popular ones is definitely www.ClickBank.com

It takes less than 5 minutes to set up an account with ClickBank, after which you can access the marketplace, check out the products and decide which ones you wish to promote. The commissions for digital products are HUGE, some even reaching up to 90%! That means you can earn $45 (over £25) for every $50 (£30) product you sell. But how exactly do you "promote" these products? Well, by sending traffic to your product. I could write another whole book about this so unfortunately it is impossible to list all the traffic methods here. My book "From Newbie To Millionaire" lists over 100 traffic methods.

292. Become An Amazon Affiliate

You sign up as an Amazon affiliate and promote your affiliate links on as many places as you can. Each time somebody buys something through your affiliate link, Amazon will pay you commission. Although commissions for physical products are rather low, it is important to remember that you get commission no matter what the prospect buys.

Why is this important? Let's say you're promoting audio CDs, and your prospect lands on that Amazon page, but he sees a related offer for a hi-fi stereo and decides to check it out and eventually buys it - you get 10% commission for that stereo.

Another great thing is that everyone has heard of Amazon, and people won't hesitate to buy from such a trusted source. They know it's not a scam, and they've probably already bought something from Amazon in the past.

Furthermore, it is important to notice that people often choose to buy more than just one thing at a time, and you get commission for all of them! You can also pick from an incredibly wide variety of products. Seasonal items, for instance, can pay extremely well when promoted at the appropriate time. You might not want to promote an outdoor pool in winter, but you will want to promote an artificial Christmas tree. However, some people want to take advantage of the lower demand for summer-themed items during the holidays. It's all about taking a few risks!
To sign up as an Amazon.com affiliate and start promoting their products, visit this link - https://affiliate-program.amazon.com. Just search for it, in whatever country you are.

293. Earn Money From Recurring Commissions - R

Apparently there is an Internet marketer who rakes in over $300,000 (£187,000) a year and all he does is sit on his computer when he feels like it and use free traffic techniques to send visitors to his recurring commissions affiliate links. His money comes in every single month without him having to get a lot of extra customers. It took him 8 years to build up his income to that level. Recurring commissions are DEFINITELY a good potential business. Visit www.lifetimecommissions.com for websites that pay recurring commission.

294. Earn Money From Mobile Phone Marketing

You will need some money to spend, as mobile marketing will cost money. But all you need to do is sign up with some mobile marketing companies and send your visitors to a landing page with your affiliate link. Mobile marketing is ideal for CPA marketing (Cost Per Action Marketing) where people have to leave their email address, or try some products for free, for you to get paid.

295. Earn Money From Pay Per Click And The Smaller Search Engines

You will need some money to spend, as you will create ads with your affiliate links as a landing page and pay search engines to show your ad. You will only pay when people click on your ad. Here's a step-by-step guide:

- Sign up with PPC (Pay Per Click) networks
- Set up a campaign with your keyword
- Find affiliate products and send people to your affiliate link

I know people who have a full-time income purely with PPC and affiliate links. You will need some start up money (I suggest between $500 and $1000 - £300 and £600), as some campaigns will lose you money but some will make you money. To start with, the income from the ones that make money might not be enough compared to your total spending, but after a few months you can focus solely on the ones that are profitable.

Important to know: Only ever use money you can afford to lose because you are very likely to set up some campaigns where you will lose all your money.

296. Viral Blogging

Join www.empowernetwork.com and its viral blogging system. You join, view their products and start blogging. You get paid commission for every sale. They have over 155,000 members.

Chapter 31. Make Money From Social Media

297. Facebook

I guess Facebook does not need introducing. People who don't know Facebook these days must have been living under a rock. No need to say it, but Facebook is extremely big.

I am personally not a massive social media fan, as I don't have the time to hang around on these sites for hours without actually doing something productive. I believe Facebook is the best thing ever for social purposes but not for money-earning purposes. For pleasure and socialising, Facebook is great, the best site ever, but I am *not* interested in exactly what time someone has a cup of tea or has a bath.

Facebook is perfect for some things: e.g. finding a lost child or a lost dog, finding a donor, donating money for a child who needs a life threatening operation in Las Vegas etc. People will share these sorts of things and Facebook can make things happen in these occasions.

Of course, **IF** you have an extremely rare product or an extremely funny video, people will share that on Facebook and you might create a few sales from the back end. **The point I am making here is that I don't think you can become a millionaire from promoting products on Facebook as an affiliate marketer e.g. you are not going to sell thousands of books on "How to train a Labrador" by selling or advertising your book on Facebook.**

From an earning point of view: I've never earned anything with social media. I put myself in my reader's shoes as I realise that a lot of readers hang out a lot on social media sites and try to earn money on Facebook. That's the reason for mentioning it in this book.

I just don't think you can believe any businessperson on Facebook as you can BUY likes and you can BUY friends. So, if someone has 100,000 likes, are they real likes? Doubtful but possible. If someone has 20,000 friends, are they real friends? Again, doubtful but possible. I watched a guru's Facebook for a while and on a Monday he had 3,000 likes and the following Monday he had 40,000 likes! Surely not possible!
People BEG other people to like them. I just don't like that. I don't wish to beg people to like me. They like me or they don't. So, if you like me, visit my Facebook Page and like me :-). www.facebook.com/christine.clayfield

Perhaps it is because I am from "the older generation" that I am not a Facebook fanatic?

On this screenshot, you can see that you can buy 2,000 friends for $69.95 / £41.

You can also buy Facebook fans and likes with "real" pictures. 1,000 photo likes for $20 / £11.

Another example: you can buy 20,000 likes for $199.95 / £119.

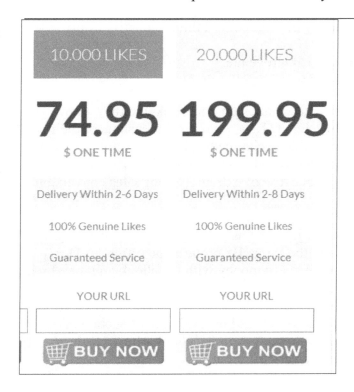

The only reason why someone would buy likes is to boast about how many friends/likes they have. From a business point of view, buying likes and friends is totallty pointless as they won't be targeted friends/potential customers so they won't be people interested in what you are selling. I suggest you don't buy likes or friends.

Furthermore, people go on Facebook to socialise or see what their friends have been up to, NOT to buy stuff. On the other hand, anyone who opens Amazon is *planning to buy* something, as you can't do anything else on Amazon but buy! You see, there is a great difference from a commercial point of view. You want to target people who have a buying attitude, NOT the ones who want to socialise. You need to sell to people who are *ready to buy*, with their credit card ready to give to you. Amazon is only one example of a site where there are "ready to buy people", but there are lots of similar sites e.g. www.udemy.com, any book selling website, any ecommerce website, etc.

A lot of business people who hang around on Facebook, do so to promote or sell their own products, *not* to buy yours. The youngsters hang around on Facebook a lot but often they don't have any money to buy things anyway therefore they are not a good target audience.

I don't know anybody who earns good money on Facebook. I think the only people who earn money on Facebook are:
- Facebook itself with their huge advertising revenue.
- People selling stuff on how to make money with Facebook.

There are people selling courses on how to make money on Facebook and they show you screenshots of their earnings BUT what they do NOT show you is screenshots of their spending. To run an ad on Facebook, or any other social media site, costs money. It's all about conversion rate. You can spend thousands on ads and earn nothing. I've tried advertising on Facebook and earned nothing because of extremely poor sales conversion rates.

Right, that's my opinion on Facebook. I know it is rare as an Internet marketer to say this but I've always believed and tell my children the same: Be proud to be different! Don't follow the crowd! Who knows, one day I might earn money with Facebook and then I will tell you a whole different story.

I don't use Facebook myself for commercial reasons but I do read about Facebook and as far as I know, people give two ways of making money with Facebook - buying ads and creating Facebook pages. Both approaches are very different.

Facebook ads serve as a way to drive targeted traffic to your site or Facebook page. They're not free, of course, so it's something you have to test over and over again until you determine that the traffic you're buying actually turns out to be profitable to you.

You can spot these ads on any Facebook page in the right column of the website. The good thing about them is that they use a cookie-technology, which means that your ad will be displayed only to audiences that have previously shown interest in whatever your site/page is about.

If you have a website and on it you have a review of a weight loss product and an affiliate link at the end, you would then buy a Facebook ad and it would be shown only to people who are already interested in losing weight. Your goal would be to convert as much of this traffic into buyers as you can, so that it covers your advertising expenses and makes you a profit.

Once you test this and determine that you're making profit, you can ramp things up and instead of investing $100 (£60) and getting $150 (£90) back, you could be investing $1000 (£595) and getting $1500 (around £890) back.

Overall, it's a pretty nice method if you've already got some capital to invest **IF** it works for you.

On the other hand, creating Facebook pages might be a better way to start if you have a limited budget, because it's essentially free. To create an FB page, follow this link: http://www.faceBook.com/pages/create/. Pick your page theme and follow the instructions: the setup is laid out in very simple terms. Once you've created your page, it's time to bring in fans - that's the whole point, right?

To do this, you must first make sure you post some good content on your page. This is important because people are more likely to "like" your page and share it with others if it's interesting.

After you've done this (written good content and boosted your 'like' count), it's time to start promoting your page and drive traffic to it. That's when things are going to get easier. People will be joining and sharing your page and some might buy.

When your page has finally become popular enough, you can start posting your affiliate links, but make sure you don't spam your page (1 link per week is already too many) and that you constantly provide free value as well. Remember, the key to a successful Facebook page is good relationship with your fans.

298. Other Social Media

Facebook is certainly not the only popular social media site you can earn money with. Here are some other ones:

www.bebo.com
www.devianart.com
www.flickr.com
www.foursquare.com
www.friendster.com
www.hi5.com
www.instagram.com
www.linkedin.com
www.meetme.com
www.myspace.com
www.orkut.com
www.pininterest.com
www.plus.google.com
www.snapchat.com

www.tagged.com
www.tumblr.com
www.twitter.com
www.vine.co
www.vk.com
www.youtube.com

299. Become A Twitter Manager - R

www.Twitter.com is useful as a promotional tool, but do you know that you can make money out of having a Twitter account?
You can offer Twitter services to a variety of companies. Do you know that most celebrity Twitter accounts are not operated by the celebrities themselves? These public figures pay professional social media specialists to post tweets on their behalf.

These specialists also operate accounts for companies while earning money on the side re-tweeting sponsored posts. On www.sponsoredtweets.com you set the amount you want to make for each tweet. You can also choose the category you want to tweet in. Advertisers will make you offers.

To get started, you need at least a working knowledge of Twitter and other social media sites, and a decent-sized following. Once you open another Twitter account for work, look for friends and followers who have a lot of followers themselves and ask them to follow your new account. This is where your credibility and ability to promote yourself becomes a huge factor.

The number of tweets you produce is also key. You have to strike a balance between updating your account constantly and producing content that looks and sounds authentic and engaging. You may even hire content writers who have expertise in certain industries to make it sound even more authoritative. Interacting with your followers is also important in this type of business.

300. Become A Social Media Manager - R

Lots of companies have social media sites but don't have the time to update their sites or Tweet or post on Facebook. This is where you come in. You can do this for those companies from home and get paid for it. A lot of famous people use social media managers.
It will also be your job to read all the comments and become a Moderator Manager e.g. rude comments to be removed, monitoring dialogues, etc.

- www.liveworld.com They have a special section on Moderation
- www.crowdsource.com They have a special section on Moderation

301. Get Paid To Socialise

A lot of companies pay people just to talk about their products online by using social media. This is different to being a social media manager as all you do here is just talk about a product or service.
www.automatedsocialmedia.net
www.cashunite.com
www.chatabout.com
www.loop88.com
www.mylikes.com
www.paidsocialmediajobs.com
www.postloop.com

302. Forum Moderator

The best way to think of this job is by imagining yourself as a prefect and all the other members are your "students". You will be someone who supervises what's happening within the forum and makes sure that everyone adheres to the rules and regulations. Regardless of what type of forum you're moderating or supervising, you'll usually be expected to perform the following responsibilities:

- Welcoming new members and offering assistance whenever necessary.
- Ensuring that policies are updated and adhered to.
- Monitoring posts and the activities of members.
- Issuing warnings and handing out penalties whenever a violation has been committed.
- Participating in all threads and moderating discussions to prevent other members from arguing.

Most magazine-style websites are likely to have forums, and they usually have quite a few job offers posted there. In any case, you have nothing to lose by asking any of the existing moderators about vacancies. Payment varies greatly for this type of job. It ultimately depends on how large its membership base is and the popularity level of the forum. Niches such as Internet Marketing are popular, and forums such as www.warriorforum.com are good places to start.

One of the ways to become a moderator is by becoming a member of a forum, and becoming active in it. Once you have established your presence and have become a well-known contributor to the forum, you will have an "authority" status, which is one of the usual requirements for being a moderator.

Make sure that you choose a forum from where you can actually earn money, because there are forums that hire moderators for free, although there are some perks provided.

303. Video On YouTube

YouTube is not only a video site; it is also a social media site where people can leave comments, like a video, etc. If you have an idea to make a video and put it on www.youtube.com and it goes viral, YouTube will pay you money as advertisers will want to advertise on your video and are willing to pay to do so.

There are probably a lot more ways to make money with social media but, as I don't know all that much about this aspect of online marketing, I won't suggest any other methods.

Chapter 32. Creative & Design Jobs

304. Drawing Objects & 3-D

It's an understatement to say that the Internet has opened art up to the world. Sites such as www.DeviantArt.com have given artists all over the globe the exposure that they need. The Internet is not just for "serious" artists though. You can create wallpapers and mobile themes for platforms as diverse as BlackBerry and Android. You may also create models using 3-D modelling software or AutoCAD. You can then upload your 3-D models on www.Thingiverse.com to get the maximum exposure for your product.

There is good money to be made from printing 3-D objects, and if you know people who are 3-D design enthusiasts but cannot afford a 3-D printer, you may offer your services to them - there are crowd-sourcing services that let you bid for 3-D printing jobs. You may either print everyday objects such as saltshakers, or specialised items such as car parts. You can even print parts for 3-D printers, making your printer capable of duplicating itself! This drives down the price of 3-D printers, making them even more affordable. The materials used for 3-D printing are no longer confined to plastic. Newer 3-D printers can now use ceramic and titanium alloy, letting you manufacture specialised parts for machines.

3-D printing could sound like a tempting prospect, but profits are not easy to come by. 3-D printing is more useful for creating prototypes, not the finished products themselves.

305. Designing Shirts

Recently, the idea of designing shirts and selling your designs online has become very popular among Internet business owners or those used to making money from the Internet. However, the market is not saturated yet so you can definitely take a healthy slice of the pie if you start now.
www.CafePress.com
www.eshirts.com
www.LogoSoftwear.com
www.shirtcity.com
www.spreadshirt.com
www.Zazzle.com
www.SpreadShirt.com
I want to make it clear that you don't have to be an artistic genius to generate income with this type of work. You can always opt for statement shirts, which require zero illustrations

but can be just as attractive. Just be unique and let your individuality shine out. Thinking outside the box when it comes to designs will help you a lot in this business.

Think about the many instances you wish you had a shirt that said exactly how you feel! Now, you have the choice of having such shirts and giving other people their own kinds of shirts. You just need to get in touch with your target market and figure out what they want.

Take advantage of your online cloud and network. Offer your services via Facebook and Twitter and show some of your designs in good photos of your work. You can also open a www.Instagram.com account for your t-shirt designs. Taking your business online will widen your market to a global level, greatly increasing your income potential. Just be sure to follow through with your plans, and show the world your best. Go one step further and contact distributors who might distribute your design. Visit www.threadless.com or www.designedbyhumans.com.

306. Designing Fonts

Fonts cost money. If a font isn't from a public domain, individuals and businesses are required to pay for the use of fonts. When designing fonts, you can get paid in various ways. Firstly, you can sell clients just the rights to use your font. More often than not, there's no limit to when and how they'll use your font once they pay this fee. On the other hand, you get paid more if you sell all the rights to one client - but that would also be the end to what you'd be earning from a particular font set. If you were thinking of long-term income possibilities, selling just the rights would be the best way to go. Generally speaking, it would require submitting your font to online font databases. People go to those first when they're looking for fonts to download and when they choose yours to use the website will earn a proportion of your profit. Make sure that your font is well designed and unique and will appeal to different kinds of industries.

307. Designing Logos

Every business has its own identity; some are more recognizable than others. Some because of the service they provide, some because of their corporate identities encapsulated in their logos, etc. A company's logo is the face it presents to the public; they can be symbolic or include the name of the organisation itself. They were first created when most people did not know how to read and write. Most of the time, the logo had more recall than the name of the product itself.

Examples of recognizable logos include those of IBM©, the Red Cross©, the BBC©, Coca-Cola©, Apple© and Google©. Some logos have stayed the same through the years, such as that of the Red Cross, because they were so recognizable that a logo change would alienate their target market. Some have changed because they were too dated or too complicated to be recognized easily. Others have changed to reflect the current situation of the company and industry, or simply to pay tribute to a figure that contributed much to history. A good example is Google ©, which changes its home page logo, often to commemorate a historical figure or event.

An effective logo is simple, versatile, appropriate to the company or organization, memorable and timeless. The Coca-Cola © logo is one example of a logo that has all of these attributes. Logo designers have succeeded in creating variants of the Coca-Cola © logo in different alphabets and languages such as Cyrillic, Chinese, Japanese and Thai, and the logo itself is an icon of American ingenuity and good taste. It is so recognizable that one only needs to see the "dynamic ribbon device" on a shop front to realize that Coca-Cola© is available there, and that ribbon device is present everywhere, including the most remote regions of Africa. Another great example of international recognition is the "M" of the McDonalds© logo.
Perhaps you'll be designing a logo for the next big thing!

308. Enter Design Competitions

www.99designs.com
www.worth1000.com
These are all websites where people are looking for a graphic design to be done e.g. a logo. You can submit your design and if you are the winner you will get a cash price.

309. Make Art

There are several websites that have art competitions for people of all walks of live. These sites are often looking for freelance artists. Have a look at these sites:
www.artdeadlineslist.com
www.artfire.com
www.avatarpress.com
www.cape-shore.com
www.crowdspring.com
www.exceltees.com
www.funnytimes.com
www.leanintree.com
http://www.oatmealstudios.com/
www.zazzle.co.uk
www.zazzle.com

Chapter 33. Use Your Computing Skills

310. Get Paid Using Your Computer or Smartphone

Now this really is an easy one: there are several websites/Apps that will pay you to do jobs e.g. taking a 'selfie' holding a product. Visit these sites for more information:
www.checkpoints.com
www.gigwalk.com
www.junowallet.com
www.staree.com

Note: some sites will not pay you in real money but in vouchers and gifts but you can sell these on auction websites.

311. Data Entry Jobs

This is relatively easy to do although the hourly pay rate is known to not be very high. Visit www.dreamhomebasedwork.com

There comes a time when you just want a job that pays well but is easy to do and doesn't stress you out at all. One such job you can find online would be data entry. It's exactly what it sounds - you'll simply be paid to type or enter data into a particular database or system. Companies offer data entry jobs because their employees are already overloaded with work, and they need to outsource what doesn't require specialised skills, just a minimum typing speed. Also, a lot of website owners hire people for data entry simply to input the alphanumeric codes requested by www.captcha.com.

Obviously, the faster you type, the more you get paid with this kind of job. One thing you have to be aware of in this line of work would be scam sites offering data entry jobs. There are a lot more of them than you think, and they are exceptionally good at luring people in.
You'll see lots of individuals complaining how the money in their account would suddenly disappear, only to find out that the company they're working for is the very one stealing their hard-earned income!
To help you get started, post your services on websites like
www.agentsofvalue.com
www.clickchores.com
www.domystuff.com
www.elance.com

www.fieldagents.net
www.fiverr.com
www.freelance.com
www.guru.com
www.ifreelance.com
www.microworkers.com
www.mturk.com
www.odesk.com
www.peopleperhour.com
www.shorttask.com
www.staff.com
www.virtualbee.com

They all have thriving communities of online data entry clerks who could take you under their wings.

You can of course look for data entry jobs in the top-ranking sites when searching for "online data entry jobs" in Google. The usual offer for data entry jobs is between $3 to $6 (around £1.70 to £4 per hour), so just remember that if an offer sounds too good to be true - like $100 (£60) for 1 hour of work - then it probably is!

312. Designing Websites

Do you want to earn money from web design? A huge chunk of the Internet these days is involved in designing and developing websites. Actually, many web developers and designers make a lot of money each year by utilizing their skills improving clients' sites from different categories of the business industry worldwide.

As you know, almost all companies now have their own websites to promote their products and services to their customers. Their own website gives them the opportunity to reach potential consumers from all over the world through just a few clicks.

Before you start offering a web design service, you must double-check your skills and qualifications. It is important for you to have full knowledge and understanding about the service that you are going to provide to your clients.

However, if you think you already have the skills and qualifications in website developing and designing then today is the perfect time for you to make money! To get started, call or e-mail some local companies, distribute business cards at the local business park or advertise in your local paper.

Apart from that, you can also try bidding for work at www.oDesk.com or http://www.elance.com. You can boost your profile by taking online tests at both these sites to get additional points and to get spotted by clients who are in need of designers and developers.

313. Design WordPress Themes

Internet marketers, resellers, and authors – the majority of them prefer to have www.WordPress.com host their blogs and sites because it's incredibly easy to use. What's not so easy, however, is customizing its design and layout. Designing a WordPress theme isn't rocket science, but it does require time and patience to learn and master: two things that not many people have in abundance. But that should be good news for you since it means a lucrative potential source of income if you are willing to learn the ropes.
I want to stress that you don't need to have a degree in programming or even complete a course in web designing to design WordPress themes.

Rates vary according to the type of theme required by the client and of course the experience and expertise level of the Wordpress designer. The longer you are in business and the more design samples you have available for viewing, the more you can charge your clients. To find out how much people charge to design a website just phone around pretending you want a website designed and see what prices you are given.

314. Technical Troubleshooting

Even though more and more people are becoming active online as time goes by, it's remarkable how an increase in one's online activities does not lead to a proportionate increase in one's technical knowledge - especially when it comes to software and hardware issues rather than just web-based tools and programs.

Your own mother may know how to use Facebook and Twitter, but if her laptop acts up and something's clearly wrong with its video card, what do you think she'd do? Most likely she'd either do nothing or do something to make it worse.

In situations like that, your mum would be desperate to get someone to help her figure out what's wrong and have it fixed immediately. Asking for a computer repair specialist or taking the laptop to the repair shop would take time. It's definitely more convenient to just either call or email for technical troubleshooting!
That's where you and your expert troubleshooting skills come in. Technical troubleshooting usually offers solutions for hardware and software on tablets, laptops, PCs, CPUs and monitors. However, some also offer expert advice about peripherals.

In any case, this can help you figure out how to best offer PC troubleshooting services online even if you don't use the same software program being recommended. Just remember that clients are more likely to stay loyal if you continuously seek ways to expand and improve your knowledge. Always treat your customers courteously and do your job quickly and reliably.

315. Testing Software

A lot of people think that testing software earns huge money - and it does even if you're only working from home - but there's a catch. You need to be backed with professional qualifications and experience.

With software testing, you need to make sure that the product:
- Does what it's supposed to do
- Does not crash randomly, frequently, or for specific reasons
- Is simple to install and user-friendly

However, not having professional experience and skills does not mean you are out of the picture entirely. You can still get paid for testing software if, and only if, you are part of the market the software company is targeting for its product.

A program similar to Adobe Photoshop would have photographers as part of its target market as well as those who are quite active on the social media front. You might not admit this yourself but - if we are honest - only a very small number of people have successfully resisted the temptation of using Adobe Photoshop to edit their photos to make themselves appear more attractive before uploading the photos online.

If you get recruited for this type of job, you will be required to familiarise yourself with every essential feature of the program. You may also be asked to note down whatever strong likes and dislikes you have as well as any other recommendations or remarks you may have to offer.

www.usertesting.com
www.top50gpt.com

316. Testing Mobile Apps

There are many app companies who pay for testing services; this allows the developers to focus on their core businesses. They also appreciate feedback from customers who would otherwise be without a voice when it comes to app development. App testers are always on the lookout for reviewers who are able to expose serious deficiencies or otherwise take note of the advantages offered by new apps.

If you have a background in development, but don't have the confidence to plunge headlong into the industry, app testing is a good alternative. One such app-testing company, www.uTest.com, allows users to sign up and create a tester profile. They are then invited to review the scope and limitations of the app according to their profile before proceeding with the test, for which they submit reports. Testers get paid every two weeks for reports that get approved. Every report they submit contributes to their rating, which affects the rate they are paid for subsequent reports.

If you decide to become an app tester, I recommend being part of an established test company. These test companies provide not just compensation but also training, networking opportunities, and exposure to the latest offerings by app developers. The training includes the latest software testing techniques, trends, and tools.
You can work from home, and have the opportunity to accept or decline apps that are assigned to you. You are only limited by your profile and your willingness to do tests. Plus, whenever you discuss the latest apps with friends, you always have the inside scoop on every developer. This is also a good opportunity to meet up with like-minded individuals who love their apps. Being exposed to the latest trends will also prove to be helpful once you decide to change careers.

317. Reviewing SEO

You've probably heard a lot about SEO (Search Engine Optimisation) as an activity that makes a lot of money, but have you ever heard of SEO review?

A SEO reviewer working either freelance or with companies such as www.Leapforce.com helps websites drive their page rankings up. You start each task by evaluating the intent of a Google user based on combinations of provided keywords and knowledge of pop culture in the user's location. You are then given guidelines to judge how the search engine results match the user's search intentions.

Reviewing SEO at home, especially with established SEO companies, does offer a steady income, but like any other job, it carries certain risks. First, going into optimized websites is like wading into a minefield - you don't know what viruses or malware there are. In this case, you need to keep your antivirus software updated.

Second, SEO reviewers need to keep an open mind, as they could be exposed to offensive content. Being a reviewer, you will be asked to determine if a website carries pornography or malware and you are putting your computer - and those who use it - at risk. Also, being exposed to keywords all the time does tend to be tedious, so you need to keep yourself motivated.

318. Editing Videos

Video editing is big business - especially because of social media. Since videos can be uploaded to sites like Facebook and YouTube as well as shared by tweeting links or blogging about them, a lot of people want to make sure that the videos they upload are of the best quality.

You do not need any kind of professional training for this type of job. You just need to have a tremendous amount of patience and determination whilst learning the ropes. That's something - again - your customers don't have, not to mention that many of them are also too busy to edit their own videos. Ultimately, they're willing to pay you good money to turn their amateur or home videos into something professional...and you know what? That's easier than you think!

Most of the time, clients want their home videos edited in the following ways:
- Adding subtitles or text inserts
- Cutting out specific scenes
- Seamlessly combining different videos in one file
- Convert to a different file format

As with anything else, the better you are at your craft, the higher your rates will be. Don't be afraid to post your videos to sites like YouTube and Video, so that you can get honest reviews from your viewers regarding your skills.

In my book "Design Free Websites" there are lots of free tools listed for video editing.

319. Converting Videos

Obviously, this opportunity may be linked with the one above but if editing just isn't in your blood, you can still earn from video converting alone. People require videos to be converted because of file requirements set by video hosting sites like YouTube. A fast Internet connection is essential since you'll be downloading your client files for conversion and then sending them back or uploading them to a particular site once they're converted.

Clients in need of video converters need to know you are speedy and reliable with your work, so be sure to mention that when promoting your services. It would also mean a lot to your clients if you include in your services uploading converted videos to requested sites. You can charge extra if they require you to upload to more than one or two sites.

It is best to start small, meaning you shouldn't charge too much. To build a small clientele, start with a lower rate, and establish your reputation as you go along. Keep in mind that as you are building your reputation, you are building your skills too so even if you start small, you will eventually earn more.

Here are some free tools for converting videos from one format to another:

- Handbrake www.handbrake.fr. Handbrake is perfect and is free. You can download it to convert almost any video format to almost any other video format.

- YouConvertit www.youconvertit.com is a free online tool where you can convert almost any media type to different formats e.g. documents, images, audio, video, etc.

- Zamzar www.zamzar.com is another free online tool to convert from one file type to another e.g. images, documents, videos, etc.

320. Editing Audio

Podcasts and audio streaming are all the rage nowadays. There are also independent artists who record their work and post it online. With the demand for high-quality sound, there is a market for people who can make audio sound better. How do you make money out of this trend?

Equipment — You need a good sound card, a pair of mixing headphones, and good speakers. If you are editing for videos, you also need a good video card and a multiple-channel mixer, especially if you want to go into the surround-sound market. Going for more expensive yet dependable brands eventually pays for itself.

Software — You also need software to help make your editing easy. The one used by professionals, Sony Sound Forge, includes tools for effects processing and exporting to Dolby Digital format. If you are just starting out, Audacity is a good program to use; it has support for multiple tracks, can convert between audio formats, and has basic effects such as echo, bass boost and fade.

Once you have the hardware and software set up, you need to determine your market. Are you doing sound editing for videos or for musicians? You need to build up a loyal client base, so it's better to stick to one industry at a time. Video producers usually have more of a budget than struggling musicians; however, the audio quality is sometimes not as good. Musicians, on the other hand, are more exact as every little hiss and pop that occurs in the studio is amplified by the speakers or headphones.

Whatever your target clientele is, you need a clear head and keen ear for things that sound off-key. You also need to be able to improvise. Doing all of these will increase your value and allow you to charge higher rates.

321. Motion Graphics

The rise of social networking and web video has made motion graphics a very lucrative online job. Motion graphics is a simple yet effective way of getting one's point across. They can be used to educate, to convince and to entertain audiences.

Wikipedia says: "*Motion graphics are graphics that use video footage and/or animation technology to create the illusion of motion or rotation, and are usually combined with audio for use in multimedia projects.*"

To get started with motion graphics, you need a computer with a good graphics adapter, such as Mac, illustration and photo editing software like Photoshop, video editing software like Adobe's After Effects or Apple's Final Cut Pro, an LCD monitor and a good eye for detail and aesthetics. You may also use animation software such as Adobe Flash, which was how the first few seasons of South Park were created. You also need a wild imagination and a compelling sense of drama to make your motion graphics animation more than just a slideshow.

It is tempting to go straight to the graphics themselves, but first, a script is needed. After all, what use are eye-catching graphics if the message itself isn't clear? Next, you have to brainstorm your concepts and graphics ideas. Once you've got that, you will create a storyboard that more or less shows how the graphics will look and how they will tie into the script.

You can now go to Photoshop and create your basic assets, such as text and illustrations, which you will then import into video-editing software. Once you have arranged them according to your storyboard, you need to record the audio or voice-over, and finally, export the file into playable form.

Motion graphics is not easy to master. You may find yourself getting too few views on YouTube, or having to create videos for a low fee. But if you're really good at what you do, you won't have any shortage of paying clients.

322. Subtitles

This is one of the easiest and definitely one of the most enjoyable ways to work online.

With this type of job, you're basically getting paid to watch films and TV shows! You just have to pause or rewind the video and write down the dialogue from time to time, but it's still a fun job nonetheless!

In most cases, you will not need any kind of special software to provide subtitles for videos. Many film companies just need you to encode the time with every line of dialogue spoken. You may have to follow a preferred format though.

In this kind of market, knowledge of different dialects and languages could be crucial. Expect to earn more if you have to translate dialogue such as adding English subtitles to a Korean film. You may also earn more by translating English dialogue into another language, but because most of the world can understand English, jobs like these are few and far between.

This job could pose its own distractions, though. You might get so engrossed in the video that you're no longer able to do your job. Even the faintest noise in the background could keep you from understanding what's being said. People with short attention spans could find it hard to do this kind of job. Whatever you're watching, it's always advisable to do this job in a quiet place where you can stay focused and relaxed.

However, there may also be times when the client will want you to manually encode or embed the subtitles in the videos. This particular task is easier than you think. Most clients just aren't willing to learn the process and would rather pay for it.

323. Second Life

www.SecondLife.com

The world of Second Life revolves around what are called "Sims" (no relation to the game of the same name), and players can buy and sell real estate. They also have the option of renting land or putting it up for lease. Second Life has its own currency called the linden, and every new member gets 250 lindens when they sign up for the game. They can design their own character and purchase clothes, accessories, body parts, movements, or even entire bodies (also known as skins).

There is no limit to what you can do in Second Life. There is never a shortage of people wanting to alter their characters' appearance, as the skins given to newbies are often described as ugly. They can also buy household items and even entire houses to put on a Sim of their choice. Their purchases are limited to the number of lindens they possess.

Second Life residents also get jobs in virtual places such as bars, restaurants, and sometimes, strip clubs as hosts, DJs, and musicians. There are also people who have found real-life love on SL.

If you wish to make a name for yourself on Second Life, you need to put in a lot of work. There are skin templates available online, and one needs a good command of image editing software to create good items. Many artists also offer free stuff in Second Life stores, and newbies often flock to these stores. Later on, when your reputation has spread by word of mouth, you can afford to put up items that sell for a lot of lindens. The great part is that lindens are actually convertible to dollars.

324. Produce A "This Is Your Life" Book Or DVD

People always look for original presents to give for a 21st, 50th, 60th, 70th, 80th or 90th birthdays. A "this is your life" book or DVD is a wonderful gift. Your customers will provide you with the pictures and a few words about them and in case the customer wants a DVD, songs can also be provided for you to put on the DVD.

You will need to put it all together and charge the customer for the end result. These days, you can produce a book like this online (but lots of people don't know that) and all you need to do is drop in the pictures and the text in a template. Search for "create photo books online"

You can do both for the same customer: a book *and* a DVD.

Chapter 34. Use Your Voice

325. Voice-over Artist

If you're like the Little Mermaid - or her male version if you're a man - in the sense that your voice is your greatest treasure, then have you ever thought about using it to make money online? Voice talents get paid an incredible amount of money for a very simple job that takes only a short amount of your time. However, competition is extremely fierce so you need to work hard on honing your voice. More specifically, you need to focus on the following:

- Improving your diction
- Trying to get rid of any distinctly regional accent
- Speaking in different accents
- Learning how to moderate the volume of your voice

Now, the big question - how much will you earn? You could get paid anywhere from $20 (£12) to $100 (£60) per minute!

If you are ready to start applying for voice over jobs, work on your audio sample. It should be no longer than ten minutes and showcase how versatile your voice is.
You can go to sites like
www.ukvoices.co.uk (in the UK)
www.voices.com (in the US)
 www.voicebunny.com
www.voices123.com
and create your own profile. These website are one of the best options if you want to start your career as an online voice-over talent. Use recording software like Goldwave and Mixcraft, create your own samples and post them under your profile. This way, clients can listen to your voice and accent, and determine whether you are a good match for their needs or not. Sites such as www.oDesk.com and www.Elance.com are also good sources of voice-over job opportunities.

326. YouTube Vlogger

Do you like talking about stuff you absolutely love...or hate? That's basically what a YouTube vlogger does. A vlog or video blog is a blog that is mostly used for videos. A vlogger is a Video Blogger. There's no limit to what you can discuss, although it's always a good idea to focus on something that you really feel passionate about. Discussions are likely to get more interesting and livelier when people have something invested in the topic. As a YouTube vlogger, you will need a high-quality video recorder. You can use Camtasia to record your screen www.techsmith.com/camtasia.html. People nowadays are spoiled with HD programming and they expect no less even from hosts of indie shows online. You should also invest in audio equipment of good quality, and while you don't need to leave your home to start shooting your video, you must be able to keep background noise to a minimum while recording.

You must have an outline or script of how every webisode (an episode of a series) will go, and every webisode per "season" must be similar in tone, format, and content. It would also be ideal if you have at least three segments in every episode. Segments may or may not be related to each other but they definitely must fall under a single umbrella theme. Let's say you want to be known as someone who vlogs about sports. The segments in your show could be the following: Game Recaps, Trade Rumours, and Sports Products. The last bit is actually very important if you'd like to make a good amount of money from vlogging.

At the start, you'll only be promoting products and services that you personally like and without any payment. But in time, when your audience grows - which is basically seen in the number of hits your videos generate - then sooner or later you will find companies knocking on your door and willing to pay actual money for you to advertise their merchandise! Most people won't mind if you do not vlog live, and that's a good thing because it allows you to do a little more post-video editing and add a few graphics and special effects. Add text balloons and picture inserts in between your lines, and interact with it or have it integrated with your discussion. Once you have your video uploaded to YouTube, make sure to get the word out to your family and friends so that they can help you promote it. You should also do a little networking beforehand and be active in online sports communities. Those people are your target market after all and if they like what they see they won't need any encouragement to spread the word. Also, remember to take the time to post replies to those who made comments on your video!

The income you can generate from vlogging is huge - and especially if you apply for a YouTube partnership. You can learn more about this following the links below:
http://www.youtube.com/t/partnerships_faq
http://www.wikihow.com/Earn-Money-on-YouTube

Basically, being a YouTube partner means you get to enjoy a share of the revenues displayed in your YouTube channel page. There are several requirements you need to meet before you can become a YouTube partner, but the one important thing is to have a lot of subscribers.

Chapter 35. Music

327. Create And Sell Music

If you are a budding composer then you can always create your own music and sell it! iTunes, without a doubt, remains one of the best places to sell your music online.
Of course, just having great music to share won't immediately promise a steady income. If you want something to go viral online, then you need to make it easy to share and you need to work on getting it enough exposure.

There are a few music-making software programs that you can use to create music of all kinds, including Dubstep, which is a highly popular genre these days. The software used to create Dubstep is available online, and you can tinker with it as you learn the ropes. Once you have created enough samples, you can start uploading them to music sites.
You can sell your music on:
www.bandcamp.com
 www.cdbaby.com
www.dittomusic.com
www.itunes.com
www.musicmagpie.co.uk
https://play.google.com
www.songstall.com
www.Soundcloud.com
www.tunecore.com

Having a sample of your music available on YouTube is a start. You should also take your chance submitting your music to traditional and Internet radio stations. All you need is just one big break, and your musical career will take off!

328. Internet Radio Station

Outside the Internet, setting up your own radio station can cost you a fortune. However, you shouldn't let something as measly as capital stand in the way of your dreams, should you? If you've always loved music, loved sharing it and would like to give managing a radio station a try, then you can do so through the World Wide Web and make money with it, too.

You can absolutely create a radio station of your own, though you will need to pay for licenses or copyright fees.

But that's just the start of your work. To earn money from it, you will need to get sponsors and advertisers. They either pay you to promote their products or services through one of your radio shows, or you record your sessions, share them through YouTube, then earn from a YouTube partnership once you make the cut.

Ultimately, the most successful radio stations are those that actually ascribe to a particular theme. You need to identify yourself with a particular genre or a target market so that listeners will know right away if they want to listen to you. Be different, and be knowledgeable about your theme. When you become an authority, people will listen to you. As with everything, be reliable and consistent, present new and unique ideas, be funny and be personable so that your listenership will grow.

www.blogtalkradio.com helps you have your own radio show or create your own radio station. You can find some prominent people here in your niche and interview them. You can then announce your radio shows on your blog, Facebook, your email list and so on. It is an easy way to create and share radio on the web. You can sign up for free and get a 30-minute show per day with 5 live callers. There are also payable options that give you a lot more possibilities. It's worth checking out.

329. Internet DJ

This kind of job is similar to owning a radio station except for a few notable differences. Firstly, being hired as an Internet DJ does not require you to care about how the radio station as a whole is doing, and secondly you don't need to pay other DJs wages.

Being an Internet radio station owner may mean bigger money, but it also means more headaches. If you don't like the challenges that come with owning and managing a business but would still love to work with music and radio in your background then you are better off becoming an online DJ yourself.

The best thing about becoming a DJ is that you don't really need professional training. Some people just have a natural gift for it. And even if you don't have one, you can learn whatever has to be learned on the job. Ultimately, what matters the most is the ability to establish rapport with your listeners. If you have that in spades, then there's nothing to worry about!

However, be aware that most Internet radio stations today do not actually offer paid jobs to the DJs they are recruiting. Does that mean all you'll get is fame and not the fortune? Not at all! Firstly, if a particular radio station wants you badly enough then they may be willing to share with you a percentage of their advertising revenue. Secondly, a free job with a popular online radio station is also a good place to start as it can give you great exposure. You can work your way up from there.

330. Podcasts

Have you ever wondered how you will get your voice heard by an audience of thousands? Podcasting is a form of media consisting of a series of audio, video, or text files that are downloaded through RSS (Really Simple Syndication) feeds or streamed directly to devices. Most podcasters use voice, as it is easier to upload and download. The difference between podcasting and web streaming is that a web stream is almost always live, while a podcast is pre-recorded. This difference aside, podcasts carry almost the same content as online radio.

Podcasts deal with a variety of topics, such as sports, politics, religion, or general discussion. Some even feature comedy and interviews with prominent figures. You may even record audio books and novels as a series, and make them available for download.

To get started with podcasting, you need all the basic requirements for recording audio: a soundproof area, a sensitive microphone, a good mixer and a decent pair of recording headphones. You also need the ability to produce good scripts, as readers gravitate towards podcasts that sound just like radio. It also helps to have good, relevant topics all the time.

You have the option of getting corporate sponsors, sign up with podcast networks, offer your podcasts for sale, offer free teasers, and beg for donations. As long as you take pride in what you do and have passion for what you stand for, you will always have a captive market of listeners.

331. Review Music

Visit www.slicethepie.com. This site has paid over 1 million dollars to reviewers. Here you get paid to review music.

Chapter 36. Artistic Jobs

332. Cartoonist

A cartoonist is different from a graphic artist in the sense that you will need to tell a story in just one or a few strips. Personal bloggers, Internet marketers, website business owners and even FTSE 100 or Fortune 500 companies would all be interested in what you'd be able to draw and narrate for them through cartoons.

Humour is the biggest selling factor in cartoon or comic strips. However, there are all kinds of humour and it's easy to offend other people with the wrong kind of joke. You also need to be tactful, especially when handling sensitive content.

In order to create the perfect cartoon strip for your client, here are a few guide questions you can ask:
- What is the client's history and background?
- What are the goals of the client? Why did the client build a blog or website?
- What makes the client unique? If you are dealing with a business, then what makes its products or services better than the competition's?
- Who is the client's target audience?

These questions should give you an idea or two on what kind of story or anecdote to illustrate.

As a cartoonist, you are just one step away from creating, say, animation shorts, which you can then share through YouTube. Be confident, perfect your craft and create samples of your work that you can include in your portfolio.

333. Edit Photos

You could offer digital photo editing and image optimization services. Just advertise your services online, on a website such as www.elance.com or www.fiverr.com

334. Restore Photos

This is very much similar to the idea of editing photos but this time you would not need to worry about adding any kind of special effects. You just have to focus on turning an old and imperfect copy into something newly crisp and shiny! You can typically charge $10 to $100 (£6 to £60) per photo but this wide range is dependent not on your preferences but on the amount of restoration work needed. Effective and regular online marketing is necessary if you want a steady income, so be sure to do the usual round of social media networking and optimize your website for search engines to get the word out.

Polish up your Photoshop skills so that you can do more in a day in order to maximize your daily earning potential. There are experts who can restore 1 photo per 5 minutes, which makes their hourly earning potential up to $500 (or £300) per hour. This can happen to you too if you continue building your skills. You can go for lower rates first if you feel like you need to establish your name and build a clientele. Always take advantage of your online network, whether via Facebook, Twitter, or LinkedIn. Offer your services to your friends and family, and in no time, you will be too busy to look for new clients.

335. Selling Arts And Crafts Products

Artists and crafters can generate income through the sites listed below and through www.eBay.com. Registering an account for these sites is free and simple.
www.artfire.com
www.artpal.com
www.etsy.com
www.folksy.com
www.zazzle.com

When selling your products, you need to write a description and upload photos, which have to be clear, sharp, and feature the product prominently. Be sure to come up with catchy product names but make sure that you are also clear about what you are selling. You will typically be asked to indicate the types of materials you have used when creating arts and crafts products or supplies. Be sure to list them all and indicate if they have been specially selected, such as in the case of eco-friendly or recycled items.

Think of ways to add competitive advantages for your products. For instance, the use of hypoallergenic materials, as well as eliminating all choking hazards, will ensure that your items are indeed safe for babies or young children to use.
Packaging is important especially if your products make great gifts. The best packaging is attractive, compact, and eco-friendly, something that a buyer won't need to gift-wrap because it's already pretty as it is.
If you browse available items in the sites above, you will notice that some of the sellers welcome the opportunity to create custom-designed products for buyers. If you are interested in doing the same, you should have a pricelist ready to ensure that you are charging fair and proper rates for customized work. You'll typically have to specify a delivery time for custom designed work and if you do, make sure you stick to it!

Chapter 37. Online Tutoring & Coaching

336. Udemy - R

www.Udemy.com is a website full of online courses, videos and tutorials and is the world's largest online learning market place. They have over 3 million students and over 18,000 courses!

Your course could be on Udemy too! All you have to do is sign up to Udemy and become an instructor, and you are ready to upload unlimited free videos. If you are an expert at languages, you can teach students from all over the world through your videos. If you play guitar, you can teach students how to play, too! You can actually make a career out of Udemy, with one user selling 5 million dollars last year!!

Just look at this screenshot of one instructor (if you are selling videos on Udemy, you are called an instructor): he has 62,900 students and he sells his videos for $99 (£62). That is 62,900 people who have bought his course for $99! That is $6,227,100 (£3,898.164)! That many sales by simply selling an advanced course on Microsoft Excel! By the way, you can probably find this information covered in these videos online e.g. YouTube but people are prepared to pay to see it all together in one course.

You think you can put a little effort in creating video tutorials if you can earn this sort of money? Of course you can!

Note: as an instructor you don't earn the total amount that you sell your videos for. If a buyer purchases your videos through a Udemy Search on their website, you get paid 50% of the sale and Udemy keeps 50%.

If a buyer purchases a video via traffic that you sent directly to your product on Udemy, you get paid 97% of the value and Udemy keeps only 3%.

You have to produce and upload your videos ONCE and you will keep selling them for years to come (providing you create a good course and use great keywords so people will find your course). Nice recurring income!

All you need to make videos that you can sell on Udemy are these three things:

1. PowerPoint presentation software. If you don't have Microsoft Office, which includes PowerPoint, www.openoffice.org is free, downloadable software and includes presentation software.

2. A good quality microphone.

3. Screen capture software to record what you are doing on your computer. In other words, record your screen. Screen capture software is what you need.

- AwesomeScreenshots http://awesomescreenshot.com/ lets you capture your page or part of it and annotate it with arrows, text, etc. You can use these screenshots to insert in a video.

- Jing is such screen capture software and you can download it for free from www.techsmith.com/jing.html. You can make short videos of 5 minutes or less. If you need longer videos, you can just record 3 videos of 5 minutes and then put them together with Audacity to make a 15-minute video.

- www.camstudio.org Not to be confused with Camtasia Studio, CamStudio is an open source video screen capture software application. Camstudio is able to record all screen and audio activity on your computer and create industry-standard AVI video files and using its built-in SWF Producer can turn those AVIs into lean, mean, bandwidth-friendly Streaming Flash videos (SWFs)

- ScreenCastOMatic is downloadable free from www.screencast-o-matic.com. It is screen capture software. You can record and save the file as MP4, AVI or other video formats.

Your video can be up to 15 minutes long but you can't edit the files.

- www.smallvideosoft.com/screen-video-capture is easy to use software for PC or Mac.

- A brilliant payable version to record your screen is Camtasia, which you can download from www.techsmith.com/camtasia.html. All my videos in www.WorldwideSelfPublishing.com are recorded with Camtasia.

- You can also use www.jingproject.com, which lets you record five minutes maximum for a video. If you need 20 minutes of video you can record four videos of five minutes. This is free of charge.

There are more free tools for audio and video in my book "Design free Websites".

Make a video totally free.

> **Top Tip:** Try this out – making a video has never been easier. You can use this method for any videos you want to make. EVERYTHING is free including all the software you will use to make the video.

Here is a step-by-step guide on how to make your own video completely free by using free pictures, free articles and free video-making software.

First step: Go to www.freeimages.com and save some royalty-free pictures regarding your niche on your hard drive. For example, if your niche is about controlling your panic attack, you can save pictures about somebody who is angry and somebody who is calm.

Second step: Go to www.gimp.org and download it free. Import the picture(s) and right-click on the picture to save it as a 700-width picture, which is a good size. Tick auto scale.

Third step: Get a PLR article regarding your niche or write a short article yourself. The latter is the better option.

Fourth step: Download Audacity: www.audacity.sourceforge.net. With Audacity you will read the article and record your voice whilst you read it.

Fifth step: Open Windows Movie Maker which you should have on your PC if you are using Windows. If not, download it. In Windows Movie Maker you can import pictures, put your voice that you have recorded over the pictures and leave your website domain name at the bottom of the video. Save the video when ready.

Sixth step: Submit your video to video sites.
ALWAYS use your keywords in the title and description when submitting a video.

The best video sites to upload your videos to are (some are payable):
www.on.aol.com
www.brightcove.com
www.buzznet.com
www.dailymotion.com
www.dropshots.com
www.fark.com/video
www.flixya.com
www.video.google.com
www.jibjab.com
www.liveleak.com
www.metacafe.com
www.screenjunkies.com
www.ustream.tv
www.viddler.com
www.vimeo.com
www.youtube.com

www.splasheo.com Creates videos, fast and easy. Free download.

337. Tutoring - R

If you have enough knowledge in you to teach someone else, you can become an online tutor. You will need a college degree to qualify as a teacher but you don't need a teaching certificate. Get more information on:
www.tutorvista.com
www.tutor.com in the US
www.tutorhub.com in the UK. Simply search for "online tutoring" to find more places to register.
You don't need to be a budding genius or even an expert to start tutoring online. Ultimately, it's just about finding your academic or artistic niche and developing just enough skills in it to help other people achieve their goals. Search online for places to register.

Without a doubt, the easiest way to become an online tutor is to offer English lessons to foreign students. It is ideal (although not necessary) to gain certification for this job. TEFL (sometimes TESOL or TESL) - Teaching of English as a Foreign Language - is the type of certification you need, and it's something you can complete online in a few months. This type of certification can help you gain access to job offers in online tutorial websites linked to prestigious schools both at home and abroad. If you need a quick revision on grammar, take a look at www.grammarbook.com.

You do not need to have actual teaching experience to work as an English tutor online. In most cases, being a native English speaker is enough. However, if you want to charge premium rates then there are a few other things you can do.

Work as a voluntary teacher online. Visit websites like www.MyLanguageExchange.com, where registering an account is free. After that you need to work on your profile and start looking for members who would like to learn English. An added bonus here is that they'd be willing to teach you their native language in return. Learning another language is actually quite helpful as it may help you teach foreign students more effectively.

Search online for free lesson plans for teaching English. Remember that these lessons are usually categorised according to age range. Also, try looking for samples of English tests that you can use to create your own exams as well.

Invest in the necessary hardware. Students prefer their online English tutors to have a quiet environment conducive to learning when offering lessons. You'll also be able to conduct your lessons more effectively with a proper headset, a speedy Internet connection and a computer or laptop that's fast enough to handle the multiple programs you'll need to use.

Most people post their services on websites like www.craigslist.com or www.gumtree.com. If you do this, be sure to specify clearly what your preferred teaching schedules are - if any - and the hardware or software requirements your student would need to meet. Let them know as well how long each tutorial session would last and what student level or age you prefer to teach.

Register with
www.tutorhunt.com or
 www.personal-tutors.co.uk
or simply search for "personal tutors" to find more companies to register with.

One of the best ways to convince students to hire you as their online English tutor is to offer a free lesson. Another way to promote your tutorial services is to create short articles, videos and info graphics that provide foreign students with valuable lessons and tips for learning English.

Keep in mind that English is not the only thing you can teach online. Other languages are of course another option as well as the following topics and/or skills, to name but a few:

- Arts and crafts, e.g. origami, scrapbook making
- Public speaking
- Creative writing
- Job skills, e.g. website designing
- Voice lessons
- Tuition in playing a musical instrument

338. Life Coach - R

You won't find any college or university offering a course for life coaching, but that's only right since life is not really something you can learn within school walls. Life is something you just have to learn by experiencing it and it's something you need to constantly adapt to.

However, some people are just better at living simply because they focus on making the best of their lives rather than just coping with it. With the latter, you are focusing on the problems while the former focuses on the opportunities.

If you are the 'cup half-full' type of person, then you already have the fundamental requirement for being a life coach. You just need to develop a coaching system to share your life-building and life-enjoying skills with your clients.

Life coaches can earn anything from $100 to $1,000 (£60 to £600) for every session, which could last up to 45 minutes or even an hour. You can talk about everything under the sun as a life coach - it's really similar to being a therapist and psychologist, but with a focus on immediate practical solutions that your client can act on.
A life coach is basically a person's cheerleader, mentor, and disciplinarian all rolled into one. That's what you will be for your client. You need to find out what your client's goals are and help them reach them by coming up with plans and strategies as well as offering verbal support and consolation during your sessions.

You may think this is just like being a friend to another person, but most friends are unable to be truly honest with each other, however you are being paid to do so - with no hard feelings afterwards!

339. Business Coach

Business coaches make even more than life coaches but again that's understandable since there are stricter qualifications for this type of job. While you do not need an MBA to be a good business coach, you do need to have actual experience managing a successful business. Otherwise, clients won't see any reason to hire you as their mentor. Popular online business coaches built their reputation from scratch, too, so it is highly possible that with the right kind of skills, determination and hard work, you can become one of them.

Start by thinking back when you were climbing the first few steps on the career ladder. If you were your own manager or mentor back then, what do you wish you could have told your younger self?

Also, put yourself in your client's shoes. What factors would they consider when looking for a business coach? This should give you an idea of what clients want. Focusing on meeting those needs will definitely help you establish your reputation as a successful business coach.

340. Teach a Foreign Language Online - R

You can use your native language to teach students online.
www.italki.com
www.udemy.com

Chapter 38. Business Services

341. Tax Preparer - R

The one thing that is probably going through your mind right now is this: don't you have to be an accountant to do this kind of job? The answer: technically... no. Consider this. Have you ever tried paying for your own taxes and doing your own bookkeeping? Yes? Now, are you a certified accountant? No? Then there you go!

Taxation is something you either absolutely love or hate. There's no middle ground for it, which is why those who do hate it are more than willing to hire someone else to manage their accounts and make sure all their taxes are paid on time and correctly.

You can work as someone's tax manager or tax specialist and do everything online since the government now accepts people filing and paying their taxes online. You can either do someone's accounts manually or you can have a computer program to calculate everything for you. Don't call yourself an accountant because that would be a deception if you are not qualified.

Paying taxes online will provide you with a good amount of access to another individual's finances, and obviously that's going to be something your client would be wary of. To alleviate your clients' concerns, you should state beforehand that you are absolutely willing to sign the necessary documents that will protect them in case anything goes wrong. However, by law, your client will be responsible should any problems occur. A big negative is that you will forever be studying the changes in the tax laws. A big positive is that it is recurring income as every year people will come back to you again, assuming you have done a good job the first time. You won't earn money all year round with this as people's tax forms all have to be done by the same date. www.intuit.com - this site hires tax preparers.

342. Online Headhunter

A headhunter is more than a recruiter. In a way, headhunters are like specialised recruiters as they work on matching specific people for specific jobs with specific companies. Most of the time, a company already has its eye on a particular individual for their current vacancy. It's up to the headhunter to figure out how to make that individual at least attend a job interview with their client - even if the individual is already employed.

You do not need to personally meet with either the client or the desired professional to do your job. You just need to contact them by phone, email, or web chat. Secondly, you need to convince the person being headhunted that switching to your client's company will be a great career move.

It's not easy to start as a headhunter as this isn't the kind of job you can actually apply for. Rather, it's all about contacts. At the start, you may have to either offer your services for free or go through your network of friends and colleagues and find someone willing to give your services a try.

How much you'll earn as a headhunter typically goes up the more "senior" the vacancy you need to fill. This means that what you'll earn for headhunting someone to work as a mid-level manager is perhaps a fraction of the commission you'll earn when headhunting a top-level executive. Also, keep in mind that most companies require headhunters to sign an agreement for which they'd only receive their commission if the headhunted employee stays with them for a minimum period of time.

343. Referring

Want to be an executive headhunter? While the majority of executive search firms have posh offices somewhere downtown, you can actually do their job, even while you're online! There are numerous positions in companies that need to be filled and companies hire headhunters to get candidates who will sit for HR (Human Resources) interviews, and pay them once the candidates are hired.

Below are some job-referral sites that could interest you:
www.WiseStep.com - This website offers jobs worldwide, and also has local listings. The site pays you per referral subject to certain criteria e.g. the person you refer may have to meet certain criteria or serve a probationary period.
www.LinkedIn.com - Otherwise known as Facebook for executives, LinkedIn is also an underrated recruitment tool. You might have a friend who wants to enter a certain company, and the HR manager for this company might have a job waiting for him. You can refer your friend as a network connection to the HR manager, and discuss the finder's fee either on LinkedIn's messaging system or by other means.

344. Virtual Assistant - R

In case you're not familiar with the term, a Virtual Assistant (VA) is basically an online employee, usually hired by an entrepreneur, or sometimes an online agency. Work is done from home or over the Internet. You will do administrative tasks such as book keeping, online research, database entries, etc.

The good thing about this is that there's always a high demand for good VAs. However, due to the nature of the job (usually repetitive tasks that can be easily learned and done by anyone), employers often hire VAs in Third World countries because they can get the same job done for a fraction of the cost.

These VAs often work odd hours to support their client. Their jobs include receiving and managing calls, message taking, appointment scheduling, customer support, sales assistance, personal assistance and other types of administrative tasks that may be performed or managed online.

However, this is NOT a rule, and there are many employers who prefer quality over anything else and don't care where you're from or how much you're charging (as long as you can deliver what they ask).

The lowest pay is around $5 (£3)/hour, and you can also work for more than one employer at once if you wish. After all, you do not have to commute to and from work. For more general information visit www.societyofvirtualassistants.com.

Some of the most popular sites where you can get a job as a VA are:
www.bestjobs.ph
www.elance.com
www.odesk.com
www.onlinejobs.ph
www.vanetworking.com
www.virtualassistantforums.com

Now, one last reminder - most virtual assistants are expected to assist their employers with Internet marketing. That being said, you need to at least understand the fundamentals of search engine optimization, particularly link building. Some - but definitely not all - would be willing to provide free on-the-job training, but it is best not to rely on such opportunities. If you want to increase your chances of getting hired as a VA, you need to invest beforehand in learning about search engine marketing.

345. Virtual Call Centre - R

If you have a phone, there are opportunities for you as an Answering Service Specialist. There are many small businesses that need someone who can answer a phone call, be professional, and take a message. This is often called a Virtual Call Centre.

Large companies can have their own staffed call centre, and companies with a large volume of calls may outsource a call centre to other countries. Smaller companies may not be able to do this, and this is where you come in. The specifications of this type of work vary. For instance, you may be asked to simply answer the phone and take messages. Or you may be expected to answer simple questions about the business. You may be asked to only work 9:00-5:00 Monday to Friday, or you may be on call 24 hours a day, every day.

The advantage of this is that if you have multiple clients, and can multi-task, you can answer their calls simultaneously. So you can contract with or bill several clients for the same hours! Often they will pay your phone bill as well.

A call centre based at home is a good option for those who don't wish to commute to work. There are other factors at play in this decision - maybe you don't like the office coffee, you'd rather be working alone, or you have things to look after at home. Whatever the reason, setting up a call centre at home is rather easy. All that's needed is a dedicated space for your office, a phone system capable of accommodating multiple lines, a computer, and furniture.

A virtual PBX (Private Branch Exchange, where your telephone system is hosted by a provider) or Skype Business ID is far cheaper and more convenient than having to install a multiple-line system. A Skype Business account will let you purchase different phone numbers and assign them as needed, while a virtual PBX system lets you enjoy all the benefits of a multiple-line phone system without requiring expensive equipment.

Don't under spend on the computer; it might just be the most important item you need. Use a separate computer for work, as this is a tax-deductible expense. It also reduces the risk of losing data and software that could happen if the rest of your family uses the same computer.

Make sure you make backups of your data daily. You also need a quality headset and lighting as well. I suggest investing in a high-end headset with a microphone attached, as this reduces the possibility of misunderstanding your customers.

You will be sitting down for a long time, so choose ergonomic office furniture. A swivel chair allows you to move easily between your phone and the computer, and the incline and height need to be adjustable to allow for maximum comfort. Getting a file cabinet is also a good idea that will ensure that you have a place for important documents and sensitive client information.

Search online for agencies offering home based call centre work. Here's one: www.liveops.com They have a very good online training program. When you work for a company and you answer the phone, a script will pop up on your screen for you to follow. LiveOp has over 20,000 people registered that work from home. You can become a LiveOp agent and you will be required to take incoming calls for corporate clients or do a variety of other jobs.

346. Earn Money Selling Leads To Call Centres

Getting targeted customers or targeted leads is not easy and the call centres know that. That's why they are prepared to pay for targeted leads. If they have to pay one employee $90 (just over £50) per day to phone around and end up with two targeted customers, they are often also willing to pay you $10 (£6) for one targeted customer lead. Contact some call centres and find out how much they pay per lead.

Example: you have a list of people who own dogs. You might have a website about dogs and people have opted-in to your list. You can contact a call centre that is working for a dog company e.g. selling dog insurance. That company might be willing to buy your list off of you as it means that the list you have are potential customers for dog insurance.

347. Work For A Call Centre - R

If you have a good telephone voice and the ability to make lots of calls per hour, you can work a few hours per day in a local call centre. Call centres are always looking to recruit new people.

348. Translator

If you are fluent or at least have skills in more than one language, then you can definitely earn a lot of money working on translations and interpretations online.

Yes, there are sites like www.translate.google.com, but have you actually tried using them? Their automated translations will work fairly well for basic sentences but are they enough to impress VIP clients or international investors you are hoping to partner up with? Not at all!
That's why a lot of people - private individuals, companies and website owners - are still willing to pay good money for professional translations.

What you could translate or interpret:
- Technical or product guides and user manuals
- Scripts for films and TV shows

- Short stories, essays, and novels
- Website content
- Business proposals and other types of business documents
- News reports
- etc.

Although having certification proving your fluency in a particular language is ideal, it's not necessary. You just need to be willing to translate some sample material provided by the client, and they'll see for themselves how fluent you are.

There are basically two types of translations you will also be expected to perform online:
- Written translations
- Oral translations

With oral translations, you may be required to listen to, or participate in, web or video chats. You may be required to either take notes and translate them afterwards or perform real-time translations so that parties involved may communicate with each other.

To start offering your services as an interpreter or translator, you can post your résumé and create ads in the usual job marketplaces online like www.Craigslist.org, www.odesk.com and www.Elance.com. However, there are also sites like the ones listed below that are exclusively dedicated to translation and interpretation jobs.

www.academicword.com
www.accurapid.com
www.berlitz.com
www.globalinktranslations.com
www.languageline.com
www.linguist.com
www.newworldlanguages.com
www.Proz.com
www.telelanguage.com
www.translationsabc.com
www.TranslatorsCafe.com
www.TranslatorsTown.com

One last reminder - don't forget to create ads and write your CV in all the languages you are fluent in!

349. Medical Transcriptionist

First of all, you may be confused about the difference between transcribers and transcriptionists. To clear any misunderstandings, a transcriptionist is an actual individual with the skills to transcribe while a transcriber is a machine or program for creating automated transcriptions.

This is one field where certification is absolutely vital, but the good news is that you can complete certificate training online. It's also quite affordable, and you can definitely earn your money back after a few months of steady work. Professional training is required as you may be transcribing documents that could have life-and-death consequences on patients if you happen to misinterpret or erroneously translate any part. Visit http://mmodal.com . According to www.forbes.com you can earn up to $50,000 - £ 31,700 per year.

Professional training is also necessary to familiarise yourself with medical terms - many of which are quite difficult to spell. Of the three types of transcription jobs, medical transcriptions typically pay the most.
Register with www.odesk.com or www.elance.con for job opportunities.

350. Legal Transcriptionist

Professional training is of course preferred but not necessary. At the end of the day, law firms would be more than willing to hire you as long as you prove competent in the job. Legal transcriptionists may not always earn as much as medical transcriptionists, but they definitely earn more than business or general transcriptionists.
Working as a legal transcriptionist will require you to be familiar with Latin terms used in legal context. Here are a few online references that should prove handy if this is the type of job you're interested in:
http://dictionary.law.com
http://www.nolo.com/dictionary
www.duhaime.org/LegalDictionary.aspx

351. Business And General Transcriptionist

With business or general transcription, expect to handle virtually any kind of document in any industry. One moment you will find yourself transcribing the minutes of a business meeting between importers and exporters and then later on you'll find yourself transcribing a job interview for childcare professionals. Anything goes with this type of transcription job. It doesn't pay as much as the other two, but it definitely has fewer requirements and it will make a good starting point for this line of work.

In any case, you will stand to earn more if you prove yourself capable of effectively transcribing minutes for business meetings. This will require you to be familiar with corporate terms - some of which will not be in English. But again, that's something you don't have to worry about because the Internet has a couple of dictionaries you can use to look up terms you may be unfamiliar with.
www.businessdictionary.com
http://dictionary.cambridge.org/dictionary/business-english
www.merriam-webster.com/dictionary/business

Where to find online transcription jobs:
http://scribie.com/freelance-transcription
www.advancedtx.com
www.mtdesk.com
www.mtjobs.com
www.ubiqus.com
www.uktranscription.com

+ any other outsourcing site e.g. www.elance.com

Be aware that many people who start out as freelancing transcriptionists eventually find their way to setting up their own transcription business. With enough clients and a reliable pool of transcriptionists, you may not find it necessary to transcribe yourself in time. All you have to do is to make sure that every client gets a transcriptionist assigned and that work is always delivered on schedule. When setting up a transcription business online, you need to prioritize the following:

- Provide clients with a safe, secure and simple way to get their files to you.
- Provide transcriptionists with an easy and efficient way to take in job orders.
- Install a system that will allow you to track job orders and ensure that transcriptions are completed on time.
- Offer clients and transcriptionists a wide variety of payment options.

352. Online Juror (US only)

Online jurors allow you to be a mock jury without leaving the house. You can register with companies such as
www.eJury.com
www.jurytest.com
www.onlineverdict.com

www.signupdirect.com
www.trialjuries.com
www.trialpractice.com

These sites pay people to sit on mock juries and give attorneys and other jury consultants feedback on cases they are handling. The cases are real cases.

353. Drafting And Reviewing Contracts

This type of work is best suited for - first and foremost - lawyers, whether you are still practicing or not. If you are a law student, a paralegal, or someone who had extensively worked or is working for law firms, then this would be a good way to make money online as well. Just make sure you state very clearly the kind of experience you have as well as the fact that you are not a practicing lawyer. Don't worry about those disclaimers, though. Like I said before, people won't care about them if they see from testimonials and the way you work that you really do have something valuable to offer.
Lawyers typically charge $200 to $500 (£120 to £300) per hour for drafting or reviewing contracts, but it's possible you will get a fixed rate for certain types of contracts regardless of their length. If you are not a lawyer then you would have to charge substantially lower than that.

Drafting contracts, to be honest, is something that even accountants and any expert in a particular field can do because there are lots of contract templates you can download and use for free. However, most of your clients won't know that - and that's a good thing. You can get paid for something that's essentially free and at most you'd only need to add a few more terms as well as tweak the wording here and there.

One last thing - another service that you can offer, even as a law student or paralegal, is to write warning and notification letters to a client's desired recipients as their "legal adviser". You see, being a legal adviser doesn't mean you are a lawyer. It just means you are advising someone on legal matters, and mostly that only means writing strictly worded letters to remind other parties about their obligations to your client.

354. Digital PR

While digital PR (Public Relations) and social media are often confused, social media is just one facet of doing public relations online. PR, whether online or offline, is all about building credibility, awareness, and goodwill. Understanding the online landscape helps companies develop strong relationships with both stakeholders and potential clients. Digital PR practitioners use SEO, social media, blogs, websites, and content development to get their clients' messages across.

Reputation management
Social media and websites can affect a company's reputation for better or for worse. Using SEO is not just an optional skill for today's PR practitioners - it is now a requirement. Should a crisis hit a company, the effects will not just be felt offline, but online as well. It is up to a digital PR practitioner to make the most out of a sticky situation. The job of a reputation manager is to make sure that online searches bury negative news down the rankings, and that positive press is on the first page of Google.

Relationship building
Digital PR practitioners also use social media to interact with people. They include Facebook, Pinterest, LinkedIn, YouTube, and Twitter. This allows the company to engage directly with their customers in order to resolve issues, get their voices heard, and to offer a more personalised service that otherwise cannot be done with the usual voice and mail-based platforms. It also offers other users a chance to see how the client deals with its customers.

Measurement
The measurement of social interactions is also part of a digital PR practitioner's arsenal. Because a lot of client-user interactions are now done online, it is now easier to keep track of them. You may use the following tools to see how your PR campaign is doing:
- Facebook insights
- YouTube insights
- Google Analytics
- KissMetrics

355. Event Planner

Like a real-time event planner of weddings or conferences, you can make money planning events online. How? The entire process is easy, especially if you are a social media guru. Planning events online and making money from it is effortless, as there are several online event-planning tools that you can use. All you have to do is find the one the fits your event and will help you get your target audience. Among the best mediums that you can use are
www.Facebook.com
www.Amiando.com
www.Eventbrite.com
www.Meetup.com

Below are brief walkthroughs of how these mediums work:

1. Facebook. This is one of the biggest and most effective tools to invite people to participate in your event. Obviously, this site offers an "invite your friends" feature, which you can use to spread the word all over the World Wide Web (based on your target audience). You can do all kinds of gimmicks to attract people such as bringing in a fun trailer of the upcoming event before the event itself. The event can also be a game, a promo, or a 50% off sale. Anything, really.

2. Amiando. This must be the biggest international event planning service tool online that supports multiple languages. It offers a better community-feel compared to other tools. And like any social media sites, Amiando also offers modules for polling, commenting, videos, and photos. Just post the details and have your tickets booked by using Amiando.

3. Eventbrite. This tool is user-friendly, keeping most of your tasks just one click away. And even if you are managing multiple event plans, this site can handle the load for you. Also, it provides easy setup for Internet marketers when promoting company events.

356. Accounting And Bookkeeping

Virtual accountancy and bookkeeping is a growing trend. You can apply here:

www.accountingdepartment.com
www.balanceyourbooks.com
www.bookminders.com
www.corptax.com
www.firstdata.com
www.intuit.com
www.tadaccounting.com

357. Lending Money

Of course I do know that his method is not for everyone, as you need a lot of money to start with. Nevertheless, it is a way of making money, so it is mentioned in this book. Many people are unable to borrow money from the usual venues, such as banks or other loan companies. Many individuals are willing to lend their money to those they think deserve it, but are apprehensive about the prospect of not getting it back. Others would like to lend to people in their circles, but have no idea about setting interest rates and chasing borrowers for payments.

There are websites that allow individuals to lend money to others while charging interest, while others make lending money to friends or family safer and easier.

www.LendingClub.com - This website lets you lend money in amounts as small as $25; the higher the risk, the higher the return. LendingClub does perform credit checks on potential borrowers. If a borrower's score is below 640, he will not be allowed to take out a loan.

www.Kiva.org - This site is aimed at budding small and medium businesses in less-developed nations such as Uganda and Nicaragua. Your money is handled by micro financing firms and does not earn interest. The payback, though, is in seeing your money help people pull themselves out of poverty.

www.VirginMoney.com - People often say it is bad business to lend money to friends and family. Virgin Money works around it by preparing formal documents, processing payments, sending reminder e-mails, and end-of-year statements. You get to keep the interest, while Virgin Money takes care of the dirty business.

www.Prosper.com - Prosper allows you to be part of the loan and offers no set interest rates. The borrower inputs the amount he or she needs, and the interest rate he or she is willing to put up with. Lenders then bid the rate down, and the potential lenders with the lowest interest rates combine their money to provide a three-year loan for the debtor.

www.fundingcircle.com is another one to check out.

Chapter 39. Trading Opportunities

> **Important:** Trading Gold/Forex or Shares involves BIG risk. Only ever use money that you are prepared to lose.
> Some people earn good money (maybe you will be one of them) but the vast majority of people don't earn a lot (if anything) with trading shares online.
> The same applies for online betting.

358. Social Investment Networks

eToro is the world's largest social investment network with over 4 million users. You can copy what other top performing traders are doing, therefore maximising your chances of making money.
www.etoro.com

359. Gold Trading

Although there's also money to be made selling, say, gemstones, it's usually necessary to have such items double-checked for authenticity and that's something only a certified professional can do. This will cost money and, as with any expense, that would have to be taken from your profit. Another thing you should also consider when investing in gemstones is that there isn't really a good marketplace online for them yet, as far as I know.

You could be better off buying and selling gold online. In the past, investing in gold and other types of precious metals was only possible if you were willing to make high-volume or high-value transactions. Nowadays, the entry barriers are much lower as you'll see for yourself when you visit sites like www.BullionVault.com, www.GoldSilver.com, or even just the Bullion Centre of www.eBay.com. For information about setting up a gold trading business in the US visit www.ehow.com/how_5942796_start-scrap-gold-silver-business.html.

360. Forex Trading

In the past, only people with thousands of dollars at their disposal would have been able to trade in the Forex (Foreign Exchange Market). Thanks to online Forex trading platforms, however, people can now start trading currencies with as little as $500 (around £300). The minimum opening balance for trading currencies varies from one site to another. You can have an idea of how much you will need to initially invest through the following sites:

www.AVAFX.com
www.etxcapital.co.uk
www.forex.com
www.forexyard.com

Forex trading is easier to learn than playing the stock market because you don't have to familiarise yourself with the entire histories of companies you don't know about. In Forex trading, you deal with factors you already know such as the USD, the Euro, the British Pound, or the Japanese Yen.

85% of trades done in the Forex market are based on the following pairs, which a lot of Forex brokers refer to as the Big Six:

- USD to Euro (EUR) and vice versa
- USD to GBP (British Pound) and vice versa
- USD to AUD (Australian Dollar) and vice versa
- USD to CHF (Swiss Franc) and vice versa
- USD to JPY (Japanese Yen) and vice versa
- USD to CAD (Canadian Dollar) and vice versa

Trades are likely to be more volatile with these pairs, but you'll also have the chance of enjoying higher profit margins from them since a high volume of trading among these currency pairs is always taking place.

The best thing about Forex trading is that you do not need to be a financial whiz to make money from it. You just have to pay closer attention to what's going on around you and the world. Start watching more news from the BBC and CNN and other news channels. Major political and economic events always have an impact on currency trading so, by regularly watching the news, you might be able to predict upcoming trends a few days in advance and trade accordingly. A dummy account basically allows you to perform mock trades of all kinds and observe results from whatever trading strategies you are testing out. Basically, your strategies will be either short-term or long-term. You can instantly make or lose a lot of money with short-term or day trading, which requires you to trade a large amount of money from one pair to another in a minute-to-minute basis. Keep in mind that you will be going up against hedge fund managers in this case as well. As someone starting out, the less volatile environment for long-term traders is more ideal.

361. Day Trading Stocks

Day trading means you buy shares and sell them the same day or even a few hours after you've bought them. It really is far too complicated to explain in a few sentences so I suggest, if you are interested in trying this, search online for help.

362. Trading In Stock

Trading in stock shares, again, is far too complicated to explain but it is possible to earn money with this - good money! You will need a lot of money to make a lot of money though. If you only buy a few shares e.g. $1,000 (£600), you will never make a lot of money.
Search online for help if you want to find out more.

363. No Risk Match Betting

You can do match betting at no risk at all. You don't gamble, you just get to know the system and play the system and it is legal. You are simply making profits from the many free bets and incentives that are offered by bookmakers. Match betting is based on a mathematical equation, not on high risk factors. The simple principle is that you make two contrasting bets and that the outcome of who wins or who loses does not affect your money. This can be done by taking advantage of the free bets offered by the bookmakers. Search online and you will find newspaper articles from people who earned money with this.
Warning: all betting/gambling can become addictive.
www.beatbookies.com
www.comparethebookie.com
www.fixtheodds.com is specialised in match betting
www.paddypower.com

Chapter 40. Other Buying & Selling Opportunities

364. Domain Flipping

Domain flipping is a very easy (and profitable) method of making money online. It's based on one simple principle - buy cheap and sell for more! If you've always had a talent for selling or reselling stuff, then just think of this as something like domain brokering!

You can earn up to $200 (£120) for a good domain. If you can buy 10 domains per week, you can earn $2,000 (£1200) per week (you need to take off some of your expenses). I have bought domains from Godaddy auctions for $39 (£23), put some decent content on them, got some more backlinks and sold them three months later for $2000 (£1200).

Internet marketers like buying domains with a lot of backlinks, as they know how much effort it takes to create backlinks. And because Google likes backlinks, it is a win-win situation. There are many domains expiring every single day and each of them first enters a bidding competition before it's finally released for public registration. This offers us a unique window of opportunity to buy a valuable domain very cheaply and sell it for more afterwards.

You can check out and download a current list of expiring domains at any time on http://auctions.godaddy.com. It costs roughly $3 (£5)/year to be able to use the Godaddy auction system, which is very affordable for anyone.

Which domains should you buy? There are a couple of very simple rules that you should follow if you want to make sure you're getting the best deal:

1. Aim for aged domains.
Aged domains have shown to have a bigger trust factor with Google, and this automatically increases their value. You can check a website's domain age at: http://www.webconfs.com/domain-age.php

2. Aim for high PR domains.
Page rank (PR) is a number between 1 and 10 that Google uses to determine the backlink value of any given web property. This is very important to people who wish to use the domain for SEO purposes.

3. Check that it's indexed in Google.

If the site is not indexed in Google, it is highly likely that the domain has been penalized or put in the »sandbox«. To check whether a site is indexed, open Google and type in: www.somedomain.com (whichever domain you are looking for). If the domain is penalized, this search will not yield any results.

4. Aim for brandable domain names.
A domain such as "www.weightloss.com" is far more valuable than a domain name such as "www.xyzabcdefhazqt.com" - you get the idea!

5. Aim for .com, .net or .org.
These are easiest to sell because they are the most common extensions that visitors have learned to trust.

Note: There are some tools that can do all these checking procedures for you, but you can also do it manually at first and then invest when you start seeing your first real profit.

Look out for websites that have very low bids in www.flippa.com, buy at a low price and re-list a few weeks/months later when other buyers will be online.

How do you increase the value of a domain?
Now that you have a potential domain to flip, it's time to up its value with a few SEO marketing strategies.

- Keywords - Look up the list of keywords that the domain has been targeting. Keywords ensure targeted traffic, which is why wrong keywords can lead the wrong people to your site while your targeted visitors remain unaware of your site. Are the keywords targeted by the domain still worth working on? Should they be improved or replaced completely?
- Content - Another way to improve the value of your website's domain is by breathing new life into it by writing fresh, original and valuable content. You can look for ideas by checking out the latest posts on competing websites as well as looking for interesting reports or articles in your industry. Just type your targeted keywords in www.news.google.com and other similar sites. There are lots of free content tools mentioned in my book "Design Free Websites".
- Income - What are the sources of income used by the previous domain owner? Are they truly effective or should you try an alternative? The primary ways to earn from a website are either by earning advertising revenue or by selling a product or service.

Where can you flip domains?

The best sites to flip domains include but are not limited to www.eBay.com, www.Flippa.com, and www.Sedo.com. Make sure to create a visually appealing and informative presentation for your domain. One glance should be all it takes to convince interested buyers to make a bid!

365. Domain Parking

Buy domain names for $8.50 (£5) and just leave them on the shelf doing nothing for years. In 5 or 10 years time you can sell them for between $100 and $5000 (£60 and £3000)! Google loves old domains so if you have good old ones to sell, people are prepared to pay a lot of money for them.

366. eBay

Making money with www.ebay.com is nothing new. At first it started out as a simple "online auction house" where you could put your own stuff for sale and bid on other things you wanted to buy. Then people realised that they could buy something at a cheaper price and sell it on for profit. This is called item flipping, and it's still very popular. There's a well-known story about a Canadian man who started out by selling his paperclip on eBay and ended up owning a house. It was all over the news...

He did it by exchanging his red paperclip for a ceramic doorknob, which in turn led to a camping stove, generator, snowmobile and eventually a two-story house in Kipling, Saskatchewan! So as you see... nothing is impossible with a little bit of creativity and imagination. Now, I'm not suggesting that you start digging up old paperclips and conspire to buy half of Manhattan via eBay, but I do want you to realize that it has more potential than you might guess.

To make money on eBay you only need two things: - an eBay account and a credit card (or PayPal). Many people think there's some "big secret" to making money on eBay, but there really isn't. You simply use eBay's auction system to add new items for sale- it's as simple as that. The amount of profit you will see is directly related to how cheaply you can buy for and for how much you can sell + the number of transactions you can comfortably handle. The good news is - you get better and better at this with experience.
Simply buy some goods at flea markets or in charity shops and sell them on eBay. It is that simple. However, that is not the ONLY way to make money with eBay. Some people choose to take the other route and become affiliates. Currently, the top 25 eBay affiliates average above $100,000 (around £60,000) in monthly commissions!

You see, eBay pays its affiliates a percentage of the sale (a commission) for every purchase that was made through their "affiliate link". Every affiliate gets his/her own unique link that he/she can promote and get instant commissions every time someone lands on eBay (via their link) and buys something. To become an eBay affiliate costs nothing and it takes about two minutes to apply for an account and be ready to start promoting your link. You can do this on forums, social media platforms (such as Facebook, Twitter, YouTube) or even on your own website if you have one. Keep in mind that although the application process itself is very short and straightforward, it may take a few days before you get your affiliate account approved by eBay.

367. Run An eBay Shop

People who have an online shop always have one problem in common: getting traffic to the shop to create sales. The solution to this problem is easy: go where there already IS traffic and create a shop there: eBay and Amazon (see next method).
If you search for a certain product on eBay, you can see how many have already sold. This gives you an idea of what type of products sell well. Let's look at an example:
I've searched for "computer cable" and this product was shown on the first page:

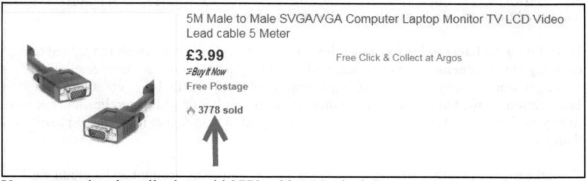

You can see that the seller has sold 3778 cables. Not bad. But we can analyse further. Once you click on the product, this screen is shown:

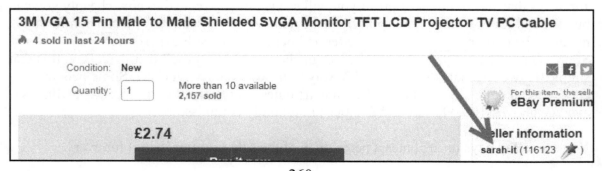

Next to the Seller Information you can see the amount of feedback the seller has, in this case 116123. Now that is a lot! Knowing that a lot of buyers don't leave feedback, you can assume that the seller has sold more than 116123 items. Now you can also find out in what period of time the seller has received the feedback by clicking on the number 116123. This reveals that the seller has been an eBay member since 27th May 2011.

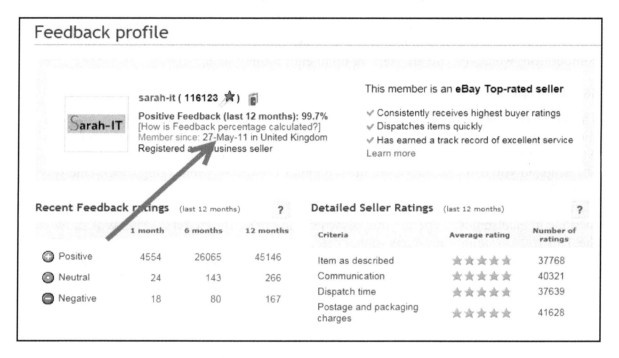

For ease of calculation, let's say he/she started selling on 1st June 2011.
It is now December 2014, that means he/she has been selling for 43 months.

116123 reviews divided by 43 months = 2700 reviews per month.
This seller has sold a minimum of 2700 products per month - on average. Simply by selling products on eBay. Not bad hey! One would think that he/she earns on average £1 per product, that is £2,700 - $4,198 per month. eBay fees have to be deducted from this total.
He/she has got a business and is earning money, just what you want to do as you are reading this book. You see, it is worth putting in the effort setting up an eBay shop and go where the traffic already IS.
Setting up an eBay shop is not that complicated and there are many shop-templates available where you can just import your products, set your prices, etc. THE most

important thing with setting up your online eBay shop is try and put as many keywords as possible in the item description so people can find your product and buy it.

You just need to find a wholesaler where you will buy your products and sell them with a profit in your shop.

There are plenty of videos online on how to set up an eBay shop and some good books too.

Another thing to remember here: when you are thinking of selling something, analyse your competition and see how much they are selling. *Always* study and learn from your competition, whatever you are starting up to earn money with.

368. Run An Amazon Shop

The same as what I wrote under the previous method applies for setting up an Amazon shop. You can, of course, list your items on both eBay and Amazon but make sure you watch your stock so you don't list items that have been sold.

On Amazon you can also check the most popular products by analysing them. One way of doing this is the Amazon Top 100. Go to www.amazon.com. This is an excellent way to identify hot new markets and is updated hourly. Choose a category from the drop down menu, e.g. electronics. Type in your keyword and click "Bestsellers". This will show you the Top 100 bestselling products in that category.

Each time you dig deeper into a specific category, it will show you the best sellers.

I have only covered eBay and Amazon but there are plenty of other online shops where you can list your products. Just search for them. As there are 1000's of different products you can sell, it is impossible to list all the shops here. I explain my experience of online shopping and the tools you will need in my book "Drop Shipping and eCommerce".

369. Become An Online Entrepreneur - R

One advantage with online selling is that you are able to sell across the entire world where sales are almost endless for the right products. The truth is that online sales are the future and the more you learn about it, the bigger your future can be.

Does being an online entrepreneur work? It sure does! I am one myself and I earn a very good living being a full time Internet marketer. I recommend it for anyone who wants to put in the work.

To read about the multiple streams of income I've created as an online entrepreneur, read my book "From Newbie to Millionaire", in which I explain which streams of income I've created.

370. Buy And Sell Coins

You can make money from buying and selling coins online. The bigger the collection of coins, they more they are going to be worth. You can buy and re-sell on sites such as www.eBay.com and www.Craigslist.org or specialist sites such as www.baldwin.co.uk and www.cambridgeshirecoins.com. You can also sell your coin collection to a pawnshop if you acquire a wide enough selection. The big advantage here is: you don't need a lot of space to store your products.

371. Buy And Sell Stamps

Buying and reselling stamps can always be done on www.eBay.com or www.Craigslist.org. To buy and sell stamps to more specialised online markets, try www.stanleygibbons.com or www.stamps2go.com. You can buy the stamps at yard sales/boot fairs very cheaply and can sell them for a large profit once you have acquired a selection. You need even less space than buying and selling coins.

372. Sell Your Old Gadgets

There are many sites that you can send your old gadgets such as computers, phones and cameras to. This can be done on websites such as www.eBay.com, or specialised markets for gadgets, such as www.gazelle.com (in the US) or http://www.mazumamobile.com/ (in the UK). You could go to markets and boot fairs/flea markets and buy stuff to sell with a profit online. I know a guy who has been doing this for 5 years and who does nothing other than buy at markets and sell on eBay.

373. Re-selling Online As An Amazon reseller

Buy books and other items at boot fairs/flea markets or online at www.ebay.com or www.madbid.com and sell them online at a profit. Sign up as a reseller on Amazon at www.amazon.com. It's simple and it's free!

If the product has a barcode, you can sell it on Amazon as a reseller. You just sign up, list your product by typing in the barcode and give the product a price. That's it. Amazon's selling machine does the rest, Amazon charges your buyer and Amazon will send you an email when you've sold something. Each month Amazon will pay you what you've sold minus their commissions and charges. I know several people who make very good money with this method, including my children and myself. Each time you've made a sale, Amazon will notify you by email. Here's a screenshot of my inbox for 2 weeks of my Amazon Reseller Account. I've sold 28 items in 2 weeks, so 2 items per day. This is NOT going to make me a millionaire but it is another stream of income, as I believe in multiple streams of income. A lot of small amounts add up to one big amount!

Amazon Services Europe	Sold, dispatch now: QZ-QVLX-	09/12/2014 10:39
Amazon Services Europe	Sold, dispatch now: 1H-ISP8-N	11/12/2014 22:48
Amazon Services Europe	Sold, dispatch now: 60-VYC8-P	12/12/2014 10:17
Amazon Services Europe	Sold, dispatch now: V4-GTHD-	12/12/2014 21:06
Amazon Services Europe	Sold, dispatch now: 1A-5BTK-L	13/12/2014 18:17
Amazon Services Europe	Sold, dispatch now: MU-TJQE-	13/12/2014 20:24
Amazon Services Europe	Sold, dispatch now: UQ-2U9M-	14/12/2014 08:48
Amazon Services Europe	Sold, dispatch now: HX-XM6H-	14/12/2014 10:50
Amazon Services Europe	Sold, dispatch now: 4X-5V0P-Q	14/12/2014 11:25
Amazon Services Europe	Sold, dispatch now: C0-NDL3-Y	14/12/2014 14:34
Amazon Services Europe	Sold, dispatch now: 5M-VMIS-J	14/12/2014 14:36
Amazon Services Europe	Sold, dispatch now: 5X-YALE-6	14/12/2014 18:03
Amazon Services Europe	Sold, dispatch now: GY-3L29-6	14/12/2014 18:29
Amazon Services Europe	Sold, dispatch now: GR-C6VA-3	14/12/2014 18:38
Amazon Services Europe	Sold, dispatch now: IB-A1WM-	14/12/2014 20:21
Amazon Services Europe	Sold, dispatch now: 0Z-LEX7-Y	14/12/2014 23:50
Amazon Services Europe	Sold, dispatch now: GC-5854-X	15/12/2014 03:37
Amazon Services Europe	Sold, dispatch now: I1-VE03-6J	15/12/2014 07:58
Amazon Services Europe	Sold, dispatch now: FY-ZRP8-C	16/12/2014 11:05
Amazon Services Europe	Sold, dispatch now: 45-2NGO-I	16/12/2014 15:35
Amazon Services Europe	Sold, dispatch now: O8-2H0N-I	16/12/2014 22:26
Amazon Services Europe	Sold, dispatch now: 5B-WHXN-	17/12/2014 22:31
Amazon Services Europe	Sold, dispatch now: WZ-UY4V-	18/12/2014 12:38
Amazon Services Europe	Sold, dispatch now: 83-HIXV-6	18/12/2014 18:13
Amazon Services Europe	Sold, dispatch now: J0-NXDH-I	23/12/2014 10:10
Amazon Services Europe	Sold, dispatch now: WI-UWOW	23/12/2014 10:44
Amazon Services Europe	Sold, dispatch now: 9D-6YM1-4	23/12/2014 13:44
Amazon Services Europe	Sold, dispatch now: KV-E8S2-Z	23/12/2014 15:29

374. Pet Merchandise Seller

The pet merchandise business is huge. You can open a store on eBay or Amazon and become specialised in all kinds of Pet Merchandise. All you need to do is find products that you can buy wholesale and sell with a profit. You can also do drop shipping. In my book "Drop Shipping and eCommerce", I explain how drop shipping works. Basically, you sell stuff but you don't have to ship anything. Ideal for a home-based business.

Chapter 41. Writing Jobs

375. Freelance Writer

If you're good at writing, you should definitely get a job as a freelance writer. The demand for good freelance writers is now bigger than ever before.

As you know, we're living in an information-based society and well-presented information can literally mean the difference between success and failure in the world of online marketing.

This is why serious marketers never hesitate to invest their money in content that will engage their visitors and help them get more sales too. For freelance writers, this is a golden opportunity to do what they enjoy doing and earn good money from it.

For starters, you need to create an account on the most popular freelance hiring platforms, such as:
www.agentsofvalue.com
www.clickchores.com
www.domystuff.com
www.elance.com
www.fieldagents.net
www.fiverr.com
www.freelance.com
www.guru.com
www.ifreelance.com
www.microworkers.com
www.mturk.com
www.odesk.com
www.peopleperhour.com
www.shorttask.com
www.staff.com
www.virtualbee.com
www.writersweekly.com

Second step is to set up your profile. This is a step that most new freelance writers skip because they think that no one ever checks their profile, which couldn't be further from the truth. Every serious employer will first check your profile to learn about your background and portfolio. Only then will he/she decide if you're worthy of working for them, so make sure you take the necessary time to do this.

Once you've done that, you're ready for the third step. The way the system works is very simple. Once an employer posts a job, freelancers (you) can start bidding on it and writing their applications. Then the employer can contact the candidates and pick the right person for the job.

Normally, there are four things that can help you boost your chances of winning the job:
- A well-structured application
- The right bid
- A professionally set up profile
- Your job history

Since you don't have any job history when you first start out, you'll have to compensate for this by writing a good application, placing a good bid (not necessarily the lowest - many employers consider low bids to mean low quality of work!) and dressing up your profile. Once you've done a few jobs, be sure to include them in your portfolio. This is how you build yourself into someone with authority.

If you become a paid Elance member you can see how much other freelancers have bid for the same job, so you know how much you need to bid to be the lowest bidder. However, buyers don't only decide based on the lowest price, as the reviews are a more important factor.

Aim for variety with your samples so that prospective clients can see for themselves how versatile your writing is. Of course, if you wish to specialise, that's up to you as well. Here is a list of the most common types of web content in demand nowadays. You'll find more detail on some of these below.
- Copywriting
- Web page content
- Reviews for products and services
- Reviews for films, books, plays, music, and all other forms or genres of art
- Essays, theses and other kinds of academic writing
- News reports
- Technical guides and manuals
- How-to guides
- Lifestyle and feature articles

- Blog posts

In time, you won't even have to worry about your applications because your job history and your portfolio will speak for itself. Then you can even start charging premium rates!

On the screenshot above taken from www.elance.com you can see that one woman has earned $392,637 (£245,800) for 1,128 jobs (in one year). That is $347 (£217) average per job. It is very likely that this person does not do all the writing herself but she outsources the writing- she has other people writing for her.

376. Writing Business Plans And Financial Reports

People who have not gone to business school create business and financial reports as well as business plans all the time. There are plenty of free learning materials and report templates you can get on the Internet and, with just enough patience and hard work, you can start offering your services to students as well as those hoping to set up their own small business.

A lot of people think that putting together these studies and reports is difficult, but it's not. If you look back on your college or university days when you had to write your final thesis, writing one was not as agonizing as defending your work - and thankfully you won't have to do the latter this time. You leave that to the client.

In writing business plans and financial reports, you can charge a fixed rate per page, though the more experience you have, the more you can charge. If you have ever owned a business, you may be qualified to be a Business Plan Writer. There are many templates available to create a business plan.

377. Technical Writer

A Technical Writer is a person who needs strong writing skills but does not have to be a creative thinker. Many organisations need help with creating technical manuals and how-to guides. Sometimes they are for customers but often they are for their own employees.

You do not need to have a technical background to write these, but you do need to be organised. Contact some local companies who work in the technical area you're most interested in and offer to write a trial piece.

378. Grant Writer

How about working as a Grant Writer? Many organisations including businesses, schools, and non-profit groups apply for grants from government, public and private agencies.

Typically there are strict guidelines on those applications and organisations will often hire someone to read the requirements and put the grant application together. For this type of work you need the ability to read and understand the instructions, gather the information and put it into the exact format required.

379. Writing Resumes / CV's

This is different from other writing jobs since it's not really something you would have learned from any creative writing you've done. Rather, résumé writing is more about learning the ever-changing dos and don'ts from experience. Having connections in human resources would also be a big help because you'll then have insider's knowledge about what recruiters are currently looking for in a résumé.

With the current economic situation, there has never been a greater need for this type of service. There are many people who are out of work and their CV is just not good enough to result in an interview. It therefore needs a fresh makeover.

Then there are people who want to move up but have never had to create a résumé before. And think of the thousands of college students and university graduates who are just entering the workforce. In any case, the goal is to write the kind of résumé that's entirely factual but at the same time written in such a way that an individual appears impressively professional, experienced, skilled, and personable.

The opportunities are wide open for someone who can put together a high quality professional résumé. If this sounds interesting but you are not sure where to start, then start with your own résumé and see how strong you can make it. Then ask other people to critique it and tell you what they like or don't like about it. Do you know someone who actually hires people and looks at a lot of CVs? Get their input and keep updating it. It won't be long before you are able to review someone else's résumé and critique it. You will quickly gain an eye for what works and what doesn't.

At that point, you are able to offer your services. Start by volunteering your services to help people create/update their résumés. If they like it, they will refer you to others. Contact the local college or university careers service offices. They are there to help students get jobs. Tell them you can assist students with their résumés and if they recommend you, it may increase your business significantly. You can also contact your local employment agencies and offer your services to their clients.

Now, there's only so much you can do to improve your skills as a résumé writer. In order to have a better competitive advantage, you should focus on improving other aspects of your work.

- Have ready-made templates for clients to choose from...templates that they won't get elsewhere!
- Include options for résumés in Pages, PDF, and other file formats.

Offer extra services like formatting photos for résumés and adding cover letters.

380. Ghost Writer

If you enjoy writing, or feel you have a natural talent for it, you can make money by becoming a ghost writer. You can advertise yourself as a ghost writer on www.elance.com (or any other outsourcing website) and earn money by writing a book, article, or website copy for your client.

I am aware that I've already mentioned ghost writing earlier. I am mentioning it here again because it is also a method to earn money online, for which you don't need a website.

I have over 200 niche books and all of these are written by ghost writers, but not my own books, as I write these myself!

381. Writing Press Releases

Companies, corporations and, sometimes, individuals issue statements known as press releases to the media as a way of making announcements. For example, some new product or service, a particular achievement or award gained or perhaps the birth of a child e.g. from a celebrity.

Reporters receive press releases all the time but if you've written one which gives all the important information they need to write a feature or news report, they're likely to use it and the organisation or person you're writing for will get the publicity they need and they'll want to use your services again.

A background in journalism is useful for writing press releases but you can find more about the format to use at www.wikihow.com/write-a-press-release. Look for opportunities on freelance sites like www.elance.com or www.odesk.com.

382. Article Writing And Article Marketing

Another way to establish yourself as an authority and an expert writer - especially when you are just starting out - is to have samples available for viewing online. One of the easiest and most effective ways to do this is by submitting original works to popular article directories.

www.associatedcontent.com
www.helium.com. These sites will pay for your articles or blog posts. Some articles on specific niches can pay out about $100 (£60).

If you don't have the money to purchase your own domain and web hosting, all you need to do is grab an affiliate link from ClickBank and use that link in your resource box at the end of your article. Be aware that some article directory websites do not like direct links to sales pages.

This way you can sit back and earn money without doing any form of web design! I have discussed article marketing already but here is a summary of the things to do:
- Write articles based on keyword research
- Put links underneath the article either from an affiliate product or your own website
- Sign up with article websites
- Publish articles to article websites
- Check account to see how much you've earned

Some popular article websites:
www.amazines.com
www.articlesbase.com
www.articlecity.com
www.articlesnatch.com
www.buzzle.com
www.ehow.com
www.examiner.com
www.ezinearticles.com
www.goarticles.com
www.hubpages.com
www.pubarticles.com
www.selfgrowth.com

www.squidoo.com
www.technorati.com
You can see the Top 50 here: http://www.vretoolbar.com/articles/directories.php

383. How-To Writer

Lots of people love to read how-to books or step-by-step articles. Websites that offer these are always looking for freelance writers to write for them. All you need to do is contact these websites and offer your services. A few examples of websites:
www.allbusiness.com
www.allexperts.com
www.answerbag.com
www.answers.com
www.answers.yahoo.com
www.ask.com
www.blurtit.com
www.businessinsider.com
www.chacha.com
www.chegg.com
www.createpool.com
www.DoItYourself.com
www.eHow.com
www.factmonster.com
www.financialhighway.com
www.fluther.com
www.howstuffworks.com
www.inewidea.com
www.justanswers.com
www.knowbrainers.com
www.makeuseof.com
www.SoYouWanna.com
www.stackexchange.com
www.statisticbrain.com
www.theanswerbank.com
www.webanswers.com
www.wiki.answers.com
+ Search for popular article directories

384. Questions And Answers Expert

Sometimes, Google doesn't hold the answers. Neither does Wikipedia. There are some things that only you can answer. How, then, can you make money out of your otherwise-useless knowledge?
The answer lies in question-and-answer websites. Questions and Answers (Q&A) websites are very popular and these websites are also constantly looking for freelance writers.

- www.Mahalo.com - This is among the first sites to pay their experts. It is rather popular both among people looking for answers, and for those who are trying to earn extra money online. It does get a bit crowded sometimes, but they offer many ways to compensate their experts.

- www.JustAnswer.com - It's just like Mahalo, only more formal. Here, the questions lean towards the professional and people expect you to have an expert grasp of the topic (you may, however, make up for the lack of knowledge with excellent research skills). The answers need to be more specific and thorough, but you can expect to get paid better than at most other Q&A sites.
Answer some questions in Yahoo Answers or Wiki Answers and you can put your affiliate link at the bottom of the answer. People ask questions and the best answers are shown on the sites. You can contact the websites mentioned in the previous method to become a Q&A expert.

385. Become A Content Writer

There are companies looking for content writers on a whole range of subjects. All you need to do is write content and you'll get paid. This is different to the previously mentioned methods, as you don't need to submit your article to sites but just deliver the content. Visit these for more information:
www.absolutewrite.com
www.blogtyrant.com
 www.constant-content.com
www.contentfocus.co.uk
www.digitaljournal.com
www.helium.com
www.listverse.com
www.mediabistro.com
www.triond.com
www.wizzley.com
www.xomba.com

www.zujava.com

386. Write Your Own PLR Articles And Sell Them

PLR stands for Private Label Rights. If you are good at writing then this is one option to consider, provided that you can find an untapped niche, as otherwise the competition will be vast. Webmasters are always looking for content.
- Find a subject to write about
- Write the articles using relevant keywords
- Write between 10 and 20 articles and package them into one article pack

Now the difficult part: find ways of selling your articles. Some PLR websites will buy your articles if they are in an untapped niche.

387. Post On Forums

You can earn money from posting on forums. Most forums compensate their users every week. This type of job is easy and you'll be hired to do it by either website owners with products and services they'd like to promote in forums, or by Internet marketers who'd like to offload their forum posting duties to focus on other parts of their work.

Ultimately, you'll get paid more if you can build or already have an established reputation relevant to what you are promoting. As you're acknowledged by other people as an authority on the subject, they're more likely to pay attention to anything you're marketing. However, let's be very clear that good forum posting never has room for outright or aggressive selling.

Register with a site like www.odesk.com or www.postonmyforum.com. To maximize your earning potential, you can register with five or more forums and write at least 10 forum posts for each site every day. There are also sites that pay referral bonuses to members that you invite to register, so you might want to try that out.

The key to being a successful forum poster is in having genuine enthusiasm for sharing your thoughts and helping people out. Avoid posting one-liners and nonsensical comments about someone else's post. Answering questions posted by another member is one thing but posting a reliable solution to a member's problem is what the forum owners are looking for.

388. Product Reviews

A lot of people are willing to pay for honest product reviews because they know how much weight that kind of review carries. You don't even have to lie if you have a very strong conscience and this goes against your principles. However, it would of course be more mutually advantageous if you did try to at least look for the best points about the product you've been asked to review.

Exceptional writing skills are not required for this type of job. You just have to focus on making yourself sound genuine on paper. It also helps if your product review follows a format that's similar to what's listed below.

- Start with an introduction. Talk about why you found yourself using the product and what it's supposed to do. Say whether you're part of its target market (e.g. you knew what it was and you found it helpful) or you're just giving it a try.
- List its features and specifications. Both are important!
- Talk about pros and cons objectively and subjectively.
- Remember to say that it's only your personal and not your professional opinion.
- Summarize key points. It helps buyers make a decision on whether to purchase the product or not.
- End with a recommendation. Giving a qualified recommendation is also fine - but only if it's absolutely necessary.

If you are an online writer, you can earn more by writing Amazon product reviews. You don't even have to use any of the products. Just consolidate the ideas already given by the feedback and reviews found on Amazon about the products.

Product reviews may pay more than regular articles, depending on the platform where you go to write for clients.

www.epinions.com
www.sponsoredreviews.com

389. Become An Online Book Critic

You can read books that are newly published and can earn money by giving people your review of the book. Search online for literary publications, magazines or printing houses.

390. Proofreading

If you prefer reading to writing, there are many organisations, writers and websites that need their documents proofread. You can have someone pay you to read over their work. Start by looking at proofreading jobs that are advertised on www.elance.com and www.Fiverr.com.

Proofreading is an art and finding a *perfect* proofreader is an even bigger art! I spend a lot of money on proofreading my own books and my niche books (written by ghost writers) but I keep finding mistakes in my books that have been proofread, no matter how much money I pay.

391. Critiquing Manuscripts

You don't need to be a professional or certified writer or editor in order to effectively critique manuscripts. At the end of the day, you just need two things:
- A genuine love of reading
- Writing and editing skills

There are two kinds of manuscript critiques you can do: general or line-by-line. With general critiques you just need to focus on the following questions:
- Are the major characters likeable and believable? Was there anything about them that disturbed you? Consider the same aspects when evaluating antagonists and supporting characters.
- Did you find the plot interesting and believable? Were there any surprising or predictable twists? Were there any plot holes?
- What can you say about the way the author resolved the main conflict? Was it satisfactory?
- What can you say about the ending? Did it leave you wanting more? Did it feel rushed?
- Take note if there are a lot of grammatical or spelling errors and typos. You don't need to point them out one by one (if you are just doing a critique) but you should mention them if they prevent you from enjoying the story properly.
- Consider the dialogue. Was it believable and appropriate? Was there too little or too much of it?
- Consider the setting. Was it described enough for you to easily imagine it in your mind? Did it contribute to the story?

Always remember that writers tend to be very sensitive about their work so you should make an effort to be tactful and constructive with your opinions at all times. You should also make an effort to give honest praise wherever and whenever it's deserved.

392. Copy Editing

If you feel you are a decent writer, there are even more opportunities available to you. Any business or person who creates content has use for a good editor. If you have knowledge of writing style guides, even better. You can offer your services as a copy editor.

Other people write the content and you then review it for style, grammar or spelling errors, punctuation, sentence structure, use of words, and other things that will improve the content. Register with sites such as www.elance.com or www.odesk.com.

393. Editing Academic Papers

More and more people are now in higher education, and research outputs are at an all-time high. With each question the academics answer, ten more questions spring up, and more academics rush to answer them. This constant need for new knowledge has spawned an entire industry devoted to publishing academic papers.

However, a lot of people engaged in research are too engrossed in their tasks to be bothered with editing their papers. Many college students are also so immersed in their experience that they forget that an essay is due tomorrow. Others simply have no clue about writing theses and dissertations - the content may be ground breaking, but the format is not correct - and they run the risk of having their papers rejected. This is where the academic editor comes in.

It goes without saying that some familiarity with the subject goes a long way, as a missing piece of punctuation or a word in the wrong place can, and will, give academic readers the wrong impression about your client's research. You could start out with short papers such as essays for college students and slowly work your way up the academic ladder. You may also give away free writing samples to friends who might be in need of editing services, and let them refer you by word of mouth.

Chapter 42. Taking Part In Surveys & Reviewing

394. Online Surveys And Get Paid To Do Something Sites

We all have an opinion and now you can get paid for yours. If going online and answering questions is your cup of tea, online surveys are a good way of making some cash.

If you want to make a full time living out of surveys you will have to sign up with 200 or so sites, as the pay-out is small, but lots of small pay-outs soon add up! In my opinion it is underpaid for the time it takes to do, but it might be something that you'd like.

It's safe and easy and sometimes free, and companies are always looking for ways to make people answer their surveys. Organisations use marketing tools to determine who receives surveys; however, not all companies have the same target markets. You might find that not a lot of surveys are applicable to you, so it's a wise decision to sign up for more than one company.

Some survey companies 'pay' in either money or credits, which can be redeemed once a threshold has been reached. Others pay in vouchers, so not in "real money".

Here are some survey companies who would like to do business with people just like you:

www.Ciao.com - Owned and operated by Microsoft and based in the UK, Ciao allows you to write reviews for products and pays you when they get read. You can earn more if you review a product first or write reviews of high quality. You even have the chance to refer friends and earn commissions reaching up to half of their earnings for the first six months.

www.valuedopinions.co.uk (in the UK) or www.ValuedOpinions.com (in the US) - These websites are totally free and easy to join. You get paid between 50 cents (30p) to $5 (£3) for each survey you complete. They offer gift certificates for well-known merchants.

www.GetPaidSurveys.com - This survey service does not only pay $1 to $10 (60p to £6) for surveys that take under 45 minutes to accomplish; it also features tips from those who actually earn a living by answering them. They also offer paid surveys for teens below 18 years old. They also offer focus groups, which pay $50 (£30) for an hour's worth of work.

Other sites:

www.2020panel.com
www.acop.com
www.cashcrate.com
www.consumerlink.com
www.fusioncash.net
www.globaltestmarket.com
www.inboxpounds.com
www.ipoll.com
www.myopinionnow.com
www.mysurvey.com Over 40 million members!
www.opinionspaid.com
www.sarosresearch.com
www.surveyclub.com
www.surveysavvy.com
www.surveyscout.com
www.swagbucks.com Members have earned over 48 million pounds!
www.zoompanel.com

395. Review Products

Lots of companies want to know what their customers think of their products. There are many sites that pay you to review their products, such as:

www.bzzagent.com
www.cashcrate.com
www.reviewstream.com
www.sharedreviews.com
www.vindale.com

You can also review products by making a video on www.YouTube.com, which can lead to you getting sponsored by the providing company.

www.toluna.com or www.uk.toluna.com is always looking for new people to test products and fill in surveys. You will get paid to give your opinion on several products and niches.

396. Review Software

www.softwarejudge.com will pay you to review various software online.

397. Read Emails

What can be easier than reading emails and responding to them? Now you can get paid to do this! Visit
www.donkeymails.com
www.inboxdollars.com

398. Become A Mystery Shopper

Large companies will pay you to buy their products from several online companies to help with their market research. Mystery shoppers may also be hired by a company interested in finding out things about its employees e.g. are they doing their job with the right amount of diligence and enthusiasm.

As a mystery shopper, you might be required to induce a particular situation to happen:
- Be rude to sales representatives.
- Buy something and then return it for a refund or exchange.

Compensation here is a little bit tricky. You will rarely get paid cash. But everything you spend while mystery shopping will be reimbursed fully. And you get to keep whatever items you bought during your "work"! Those items are basically your income, and you can either use them yourself or sell them for 100% profit e.g. as an Amazon Reseller.

Being a mystery shopper is attractive for those who are compulsive shoppers, as they can shop and get paid to do it without spending their own money. However, you should also be wary of scammers - there are lots of them online. Try:
www.aboutfacecorp.com
www.customer-1st.com
www.dataquestonline.com
www.marketviewpoint.com
www.mystery-shoppers.co.uk
www.mystery-shoppers.com
www.restaurant-cops.com
www.marketforce.com or
www.uk.marketforce.com
www.secretshopper.com
www.servicecheck.com
www.shopperscritique.com
www.tnsglobal.com

or search for "mystery shopping".

If you secret shop at a restaurant, your meal will be free so not only do you get paid to do the job but you will save money as well.

399. Join A Focus Group

Lots of companies are willing to pay people to provide feedback on their products. This is often done with focus groups. Visit:
www.findfocusgroups.com
www.focusgroups.com
www.paidfocusgroup.co.uk
www.plazaresearch.com

400. Get Paid To Buy Alcohol

On www.servelegal.co.uk - you get paid to buy booze! ServeLegal pays 18- and 19-year-olds to buy age-restricted products from supermarkets and bars e.g. tobacco and alcohol. The aim here is to test if the places you buy the age-restricted products from ask for your ID.
You get to keep the alcohol you buy!

Chapter 43. Other Ways To Earn Money Online Without A Website

401. Earn Money Playing Games

Believe it or not, a lot of people are willing to pay real money just for you to play a game. There are a number of sites where you can get paid to play video games. Some include
www.gamesville.com
www.gamesradar.com
www.game-testers.net.

Generally speaking, these games can be categorised as either RPG (Role Playing Games) or MMORPG (Massive Multiplayer Online Role Playing Games). In many cases, you need actual experience and expertise in playing the game to get hired. You may also need to play a sample game in front of the potential employer to prove that you have what it takes.
Another way to earn from playing this type of game is by creating a strong "character" in such games and then selling your account to another player: a lot of these accounts can sell for hundreds of dollars! Rare items in these games also sell for a hefty amount.

As for which games you should "invest" your time in, it's best to choose something popular but at the same time something you'd actually have fun playing. In recent times, online multiplayer shooting games have gained in popularity. The income potential of these games is still at its budding stages, but you can still earn a respectable amount of money occasionally by building strong characters or accounts.

402. Refer A Friend

On www.refermehappy.com you can refer a friend who is good at a particular job and you will receive a referral fee should your friend get hired for the job.

403. Earn Money Just Searching The Web

If you, just like me, constantly search the web, you can get paid for it. Qmee pays you. You need to install an add-on to your browser and when you search, you will see sponsored search results as well as normal results. Each Qmee result has a cash award attached to it when you click on it. You won't become a millionaire with this method but every little helps....For more information:
www.qmee.com

404. Earn Money Reading Emails

Some companies are prepared to pay to find out what people are saying about their website/services/products. www.htmail.com is an email marketing company with customer feedback. Most sites will pay you between one pence and 10 pence per email that you read. It will probably never earn you a lot of money.

You might earn up to $100 (£60) per month, which would be a lot for this type of email marketing, but www.htmail.com also has a referral program where you get paid commission for every friend that you refer to them. That's when the money can add up.

www.Donkeymails.com is a reputable company that pays well and on time. They pay you for reading e-mail and click on ads (rates starting at 1 cent per click). It offers upgrades and a referral program. See also www.wowearnings.com.

405. Earn Money Viewing Adverts

Head over to www.qustodian.com, download the App, and you will get paid to view adverts.

406. Earn Money Watching Advertisements

While big money has been spent on producing adverts, advertisers have not gone around paying viewers for watching them. Start-up www.YouData.com changed all that. YouData believes that advertisers should pay you directly for giving them the attention they need, and that promoting a product is more successful when the marketing effort is targeted at a specific clientele.

Here is how you get started with YouData:
- You register and create a "me file" at YouData.
- You answer a set of questions about yourself. These determine the type and number of commercials that you will receive.
- Advertisements that fit your profile are sent to you, along with the amount that the advertiser will pay if you watch it.

YouData offers payment for watching commercials and gives away incentives to users who get more people to sign up. While the compensation is small (usually 65 cents per video), the videos are usually short, and these could add up to a pretty substantial sum by the time you're done watching.

You will also be able to look and be paid looking at banner ads; it all depends on the information you submitted in your "me file", and the number of advertisers who use YouData in your region. If your "me file" is similar to those of other users, more advertisers will use YouData and you will get more opportunities to get paid.

YouData pays you instantly via PayPal. While the amount they pay might be chicken feed (as little as a dollar per day), loose change can add up to a fat account if you keep plugging away. You also have the option to donate a portion of your earnings to charity.

407. Earn Money Clicking Ad Links

If you're looking for a quick, easy source of money, you can go to websites that pay users to click ad links. These are known as "Get-Paid-to-Click" sites.

- www.clixsense.com - Pays you between 1 to 40 cents/40 pence per click. A lot of the higher-paying advertisements are available to premium members and an upgrade is available for $10 (£6).
- www.bux.to - Bux pays you for visiting websites and clicking ads. You just view a site for 30 seconds to get paid. You may even earn more for referring friends. Rates start at 1 cent / 1 penny per view and 1 cent / 1 penny per referral. You may withdraw your payment daily using PayPal or AlertPay.
- www.fusioncash.com - (US only) Pays you to click on ads, check the weather, read the latest news, play games, and answer surveys. Each action is paid a different rate. You may withdraw a minimum of $25 (£15) using a wide range of options, including PayPal.

408. Earn Money From Fiverr

www.fiverr.com is a great little site. For just $5 (£3), you can order almost anything you can imagine - from graphics and design to videos, articles, programming, music, even gifts and all kinds of other crazy things!

It's a very popular site and it's growing rapidly. If you think you have a talent of some sort, or would be willing to offer a service for $5 (£3), this is definitely a place to start making quick money! No bidding or no membership fees. It is very easy to use and free to sign up. You just have to register an account (for free) and you're ready to start posting your offers. You can post as many offers as you like, but it's a good idea to check out first what's in demand and then tweak your offer so that it's just a little bit better - this is how the pros do it.

You may think that $5 (£3) is not much, and you may be right. However, if you can semi-automate your service or perhaps even completely automate, you can earn decent money. Some people earn a full-time monthly income this way. A few people are aware of this, but sellers are ranked according to different levels. Achieving a higher seller level and getting your offer featured is based on a variety of factors including, but not limited to, the volume of orders delivered satisfactorily versus the number of cancelled and delayed orders as well as your average income. Feedback or reviews from buyers are taken into account too.

Once you "earn" Top Rated Seller status, you will be able to offer extras and prices at more than $5. For instance, one top-rated seller offers his services for creating a 5-slide Power Point presentation at $5 (£3). However, the seller also offers the option for buyers of an additional 7 slides for $5. Rush orders for delivery within 24 hours may be made for an additional $40 (£24).
All services start as $5 for one gig, but almost every time there is an upsell e.g. someone will create a video for you for $5 but they charge an extra $10 (£6) to deliver it to you within 2 days.

Another common strategy that the most prolific sellers use is to offer incentives or promotions for buyers to shop in bulk. For instance, some sellers will offer a free order for every four orders purchased. Others offer a free complementary service in exchange for a particular number of order requests.
Whatever it is you are selling, just remember to always ask for reviews or feedback as this can greatly help in improving your seller ranking.

But there's a way to leverage Fiverr to earn much more than $5 (£3) ... and most people don't even think about it! It's super sneaky and it includes reselling cheap Fiverr services for big money on freelance platforms like Elance or Odesk.

For example, you may offer a logo design service on Elance and get a job for $60 (£35), which you can easily outsource to someone on Fiverr for $5. Your profit - $55 (£32)!

This is a method that a lot of people use - buy cheap and sell for more. It can be scaled very quickly and, if done properly, it can potentially earn you a lot of money. There is, in essence, nothing wrong with doing this because the buyer (the person who needs the logo) is happy to pay $60 (£35) whilst you can get it done for $5 (£3)! It's called doing business.

409. Miscellaneous Freelance Work

On www.Clicknwork.com you can do freelance work and you'll get paid per hour. Depending on the job, you could earn up to $150 (£90) per hour. You will work for professional companies so you will need to go through a test to be accepted as a freelancer.

Browse other freelance sites for all sorts of jobs you can earn money with:
www.agentsofvalue.com
www.clickchores.com
www.domystuff.com
www.elance.com
www.fieldagents.net
www.fiverr.com
www.freelance.com
www.guru.com
www.ifreelance.com
www.microworkers.com
www.mturk.com
www.odesk.com
www.peopleperhour.com
www.shorttask.com
www.staff.com
www.virtualbee.com

The beauty of these freelance sites is that you can work from anywhere in the world for anywhere in the world e.g. you can be based in the UK and do work for somebody based in Australia.

410. Earn Money From Swapit

www.swapit.co.uk This is an auction site mostly for children and teenagers. The whole thing is based on "swapits" - virtual currency. You swap online, sending the items you want to swap to the site. You can earn swapits by trading, and then use these to buy new items. This is effectively earning money, because you can now sell these new items on eBay or on Amazon as a Reseller, earning real money.

411. Become A Seller Assistant

There are many people who don't know how to sell items online and aren't interested in trying, while others simply don't have the time. A lot of these people are "the older generation", the not so savvy computer users. Whatever the reason, you can make money from selling these people's items. As a 'seller assistant' for other people's goods, you need to take a picture of the item, write the description, and handle the payment and shipping. The owner will charge a small fee for this, or the owner can pay you in commission. You can sell their stuff and charge a percentage of what you've sold. You can list all the products they have to sell and take care of the whole sales process as well, charging extra

for this.
Once you find owners who give you stuff to sell, you can list the items for sale on websites:
www.craigslist.org
www.ebay.co.uk
www.ebay.com
www.etsy.com
www.folksy.com
On Amazon as a reseller
- etc.

412. Virtual Farming

The World of Warcraft is a phenomenon; it is a multi-player online role-play game. Gold is the main currency of the game bit it takes time to earn gold. So, people all over the world are playing the game with the aim of making gold and selling it in the game for real money. Why not give it a go.

413. Become A Local Expert.

If you know a town or place really well you can become an expert and sell your knowledge. On www.vayable.com you can create money from your wisdom as you can create tours and sell them.

414. Become A Grandma

Lots of people are looking for someone they can trust to do all sorts of job e.g. caring for children, cooking, housekeepers, special need care, etc.

On www.rentagrandma.com, you can register and create a profile and negotiate the terms of the job directly with the families you will work for.
If you have the money, you can even become a Rent A Grandma Franchisee.

415. Sell Unwanted Gift Cards.

On www.giftcardgranny.com you can get money for your unwanted gift cards.

416. Become A Friend For Someone

On www.rentafriend.com you can become a friend for somebody who needs a friend for a party, a wedding, a social event, a trip to a restaurant, etc. There are over 526,000 friends registered available to rent worldwide.

Of course, you get paid to be a friend for an hour, a day or perhaps even a week or two!

417. Get Paid To Watch Ads

On www.clixsense.com you get paid to sit and watch an ad a number of times. The advertiser will be interested in what your reaction is to the ad.

418. Crowdfunding

People who have ideas to start a business but don't have the money list their idea on Crowdfunding websites.
Crowdfunding is where you explain your idea to people and people will invest in your business (giving you money) in return for something e.g. a share of the profit the business will make. The crowd funding industry is a billion dollar industry!
If you have the money, invest in a few ideas and perhaps you will earn a lot of money.
www.crowdcube.com
www.crowdfunder.co.uk
www.crowdfunding.com
www.gofundme.com
www.indiegogo.com
www.kickstarter.com
www.venturefounders.co.uk

419. Sell Your Photography

Nowadays, you don't need to actually complete a photography course in order to produce beautiful photographs. Rather, you just need to use high-quality or professional-level equipment (an SLR camera with various lens options would do for starters) and then you can learn everything else you want to know from the many guides and video tutorials available online.
Basically how it works is as follows: you upload your photos to stock photo websites and when someone buys your photo (to use in their books or on their websites, etc.) you get paid.
If you are a good photographer you can sell your photos on the web. There are thousands of people looking for specific pictures. Those people type in keywords in stock photography sites and buy the pictures that they like.
Once you have a ready set of photos to sell, you can then upload them to online photo libraries like the following:
www.bigstockphoto.com
www.dreamstime.com
www.fotalia.com

www.gettyimages.com
www.istockphoto.com
www.shutterstock.com

A lot more stock photo websites are listed in my book "Design Free Websites".

420. Find Freebies And Discounted Products And Sell Them

There are a lot of websites that give away things for free or sell items at heavily discounted prices. Get your hands on these and simply sell them. Visit these websites to find products:
www.groupola.com
www.groupon.com
www.gumtree.com
www.mightydeals.com
www.wowcher.com
Make sure you check the terms, as sometimes a product will say you are not allowed to resell it.

421. Make Money Sharing Files

There are plenty of sharing websites where you can download files for free. If you have something that people can download, now you can get paid for it.
www.cpalead.com
www.sharecash.org
Upload your files, promote them and each time somebody downloads the file, you get paid.

422. Enter Competitions

Comping or entering competitions is done by thousands of people and some have given up their day job just to "comp" (so I've read in a newspaper article a while ago). There are thousands of competitions online every day so if you enter a lot of them, you stand a chance of winning some really good prizes. Search for " taking part in online competitions" to find out more.

423. Become A Web Hosting Reseller - R

There are lots of web hosting companies that give you the possibility to become a reseller. It would be very expensive to start up your own hosting company but as a reseller there is no need to for the high expenses.

You can buy web hosting at a wholesale price and sell this to your customers at a higher price. If you are successful, this can be a very lucrative business, as your customers will pay you every month for their hosting.

These hosting companies offer reseller packages:
www.1and1.co.uk
www.1and1.com
www.fasthosts.co.uk
www.heartinternet.co.uk
www.hostgator.com

424. Sell Coupons

Lots of companies e.g. coupon companies and special deal companies pay you money to share deals and coupons. Visit www.couponchief.com for more info.

You can also upload your own Coupon and get paid each time somebody uses your coupon.

Chapter 44. Self Publishing

425. Publish A Book - R

Have you been thinking about getting your book out there? Well, it has never been easier and nowadays it is very affordable to do! These days you hardly need any money to publish a book. For approx. £42 / $75, you can publish a book with worldwide distribution. You don't even need to print any books or hold stock of any books. You don't even have to write the books. I outsource the writing of my niche books (I have over 200 niche books now) and I can teach you how you can do this too.

In my product www.WorldwideSelfPublishing.com, I explain in video tutorials EVERYTHING from A to Z about how to self publish books in various formats to create multiple streams of income. The videos include how to get your hard copy book to number 1 on Amazon and hundreds of other book selling websites. The best thing: your book will stay number 1 for years if you follow my publishing methods. One book will give you income, each month, without ever touching it or sending traffic to it. It is not possible to give you a detailed step-by-step guide in this book. I explain everything very detailed in my Self Publishing Video Tutorials.

It is important for you to have a look at this product if you want to earn money self-publishing books because it is THE BEST product out there about self-publishing. I know, because I bought all the other products available.

In the video tutorials, I teach you how to publish your book in all these different book formats:
- Hard copy book (paperback)
- eBook
- Kindle book
- All other eReaders
- Audio book

Self-publishing niche books is THE BEST thing I have ever done in Internet marketing. It truly is recurring, automated income. Once the book is published, you don't have to do ANYTHING to earn money as the enormous distribution power of the Internet takes care of the sales.

All you need to do, once the book is written, is three things:
1) Format the book ready for publishing (I show you how)

2) Publish the book (I show you how)
3) Bank the money at the end of each month. You don't even have to do anything for this as it is paid directly into your bank account. So, in essence, all you have to do is two things!

An absolutely brilliant system to earn money from home!

Note: my publishing video tutorials focus on self-publishing niche books, not novels. You can however use my publishing system in exactly the same way for self-publishing your novel, fiction, nonfiction, diary, etc.

The book you are reading now is published with my self-publishing method. You have found the book and bought it, that means my methods must work :-).

When You Use My Self Publishing Training To Publish Your Book

- You <u>DO NOT</u> need to develop your own website.

- You <u>DO NOT</u> have to write a book (outsource it)

- You <u>DO NOT</u> need to spend hours or days sending traffic

- You <u>DO NOT</u> have to spend hours or days getting back links

- You <u>DO NOT</u> need to worry about ranking in Google

- You <u>DO NOT</u> need to invest in stock of your books

- You <u>DO NOT</u> need to print any books

- You <u>DO NOT</u> need to ship any books

- You <u>DO NOT</u> have to speak to anybody

- You <u>DO NOT</u> have high set up costs

- You <u>DO NOT</u> have to worry about customer services

- You <u>DO NOT</u> have to beg publishers

- You <u>DO NOT</u> have to buy barcodes for your book

- You <u>DO NOT</u> have to possess any publishing knowledge

- Everything is done online, without you ever have to leave your comfi-chair.

Part 4) Make Money Online - Your Own Website Needed

In this part of the book I will cover some methods that you can earn money with, from home, but you will need your own website. This means you will have to buy your own domain name and you will have monthly recurring expenses e.g. hosting.

Building a website doesn't have to be expensive: in my book "Design Free Websites" there are over 300 free tools and resources you can use to design a website completely free.

Chapter 45. Online Writing And Publishing Ideas

426. Earn Money From Your Own Blog/Website

If you want to do something that allows you to be creative, you can start your own blog. If you create a blog that shows your personality and writing style then after a while it could become a portfolio that you can use to help you get other types of writing jobs.

Blogging can be compared to an online diary, only this kind of diary is available to the eyes of the public and you're not the only one expressing your thoughts -people can leave their comments as well.

Websites like www.wordpress.com allow you to start your own blog for free. No programming knowledge is required. Once you've set up your blog, you can start writing and publishing content within the Wordpress dashboard (a very simple blogging visual interface). The goal is to get as many loyal readers as you can, so it's your job to write interesting and thought provoking articles - content that people will want to share and comment on! This is best done by choosing to enter a popular niche. Promotions, recommending goods, your own products etc. can make your blogging produce revenue.

Remember, by writing about popular topics, your content will get automatically picked up by Google and people will be finding your blog naturally via search results, if good SEO is applied. This sounds easy but it isn't. To rank a website on the first page of Google with SEO only is not easy at all but possible.

 I'll prove to you that it IS possible: this is one of my own websites: www.micropigshed.com. I personally built this site over three years ago. This site creates income from book sales and from Adsense. It ranks on the first page of Google for the following targeted keywords:
- Looking after a micro pig
- Micro pigs care
- Micro pig care
- Micro pig
- Micro pigs
- Keeping micro pigs
- Micro pig diet
- How to keep micro pigs

- How to keep micro pigs as pets
- Micro pig food
- Micro pig food UK
- How big is a micro pig
- Micro pigs book

Well, I hope these keywords are still ranking well when you are reading this book. They were when I finished writing this book you are reading now (December 2014).
This site is proof that a website that ranks well does not need to be complicated or designed with all the bells and whistles. This is a very simple site that does the job it was designed for: rank high in Google to sell my Micro Pig books.

It is never a good idea to rely on a single source of traffic, so you should always use other methods of promotion to get your blog out there. The most common method used by bloggers is commenting on other people's blogs that are related to their own. This way, visitors of that blog will see that you also have a blog and will be inclined to check it out.

Once you've built a steady stream of traffic, you can put Adsense and affiliate links on the site, which can make you money. You can also decide to create your own product and sell it, or better yet - give it away for free to people who subscribe to your blog. This way you'll be building an e-mail list, which you can use to make serious money with.

427. Set Up A Wordpress Blog That Updates Itself ("Autoblogging")

With a program like Wordpress Robot you can set up a blog in a matter of minutes and then never touch it again!

You give the easy to use bit of software a few keywords that describe your niche, and then it goes and finds content all over the Internet to post on your site - it really is as easy as that.

You can tell it:
- How often you want it to post
- Where you want it to get content from - article sites, ClickBank, YouTube, Yahoo! Answers and so on
- What kind of ads you want to display - AdSense, eBay, Amazon and so on
- How to lay out the content

You can literally set up your blog and forget about it while it grows and grows and earns you money! Read more about Wordpress Robot here - http://wprobot.net/

The downside of this is that some people consider this as dangerous, although it is done by many website masters in different niches. A word of caution: the content will not be unique content if other Internet marketers in the same niche as yours also have auto blogging on their website.

428. Guest Blogging

Blogging is one of the biggest trends on the World Wide Web these days. You can simply describe it as your personal leisure pursuit or side-line if you have your own blog where you write your day to day experiences, post your photos or your do-it-yourself home improvement tips.

How about guest blogging? If you have heard about it, then maybe you are familiar with its background. If you have also contributed blog posts on several sites before, then that is quite a way of gaining traffic to your own blog site. However, are you aware that you can be paid as a guest blogger on several sites that accept guest posts, too?

Yes! Guest posting is actually one of the most cost-effective and advantageous ways to make money online these days. If you are also a freelancer and not just a blogger, this is a big opportunity for you to be a guest blogger on popular sites that pay you for each blog you contribute that meets their standards.

Remember, these sites that accept and pay guest blogs are also aiming to become more popular and to get higher rankings on Google. They gain traffic through paid guest posts where they can have hundreds and thousands of readers reading the contributed blogs every day. You can search on the Internet for sites that pay guest posts. Then, you have to read their guidelines, and after that, contact and inform them that you are willing to contribute a piece. You must wait for their response before starting your article.

In order to get approved and paid for your guest posts, you have to write articles that are concise and directly related to the topics of the site you are writing for. Make sure that your blog article contains a back link to your blog too (if allowed by the webmaster).

429. Creating And Marketing An Informative eBook

You don't have to be the next JK Rowling to write a book. If you enjoy writing, have expertise in a certain subject, or you can learn about something and write about it in your own words, then you can produce something valuable and sell it online by creating an informative book/eBook.

For example: you have investigated a new niche and come to the conclusion that there is no eBook on "How to make a rabbit cage". This could mean two things: either there is not enough demand for such a book or yours will be the only one on ClickBank, so it will sell like hotcakes and lots of affiliates will want to sell it. If your keyword research has shown that there are a lot of searches and there is no eBook available at all on making a rabbit cage, it might be a good idea to write an eBook and put it on ClickBank for others to sell for you. Anybody who has a website about rabbits could put your book on their site and sell it.

I've mentioned my self-publishing video tutorials already but this method is about writing an eBook (not a Paperback). In order to sell an eBook, you will need a download page for people to visit after their purchase. On that download page, your customers will be able to download the eBook they've purchased. So for that reason, this method is in this part, where you do need your own website to make money. If you want affiliates to sell your eBook, you will also need to create an affiliate page.

If you have decided to make your own eBook, you could make a 'one-page sales wonder'. This is a long, one-page website usually between 3000 and 5000 words of sales copy (or selling tactics). Usually they are 10 to 30 pages when printed on A4 paper. The sales copy on these sorts of websites needs to lead people to click the "Add to Cart" button. That's where the name comes from: they do "wonders" with their high conversion numbers because of the very good sales letters. You have already seen some of my examples earlier in this book.

Downside of this method: Google does not like them as they do not have any content on the page, so you need to spend a lot of time sending traffic to your site or let affiliates do the work for you. You can develop a site with a lot of content on and make the one-page sales wonder page a separate page within your website, with internal links to that page. In this case you can rank in Google.

Do one-page sales wonders work? Yes they do: www.ClickBank.com is full of one-page wonder sales pages and ClickBank sell a product every three seconds! That tells you that they do work.

Unless you hire a qualified sales copywriter, it is very difficult to write a one-page wonder yourself. Help is available for writing on any of the outsourcing websites.

What about the competition?
Search several eBook websites and see what the competition is doing and what the price is for their eBooks. Search for "your keyword" + " eBook"
www.abeBooks.com
www.bn.com
www.eBooks.com
www.ebooks.com
www.waterstones.com
You can also search Amazon Kindle books.

The cover of your eBook will determine your sales. Covers sell books. Get it done professionally if you cannot do it yourself. For eBook cover help try:
www.20dollarbanners.com
www.absolutecovers.com.
www.coverfactory.com
www.designgururyan.com
www.eBookcovercreator.com
www.fiverr.com
www.groups.yahoo.com/group/eBook-community
www.killercovers.com
www.logocreator.com create a two-dimensional image of a book in minutes

430. Transfer Public Domain Into An eBook

Find a Public Domain book and change it into an eBook, put the eBook on ClickBank and let affiliates sell the eBook for you.

You can duplicate the content from a Public Domain book and keep all the profit when you sell it as an eBook. Is there an easier way to write a book? And it gets better: you can change the content, add stuff to it and then sell it as your own book. If you sell an eBook, you will need your own website. That's the reason why this method is listed in this part of the book. However, you can also publish and sell eBooks without your own website. My course www.worldwideselfpublishing.com explains it all.

431. Start A Digital Publishing Company

Why not start a digital publishing business? Publishing books has never been easier. You can publish your own books and you can publish books for other people and charge a one-off fee for doing this.

In order to become a successful Digital Publishing Company, you *will* need your own website as there is a lot of competition. You will have to sell your services to your customers via your website as that is likely the first thing they see about you. That's the reason why this moneymaking method is listed in this part of this book.

At the moment there are numerous platforms for digital publishing, but the most commonly used ones are listed below.

- Smashwords

For most people, www.smashwords.com is one of the best places to sell eBooks, as it is a one-stop digital publishing site. If your eBook passes the formatting and publishing standards of the site, Smashwords can distribute your eBook and have it appear in other popular online bookstores - including some of the websites listed below. However, one thing it cannot do is have your eBook show up on Amazon as well.

- Kindle Direct Publishing (from Amazon)

https://kdp.amazon.com/ is inarguably the most popular and comprehensive bookstore online, which is why a lot of people are willing to sign up with KDP Select (Kindle Direct Publishing). This program requires you to exclusively sell your eBooks for ninety days with the site. In exchange, you get to offer your eBook for free to Amazon's millions of customers up to five days. By including your eBook in Amazon's lending library you also get to earn royalties every time an Amazon Prime member borrows your book. You can also list your Kindle book without giving exclusivity to Amazon - that's what I do with most of my books.

- Pub It (from Barnes & Noble)

As www.nookpress.com is also owned by Barnes & Noble, it goes without saying that this particular eReader primarily relies on getting its eBooks from the B&N store. Read In Store is the site's equivalent to Amazon's KDP and as such offers several perks for members.

- Lulu

Before bookstore giants like Amazon and Barnes & Noble created their own publishing platforms, www.lulu.com used to be the place for self-publishing authors and digital publishers to go to. Even though its popularity has waned in recent years, it's still a good place to have your book on display and especially if you would like to create your own book covers. Lulu's cover design program allows you to drag and drop items with ready-made templates for book covers. The site offers both eBook publishing and POD (print on demand) services.

- Create Space (Owned by Amazon)

KDP is where you go to if you want to publish an eBook on Amazon, but if you think it is time to create paperbacks, hard covers, or even box sets for your books then you need to head out to www.createspace.com instead. When using Create Space, you would need to tinker with the design of your cover and your manuscript's formatting to ensure that production costs are low enough for you to make a profit.

- iTunes Connect (from Apple)

Apple's digital bookstore, https://itunesconnect.apple.com, is the newest and youngest in this list, but it's steadily growing in popularity. Having your eBooks available in iTunes is also a great opportunity to sell more copies, as it immediately connects you with Apple's millions of users.

How to Find the Best Manuscripts?
There are two ways for you to find manuscripts worth publishing: you either look for them on their own or you get authors to approach you on your own. However, if you want what's best for your future digital publishing house then you should consider using both approaches.
To find manuscripts worth publishing, you can start with the following websites:
- www.fictionpress.com
- www.fanfiction.net
- www.wattpad.com

As hundreds of stories are added to these sites each day, it's not possible to read each and every story you come across. Instead, consider the following tips for a more effective search for manuscripts with potential to become future bestsellers:
- Stick to stories in your favourite genres.
- Search for the Most Popular stories - the ones that have the most number of followers, comments, and likes.
- Search using keywords that indicate the type of plot you like, e.g. ghosts, Alpha male, Gods, etc.

- Search using authors and titles of your favourite bestsellers (e.g. Stephen King, E L James, Stephanie Meyer) because many writers often compare their works to the most popular books in their genres.

For aspiring authors to voluntarily knock on your door, you need to do the following:

Create your own website and blog

First of all, choose a name for your digital publishing house and use it when buying a personalised domain for your site. On your website, you will need to spell out the various reasons why an aspiring author would do better working with you than on their own.

- Book covers - Promise to give them a professional book cover (designs for front, back and spine) that includes not just fancy fonts for the title and author but real-life images as well whenever necessary.
- Marketing - Authors can finally concentrate on what they do best - which is to write - and leave it to you to do the marketing. This means coming up with a marketing plan that should include both free and paid advertising strategies.
- Publishing and Formatting - A lot of authors also have a hard time figuring out how to effectively format and execute the perfect book layout for their manuscripts. If you can promise to take that burden away from them, then that's yet another reason for authors to work with you.
- Pricing - There are two ways for you to earn as a digital publisher. On your part, you stand to earn more if you pay an author a manuscript fee. It means a bigger initial investment, but it also promises a more lucrative income that's completely yours if the book proves to be a bestseller. However, most serious-minded authors - those who think of writing books as their ideal long-term career - would rather share royalties.

Start marketing

Once your website and blog are up and running, it's now time to market your services. Make the usual rounds of social promotion.

- Submit articles to directories discussing the advantages for authors to work with digital publishers rather than doing everything on their own, e.g. more time to write, less need to worry about non-writing aspects of their work.
- Create a Twitter account and Facebook page. Offer contests and promotions for authors to know about your site and for readers to know that you'll soon be offering high quality reads.
- Participate in forums dedicated to writers like you would find on the likes of www.absolutewrite.com, www.writersdigest.com . Writers use these sites to gain feedback about their work so the best way to get friendly with them is to post

quality reviews or constructive criticism on their work. At the same time, you should also mention on your profile and signature that you are a digital publisher, together with a link to your site.

- Register for an account in websites like www.querytracker.net and www.WeBook.com, both of which are used by writers hoping to be traditionally published. Those who have been rejected repeatedly by publishers and literary agents may be willing to consider a new avenue of publishing, given the right incentive.

Turn the manuscript into a book ready for publishing

As a new publisher, you may have to outsource the first few steps in polishing the manuscripts you have acquired.

- Book cover designing - In the past, you had to spend as much as $100 (£60) just to have a plain book cover for your manuscript. Nowadays, however, you can easily get one done for $5 (£3) through Fiverr or you can even make one yourself by buying photos from stock photo websites.
- Editing and proofreading - If you don't have the skills for both then you may have to hire someone to ensure that your manuscripts will make a great reading experience for your readers.
- Layout and Format - You may need to come up with different formats and layouts depending on what kinds of forms or file types you want your manuscript to be available as (e.g. PDF, EPUB, MOBI).

Everything about different book formats is explained in my video tutorials www.worldwideselfpublishing.com. Sorry I am referring to my product again but if you are *really* interested in self-publishing books or becoming a Digital Publishing Company, it really is a superb product. I have several students earning a full-time income from self-publishing niche books.

Start advertising the book

This part is where your skills as a publisher would be really tested. As mentioned earlier, it's best to rely on a combination of paid and free advertising strategies when promoting your book and your author.

Advertising strategies for promoting your book:

- Author promotions - Amazon and other online bookstores allow their authors to create an Author Page on their sites. Your author should work on his or her Author Page as well as create a Twitter account and Facebook page. He or she should use all these to regularly connect with readers.

- Book reviews - Email book bloggers and ask them if they are willing to review your book. Keep in mind that you are offering a free copy of your book in exchange for an honest review.
- Forums - Look for forums where online readers gather and where you can promote the books you are publishing.
- Programs for publishers - Think Kindle Select of Amazon. Check out what on-site tools and services they have that you can use to effectively promote your book.
- Website advertisements - Aim for targeted exposure from website ads and preferably on the dates that your book will be officially released in the market. As such, it's best that you manually search for websites of popular book bloggers that take in advertisements. For website ads, it is sufficient to tinker a little with your book cover photo to include its official release date and on or below it a blurb about what to expect from the book.
- Giveaways - You can hold this yourself on your own website or you can have authors hold their own contests for promoting a book. eBooks and Amazon gift cards are the most common prizes given away when promoting a new book.
- Book trailers - You are likely to need a professional's help to ensure that you have a high-quality book trailer worth watching.

It's only at the start that you'd need to feel your way through, but once you've perfected a system for publishing it will be a rinse-wash-repeat method you can use for your other books and other people's books.

Chapter 46. Setting Up Forums, Websites And Membership Sites

432. Start Your Own Forum

From earlier sections in this book you now know about earning money either by moderating forum boards or by posting messages on such forums. If these don't appeal to you, does that mean you should leave online forums completely out of the question? Not at all! Maybe you are meant to work behind the scenes instead. How about setting up your own forum? With web forums, you earn an income from advertising revenues. A lot of people confuse web forums with membership sites because both of them require people to sign up and provide a place for people with shared interests to hang out online. Although the latter can generate income as well, they do so with membership fees. Right now, we need to focus on setting up a forum online, and the first thing you need to remember about it is that the most popular and successful online forums are free to join!
Here are a few examples of where you can start your web forum at zero cost:
www.forumotion.com
www.proboards.com
www.prophpbb.com

You have many other options so do take your time choosing which site should be hosting your forum. Familiarise yourself with their varying features and make sure that you choose one with features you'll actually need and not just because someone recommended it to you. If you have a website currently hosted by, say, justhost.com or hostgator.com, you can just buy a new domain name and then make it into a forum. Make sure that you have a clear idea as to which niche would you like to target so that when you start building your forum you won't have to correct a lot of errors.

433. Start A Membership Website - R

People are willing to pay good money to join a membership site for two primary reasons: you have something they want that they can't get elsewhere and your site offers exclusivity and that's exactly what they like.

Exclusivity is the operative word when it comes to membership sites. Cheap membership fees are not what the most successful membership sites have in common. In fact, money won't even be an option as long as they can see for themselves that what they're getting from your site is something non-members envy them for.

There are several ways to offer unique and exclusive content for your members:
- Make your own content.
- Compile all resources from the web and turn your site into a one-stop shop for all your members' needs.
- Be stringent with membership requirements so that you have a unique, tight-knit community to offer.

Keep in mind that unique, fresh and interesting content is the key to generating income from a membership site. Your visitors will register because of the information that you have to offer in the first place, so present the information and new ideas in an interesting manner. You can create a recipe website or a travel website to get started. To start a membership site: Search for "keyword"+"membership" to see if there are any membership sites available in your niche. If there aren't and your research tells you that there is a lot of demand for your niche, a membership site is certainly something you could consider. It will be hard work, as you have to make sure that you have something to tell your members each month, but the spread sheet below shows what your income could be.

Membership at $19.99 per month.

MONTH	MEMBERS	TOTAL MONTH	TOTAL YEAR
$19.99	10	$199.90	$2,398.80
$19.99	20	$399.80	$4,797.60
$19.99	30	$599.70	$7,196.40
$19.99	40	$799.60	$9,595.20
$19.99	50	$999.50	$11,994.00
$19.99	60	$1,199.40	$14,392.80
$19.99	70	$1,399.30	$16,791.60
$19.99	80	$1,599.20	$19,190.40
$19.99	90	$1,799.10	$21,589.20
$19.99	100	$1,999.00	$23,988.00
$19.99	200	$3,998.00	$47,976.00
$19.99	300	$5,997.00	$71,964.00
$19.99	400	$7,996.00	$95,952.00
$19.99	500	$9,995.00	$119,940.00
$19.99	600	$11,994.00	$143,928.00
$19.99	700	$13,993.00	$167,916.00
$19.99	800	$15,992.00	$191,904.00
$19.99	900	$17,991.00	$215,892.00
$19.99	1000	$19,990.00	$239,880.00

Membership at $7.99 per month.

MONTH	MEMBERS	TOTAL MONTH	TOTAL YEAR
$7.99	10	$79.90	$958.80
$7.99	20	$159.80	$1,917.60
$7.99	30	$239.70	$2,876.40
$7.99	40	$319.60	$3,835.20
$7.99	50	$399.50	$4,794.00
$7.99	60	$479.40	$5,752.80
$7.99	70	$559.30	$6,711.60
$7.99	80	$639.20	$7,670.40
$7.99	90	$719.10	$8,629.20
$7.99	100	$799.00	$9,588.00
$7.99	200	$1,598.00	$19,176.00
$7.99	300	$2,397.00	$28,764.00
$7.99	400	$3,196.00	$38,352.00
$7.99	500	$3,995.00	$47,940.00
$7.99	600	$4,794.00	$57,528.00
$7.99	700	$5,593.00	$67,116.00
$7.99	800	$6,392.00	$76,704.00
$7.99	900	$7,191.00	$86,292.00
$7.99	1000	$7,990.00	$95,880.00

As you can see, you "only" need 200 members paying you $ 7.99 per month to earn a living.

Whichever type of membership you choose, remember:

- Make the sign-up process simple, quick and easy. If there are too many pages to fill in, people will leave in the middle of the sign-up process.

- Make sure you choose one with a drip-feed possibility: this means that every week you can allow new members access to some new content on your site. If they can see all the content at once, they've no incentive to return and will want their money back after a week or so. If they know there is fresh stuff to come every week, they are more likely to stick around.

- Make it interesting to sign up for a $1(0.60p) trial. A $1(0.60p) trial is better than a free trial. After 7 days of the $1 trial, their card is automatically charged the first monthly fee, unless they've asked for a refund.

- Great and unique content is essential if you want to keep your members.

- You must give the members their money's worth each month.

- The more you give the more you get: if you give a lot of good stuff, your members will stay longer.

- Most members love video content so give it to them. PLR videos are available in a lot of different niches, simply Google "your keyword" + " PLR video". Although the content of these videos is not unique, your members will not know this. People who are not Internet marketers don't even know what PLR means. There are actually good PLR videos out there. Of course, don't always give your members PLR videos. Make sure to watch the videos first to judge the quality of them. It is always best to do your own videos but PLR videos can help you out now and again e.g. if you really didn't have the time to create fresh content to give to your members.

- If your membership site is a success and you get lots of members, you must be prepared to give customer service. Set up the site accordingly with telephone numbers and support email addresses. You can get Helpdesks to sort this out for you (just Google help desks).

Important: members will come and go so you will *always* have to work on finding new members, this is a big downside of a membership site.

You must spend a lot of time evaluating each membership site before you purchase because they all give different possibilities. Here are some sites you can evaluate:
www.amember.com
www.easymemberpro.com
www.membergate.com
www.memberspeed.com
www.wishlistmember.com
Wordpress also has good plugins for membership sites.

Information about memberships:

www.membershipacademy.com

Wordpress membership scripts are available at www.memberwing.com

434. Start A Dating Website - R

Dating websites are booming! Millions of people go online to find the right partner. You could even start your own dating site: www.whitelabeldating.com and have recurring income from your members as they will have to pay a monthly fee.

www.whitelabeldating.com is a dating site where you are able to set up your own dating site free of charge. All you need is a domain name. They take a percentage of your takings.

Chapter 47. Various Online Ideas With Your Own Website

435. Get A Free Website And Drive Traffic To It

Visit www.homewebsitecenter.com. This is a great website. Here you can have your own website with an eBook to sell in three easy steps. Simply fill in your PayPal address and your website is ready. There's a choice of several niches. There are several upgrades possible but even with the completely free version your website is created in less than five minutes. Simply drive traffic to your site and start earning money. It's highly recommended for newbies who want to test out driving traffic to a site. The paid version gives you a bunch of website statistics as well. You can also visit www.weebly.com for free websites.

There are over 300 free tools and resources, including free websites, in my book "Design Free Websites".

436. Earn Money By Building A List With A Squeeze Page

This is a very popular method. Put very simply, it involves giving away free stuff in exchange for an e-mail address.

The reason this method is so popular is because it's very simple to do, and the income you can generate is virtually limitless! OK, so here are the basic things you will need:
- A domain name
- Hosting
- A squeeze page
- A freebie
- An auto responder
- Follow up emails

A squeeze page is a very simple page, which basically consists of a headline and an opt-in form (a box where people fill in their email address). The opt-in form takes the visitor's email address, saves it in your email list and automatically sends out the freebie to anyone who joins. The freebie can be anything you're most comfortable creating - a short report, a video, a recording, anything that's valuable enough for people to input their email! I have covered opt-in forms already in this book but I am repeating it here because of its importance.

Here's an example of a squeeze page. Note the arrows above the opt-in box. They work very well and convert better – according to research and split testing - than the no arrow-opt-in boxes.

Once people input their e-mail, they're automatically added to your list and they receive the freebie in their inbox. The software that creates the opt-in form, holds your list and sends out emails automatically is called an auto responder. A very popular auto responder is Aweber, and you can get the $1 (£0.60)/month trial here: www.aweber.com.
Other auto-responders:
www.1shoppingcart.com (expensive)
www.constantcontact.com
www.getresponse.co.uk
www.infusionsoft.com (expensive)
www.listwire.com
www.mailchimp.com

You can buy pre-made landing/squeeze page templates at very affordable prices:
www.buylandingpagedesign.com
www.instapage.com
www.landingpagemonkey.com
www.leadpages.net - recommended
www.semanticlp.com

Once you've set that up, it's time to write a follow-up sequence: in other words pre-written emails which will be automatically delivered to your email list day after day upon joining - like a newsletter. These emails are designed to engage your list, deliver value and ultimately send monetised offers.

The whole idea is to have everything automated so that when you set it all up your job is only to get traffic, and the system will take care of the rest (deliver freebie, send out emails and product offers).

Getting people on your e-mail list is relatively easy since you're essentially giving them free stuff. One way of getting people on your list is with solo ads. Solo ads are emails that you can send to other people's email lists to promote your own. For example, you can find an individual in your niche that has a list, and you pay him $100 (£60) to send out a promotional email with a link to your squeeze page. His subscribers then visit your squeeze page and opt in to your list, and therefore become your subscribers. It's not free, but it's worth it if you do it right. It's also a very rapid method of building subscribers, but you need to do a little maths.

You have to make sure that your returns are bigger than your investments. So if you pay $100 (£60) for 200 subscribers, you need to make sure that those 200 subscribers are well worth your $100 (£60) in the long run. This is done by properly structuring your follow-up sequence. List building is an awesome way to make money because it allows you to generate a big recurring income with just a few hours of work per day (once you set everything up). It is estimated that 1 subscriber is worth $1 (£0.60) per month on average, which means that if you can get 10,000 people on your list, you'll eventually be earning $10,000 (£6000) per month!

Add a great headline to your squeeze page and tell people the benefits of opting in, why they need your freebie and what exciting information you're going to send them over the next few months. You can promote Amazon links, CPA offers, affiliate links and so on to your opt-ins and earn money just from having a list of email addresses! Google generally does not like squeeze pages (there is no content on them) so the only way for you to get people to opt-in is to send traffic to your page.

437. Earn Money By Selling Advertising Space - R

Once you have mastered how to get traffic to your site, you can make some extra easy money. At first glance, trying to sell advertising space on a website with low traffic seems a bit dumb. After all, advertisers are more interested in getting their product featured in high-visibility sites.

However, there is still reason to be optimistic about your chances. You need to remember that high traffic is not everything: conversion rates are as important, if not more important, than traffic. There are websites that have low visitor numbers but have a lot of advertising. They succeed because they are able to deliver ads to people who are more likely to buy from the advertiser. In other words, they provide a target market.

You can contact website owners in your niche or even businesses who do not have a website and ask if they are interested in placing a banner ad on your website. If you cannot design a banner yourself, you can outsource it: www.elance.com. You can also go to www.20dollarbanners.com and have some made. All you need is a picture and when somebody clicks on the picture, the visitor goes to the advertiser's website. Don't forget to make sure that the advertiser's website opens in a new browser window so your website stays open.

To make a simple banner all you need is the free graphic editor software www.paint.net. A standard size horizontal banner is 468x60. A block ad format can be 250x250. Whatever you use to make the banner look nice, do not use annoying flashing banners and do not use clashing colours. Your banner can be just text, with or without a border, but it must be eye-catching. You could sell banner space to 10 different companies. For one banner you can ask for approximately $200 (£120) per month x 10 banners per site x 10 companies = $20,000 (around £12,000) per month for doing nothing.

Before going off to make an offer, take a look at your website first. What is your readership like? What kind of articles attract the most traffic? What do people say about your website?

There are many ways to do this. First, you can use Google Analytics or www.Clicky.com, which offers real-time numbers. You get to know what the most popular posts are, how they find your website, and how long they stay there.

You may also start polling your readers. Make the poll short and consider giving away free items as an incentive. People rarely do surveys without something in return. You could also check Twitter and Facebook. Twitter allows you to track mentions of your website, and Facebook has a "X talking about this" feature on their fan pages. Google Analytics also keep track of websites that lead to yours. Also, look at websites with content similar to yours - you might be surprised at the advertisers they attract. Armed with this information, you can now go to the advertisers and show them that your page can get them the clicks that they need.

Selling banner space is a little bit of work to start with but can work really well. The money it brings in even with just one banner can pay for a full-time freelancer who can do a lot of other IM (Internet marketing) work for you.

438. Earn Money With Adsense only

I bet you have come across websites that basically have a little bit of content on their pages and the rest is ONLY Adsense. Well it is indeed an easy way to earn money but you don't get paid all that much. To earn $200 (£120) a month you would need about 200,000 page views! However, there are niches for which you can earn as high as $200 (£130) per click, but these niches are extremely difficult to rank for e.g. insurance, loans, mortgage etc.

As an alternative to Adsense, you also need to check out other platforms, for instance www.adbrite.com.
Many people say putting Adsense on your website no longer works but here's my opinion on it: if Google never showed websites with Adsense in the first rankings, Google's income from Adsense would stop. Of course, Google being a commercial institution, they will not stop showing sites that have Adsense, otherwise they would lose that income.

439. Earn Money With CPA (Cost Per Action)

You can use the smaller search engines to place ads and send them directly to a landing page with a CPA-offer on it. This method will cost you money to advertise but once you have found a niche that works for you, you can make money.

440. Misspellings Opportunities

There are still some opportunities in the misspelling/typo market. People who type in a misspelled word land on your website and you sell them your stuff or some affiliate links from the misspelled word niche. Although Google autocorrects misspellings nowadays, some people ignore this and click on the sites with misspelled words. Your website could be: www.artritispainrelief.com instead of www.arthritispainrelief.com. Don't worry about it not being professional as only the people typing in the misspelled word will get to see your misspelled domain name and they probably don't even know they've misspelled it. Needless to say, you would spell all the words correctly on all your pages once people have clicked on your domain name.

441. Aggregating News

The latest Google updates (Panda, Penguin and Hummingbird) have brought relevance and great content back to the Internet. In the past, you could practically write anything, sprinkle it with the right keywords, and see your site rank high on the SERPs (Search Engine Results Page). Not anymore. Google has made sure that your content needs to be tiptop.

In order to bring heavy traffic to your website and make some good conversions, you can start aggregating news. The process is totally uncomplicated. The trick is to be able to curate the right stories each day and publish them strategically on your site. You will be able to create a better connection with your audience if you begin aggregating news, plus you should be way out of trouble's way with Google's algorithms. First, you have to establish yourself as the go-to source for the latest news on things that are related to your niche. You can do a little market research in order to capture existing audiences from a totally different platform and that would be easy to do. In the event that you are starting from the bare bottom, take a close look at the competition and search for the demographics that seem to be underserved. Target these demographics and you've got yourself a captured market already.

Keep your news fresh and updated. Do not publish anything that is 3 weeks old. If you want to truly engage your readers, you need to come out with fresh and helpful content consistently, information that they would not have a chance to see in other online publications.

442. Sell Resell Rights Products

Some good websites to visit if you want to earn money this way:
www.master-resale-rights.com
www.theplrstore.com
or search for "your keyword + resell rights".

Some of the PLR sites will buy your PLR product and put it on their website and pay you a commission when they've sold some.

443. Earn Money With White Label Strategy

White Label Strategy is when you can turn a product or service into your own and brand the product as your own. It is the same principle as in the food/car/computer industry: a computer called XYZ might use exactly the same components as the computer brand ABC, they're just branded differently. But because it is "White Labelling" nobody knows that XYZ and ABC is actually the same computer. There are plenty of white label products. Just search for "your keyword +white labelling". All the design work is done for you. All you need to do is get traffic to your site. You will however need some money to buy your products to sell, usually in fairly large quantities.

444. Top 10 Reviews Websites

Buy a domain name "Top 10 best music recording software" or "Top 10 – your keyword-here" and put some decent content on your website with your affiliate link to buy the products dotted all over the pages. Eight years ago I used to believe Top 10 websites. Now I realise that very often the first one in the Top 10 listed products is the product the website developer makes most money from. Always be honest with your reviews!

445. Join New Product Launches Websites

Join www.jvnotifypro.com and www.imnewswatch.com. When a new product is being launched you build a website e.g. "keywordhere-review.com" or "keywordhere-scam.com" and describe the pros and cons of the product, with your affiliate link dotted all over the page.

446. Online Stylist

Do you have great fashion sense? Do people come to you all the time seeking advice on what they should wear for this or that occasion? Or do they want to know what you'd recommend so that they'd look, say, slimmer, darker, or taller? Clothes may not always make the man - or woman - but they always help make a superb impression on others, which is nothing to scoff at. It used to be that only celebrities had the need for stylists and image consultants, but not anymore. Considering how anyone can have their fifteen minutes of fame with photos uploaded to Instagram, Facebook, and even entire videos to YouTube, it's important that you look your very best when you know all eyes are on you!

Unfortunately, not everyone has your skills. Not everyone can instinctively come up with an outfit that's guaranteed to knock everyone's socks off for any occasion, which is why you shouldn't think of this as a shallow job. You're actually doing people a favour by helping them improve their image.
To start working as an online stylist, you need to prove your worth with a "look book", which consists of your different "looks". Have someone take photos of your best outfits, but they can't just be fabulous-looking outfits, though. Everything - from your hairstyle to your clothes and footwear and accessories - needs to be chosen with one theme in mind. Think themes like "Damsel in Distress", "Winter Wonderland", and "Happy Holidays". You get the idea? Descriptions of all items you've used to create your look must be detailed and accurate.

You can upload your photos in www.Lookbook.nu and www.Fashiolista.com . Now,

celebrity stylists can earn six-digit figures advising their famous clients on their red-carpet looks. That could be a part of your future once you start building your reputation.
One last point: if you are not catering to local clients alone, it may be a good idea to focus on items that your clients can purchase easily from product catalogues or on the Internet.

447. Makeup Artist

Here's another way you can make money just by helping other people appear more attractive. There are several ways you can earn as a makeup artist from the Internet, and most of these will be in combination with ideas we've previously discussed.

- Start blogging about makeup products you've used and recommend. Include tips, video tutorials, and photos in which celebrities and other famous figures are shown using the same makeup. Include links to where they can buy the products on Amazon and earn commission as an affiliate.
- Focus on building your subscription base with regular makeup tutorials and earn commission as a YouTube partner.
- Offer webinars so that you can teach people makeup techniques in real-time.
- Build a list and make money with email marketing

448. Online Travel Agent

Have you always been the designated planner every time you join your family or friends for a trip? Do they trust you because you're reliable, organised, and able to find the most affordable options for tours? If so, why not extend your services to other people who greatly need your help and would be willing to pay for it?

Now, you are probably wondering why clients would opt for your services when they can easily book a holiday online themselves. The answer is simple: a lot of people don't have the time or the need to plan their own trip. They prefer to enjoy hassle-free travelling and they're willing to pay someone else - that would be you - to plan the entire trip according to their own specifications. A genuine love for travel is essential for this type of job. More likely than not, if you are passionate about travelling then you will probably derive a lot of pleasure just by coming up with a suitable tour package for your clients. You're able to enjoy their trips vicariously through them, and that's a good thing because it will motivate you to get the best deals for your clients while getting paid for it at the same time.

As an independent travel agent, you will rely on the most popular websites that you might have used in the past for your personal travelling needs.
Lastly, you need to come up with alternatives for tours or travel itineraries as well as options for round trip transfers from airport to hotel. To do this, you need to look for the

cheapest tours and packages online and simply mark them up. Another option is to use the Advance Search tools on Google to ensure that your search results are restricted to local listings.

Let's say you are looking for "food and wine tour Italy". After searching for it on Google, you'll notice there's a 'settings' button in the top right part of your page. Click that and click *Advanced Search*. After that, you will be presented with a variety of options for modifying your search. Since you are looking for tours in Italy, it is best that you click the drop-down menu for Region to restrict your results to Italy. Since you want to make sure that you're also getting the latest results, you can configure the Last Update option to Last Year. Click *search* again and you'll see that the results you are getting this time are straight from Italy-based websites.

449. Medical Assistance

If you work in an actual healthcare facility then that typically means multiple shifts in a day, with few hours of sleep and lots of stress to deal with. Now, how do you feel about taking a more laidback approach to work while earning just about the same amount of money? Even better, you can actually work from home and thus spend more quality time with your loved ones. That's exactly what you can do when you start working as a RN (Registered Nurse) available for providing on-call medical assistance and advice on the Internet. There are two ways to do this: you can look for healthcare websites looking for RNs to work for them and for which you'd be paid standard wages. On the other hand, you can work independently by coming up with your own website and virtual office. You can even create your own blog where you can provide information and medical solutions to your visitors.

According to www.forbes.com you can earn $1,000 - £ 630 per week.

450. Create A Specialised Auction Website

You can create your own auction website for people to sell their goods on. It is better to focus on one niche of items, e.g. antiques. You can offer products to a specific market, all in one place, which will make them keep coming back rather than searching with the competition, like eBay. You can also charge lower fees to compete with competitors e.g. you can build an auction site only for car parts or only for boat parts, etc. Use your imagination.

Of course, you will need to spend a lot of money building the website and incorporating payment facilities but you can outsource this if you can't do it yourself.

Chapter 48. Technical Jobs

Chapter 48. Technical Jobs

451. Website Maintenance - R

Website maintenance requires you to master at least the basics of building and developing a website. If you know how to create one, then you'll have an easier time detecting what's wrong. With website maintenance, you need to consider both the front and back end of operations. More specifically, you will need to look into the following:

- Check if all links are working.
- Check if all email addresses associated with the website are still applicable and working.
- Monitor and review traffic and SEO statistics then write a report for the website owner.
- Take note of expiry dates for hosting and domain names to make sure that no one ends up buying them from right under your nose.
- Get the posting schedule for content and see if it's being followed.
- Compile a report.

You can perform this type of work from home because all you'll need are the login details for the website. Most website owners are willing to pay you a fixed monthly rate for this type of job - even though your work will only take a few hours at most each day.

Sites such as www.Elance.com and www.oDesk.com often post job vacancies for remote website maintenance specialists, so you can apply there. When applying, it's good to showcase your past experience related to the job, or if you don't have any yet, but are comfortable with maintaining websites and any other IT work, let your potential employer know that you are highly trainable and will quickly learn the ropes of the job. Go for a lower pay first and gather experience. As you gain further experience, you will be able to ask for a higher rate.

You will need your own website to show people you can maintain your own site, therefore this method is listed in this part of the book.

452. SEO - R

SEO stands for Search Engine Optimisation, in other words, it means ranking a website in search engines such as Google, Yahoo and Bing for free targeted traffic. Many individuals who start out as Virtual Assistants eventually work their way to becoming independent SEO marketers or consultants.

317

SEO traffic can be very profitable and that's why many companies pay thousands of dollars per month for their SEO work. Imagine what it means to be #1 on Google for the search "T-shirts New York" if you own a store in New York that sells T-shirts.

Or if you're doing affiliate marketing and you're promoting a weight loss product you would be banking BIG TIME if you managed to rank for the keyword "how to lose weight", especially knowing that it brings in roughly a few hundred thousand unique visitors per month (and these are VERY HOT leads!)

Of course, to rank for such a keyword you'd have to spend a lot of time and money, because the competition is just ridiculous. But the good news is new keywords are emerging every day and there are still thousands of untapped keywords that have little or no competition at all. But the potential of SEO doesn't end here. There are a huge number of offline businesses that would pay a lot of money to be ranked on Google for their city/state. For example, a dentist in Chicago would be happy to pay several thousands of dollars if you could get him on #1 of Google. He'll re-cover those costs with only a couple of new regular clients.

Maintaining SEO for clients is recurring income because once you get your client's site to the first page of Google, they will want to stay there and they will pay you a monthly fee for you to keep watching their website and tweak it, if need be. A site that is number one today might not be number one tomorrow, so sometimes the sites need tweaking or will need a few back links to get back to the top. You can easily charge $50 (£31) per month, per website so if you "only" have 30 clients, you would earn $1,500 (£935) per month.

So how exactly do you "do SEO"? It would be impossible to answer this question with 100% precision, for two main reasons:

1) No one knows the "exact" algorithm that Google uses to rank websites.
2) The algorithm is updated and changed quite often.

However, there are some rules that haven't changed for years. These rules are divided into two main categories: on page and off page SEO.

On page SEO basically means placing your keyword inside your title, meta tags as well as H1 and H2 tags on your web page. There are also many other changes you can make such as adding your keyword inside image alt tag, linking to authority websites inside your niche, etc. Off page SEO is performed by building backlinks to your website. There is a lot of controversy about this topic as to what is considered "blackhat" or "whitehat". Just make sure you're building white hat backlinks regularly and properly otherwise Google might penalise your site and never show it again.

453. Hosting Websites - R

Ever wonder where websites are stored? A lot of them are located in "server farms" - facilities that house a lot of servers and storage spaces for data. However, cheaper servers and storage systems have made it possible for ordinary people to host websites from their own homes. You can also host a website on your PC!

Here's what you need:
- A fast and reliable Internet connection.
- A static local IP address. You can check with your Internet service provider for more details.
- A fast computer that's plugged in all day, every day.
- Server software such as Apache.
- Storage space. A one-terabyte hard disk is too small to contain all the data you will have to store. This includes not just the website itself, but also information related to those who visit it. There are cheap systems available, which boast not just storage space but also back-up systems in case one of the hard disks fails.

Hosting services offer packages of up to $20 (£12) per month for small businesses. Costs for bigger websites with multiple pages will be considerably more.

You could offer round-the-clock support for an additional fee. While the initial investment may seem large, the return on investment will give you a reason to smile. So, go out, seek professional advice, buy your hardware and software, have an Internet connection at the ready, and start hosting websites for a fee!

454. Webinars

Webinars are basically online seminars, and conducting or organising them for yourself - or for other people - can definitely earn you a good deal of money. If you are the one conducting the webinar, the bulk of your income would come from how much you'll be charging interested participants for joining. If you are organising one for others, you'll be paid a service fee and perhaps earn a percentage as well from the joining fees charged by your client.

A lot of Internet marketers don't charge any money to attend the webinar but they are selling a product at the end of the webinar so they make their money that way. If you have a product to sell, find some websites in your niche that have an opt-in box. Those websites are likely to have a list. Ask the website owner if they are interested in doing a webinar. In this case, you would share the profit of your sales, usually 50/50 split.

Important: good webinar software is expensive though, so you will have to invest in that. However, you can also use somebody else's webinar software and be a presenter.

When organising a webinar, you need to consider the following:
- Program - Every minute should be accounted for and spent wisely so that participants will feel they've had their money's worth. For daylong or multiple day webinars, remember to allocate sufficient time for breaks.
- Guest speakers - This will increase the value of your webinar, but unless you'll be getting the guest speaker's services for free, it may also mean sharing a percentage of your profit with them or paying them a fixed rate for their time.
- Interaction - Little interaction is needed when participants are only required to listen and take notes, and in this case you can accommodate as many as your site can handle.
- Materials - People also have a greater liking for webinars that offer them a lot of free resources and materials to work with before, during and after the session. Think of study guides you can share and try to come up with modules and tests they can use during the webinar itself. Make sure that a download link for the entire webinar is also made exclusively available to the participants afterwards.

People are willing to pay for webinars because they are convenient. People prefer webinars over seminars because they offer the same value at a more affordable price.

455. Building Apps

It may not seem likely right now, but you could create the next big thing after popular mobile games like Angry Birds or service apps like Foursquare! And again, you do not need to have a degree to build your own app. It's just a matter of finding essential learning resources online and applying what you've learned.

Now, the two most powerful platforms today are of course Google's Android and Apple's iOS. When building an app, it's best to target both platforms even if it means taking more time with developing your app. What are a few more weeks or months of creating alternate coding for your app if it means earning from two massive income-generating markets, right?

Having a great idea is always a good start for building a mobile app, but you need to improve on that idea to make sure that it answers the market's needs or demands. Mobile gamers obviously prefer games that are free to play, but most of them are willing to pay real money if you give them good reason to. One site where you can build apps is www.seattleclouds.com

You can also outsource the building of the Apps on www.elance.com or any other outsourcing websites.

456. Bring Out Your Own Software - R

This sounds complicated but it really isn't because you don't have to develop the software yourself. Let me give you two of my own examples:

My Break Reminder Software
I have to try to reduce the time I spend on my computer due to a neck injury. I used to use www.workpace.com, which is software that forces you to take breaks while on your computer.

Because I couldn't find a really simple version, without all the bells and whistles, I had my own, simplified version developed, which you can buy here: www.BreakReminderSoftware.com. I had the software developed on www.elance.com, for $85 (£53)!! Yes, that low! I sell it for $47 (£29) so I only had to sell two to get my money back. This software doesn't earn me millions but I do sell, on average, about 8 per month. All these little amounts add up! I have already mentioned that I am a strong believer in multiple streams of income. This is another example of this.

My Print Screen Software
When I was looking for a very simple print screen software application I couldn't find it, therefore I had my own developed. I use it every single day and don't know how I could ever be without it. You can buy it here: www.PrintingYourScreen.com.

I had this software developed on www.elance.com for $120 (£75) and I sell it for $19.97 (£12). Again, this does not make me millions but I do sell a lot of this software per month.

The beauty with bringing out your own software is that you have a one-time expense for developing the software and after the investment is paid back, all the following sales are pure profit. Once somebody clicks the order button on my sales letter for the software, ClickBank charges the customer and the software is delivered automatically after a successful payment.

Surely you can do this as well!

Chapter 49. Creative Jobs

457. Graphic Artist

I have put this in the 'website needed' section of the book as these days you will need a website showing your own work in order to get work. However, you can also make money on Elance as a graphic artist and in this case you don't need a website as you can just show your portfolio on your Elance profile. Graphic artists have it lucky, as their skills can prove handy in a wide variety of fields. After all, no matter what industry a client is in, it's likely that their business will have an occasional or even regular need for graphics. These graphics may be used on their company website, product brochures, or sales material.

The best thing about working as a graphic artist is that you only have to invest in the right software programs – you could be earning hundreds each day just with Adobe Photoshop - and with the right amount of creativity, you're good to go.

The first step in working as a graphic artist online is to have your portfolio ready for viewing on the Internet. The best place to have your artwork on display would be www.deviantart.com, www.artgallery.co.uk, www.artweb.com. You'll find a lot of fellow artists here and some may even be able to recommend jobs to you. Once you have your artwork on display, it's time to get the right people to see it.

One of the best ways to do so is to share your work through image hosting and sharing sites like
www.instagram.com
www.pinterest.com,
 www.tumblr.com.
Naturally, you should also share them through the usual social media channels like Facebook and Twitter.

Why do people need to hire a graphic artist?
- Private individuals want their headshots and photos professionally edited so that they look their best.
- Business clients need graphics to promote their websites, products and services, and to use in existing or future marketing campaigns.
- Authors also require graphics for their book covers, website banners, Facebook cover photos and designs for items (e.g. bookmarks) that they give away to their readers.

- Exhibition signs
- Leaflets
- Company brochures
- Packaging
- etc.

More and more blue chip companies hire freelance workers for their graphic designs. All you need to do is email companies to offer your services. You just send them an invoice for your work, they pay you and the job is done.

Artists - and as a graphic artist you are definitely one of them - have the reputation of being temperamental, which is why proving people wrong by being able to work efficiently and effectively will definitely help you become everyone's number one graphic artist.

Being professional means:
- Using an organized system for working. Clients prefer working with graphic artists who use a well-planned system for designing graphics. Phase 1, for instance, may include brainstorming with the client while Phase 2 may include showing the client the initial draft of your design and incorporating any additions or changes they may want done.
- Not flying off the handle just because the client didn't like your first draft. Remember: they are paying you money to create the kind of graphics *they* want and are not really interested in what *you* like.
- Delivering your work on time. That you find yourself "lacking inspiration" is not a valid excuse. Set a reasonable delivery time for your work and stick to it! Your delay could cost your client money. If that happens their negative feedback is sure to hurt your reputation!

It would also help if you offer them a clear-cut system for payments. Unless you are offering your services through oDesk or Fiverr, most freelancing graphic artists today require an initial 50% deposit or down payment upon accepting a project. The remaining balance will then be paid once the project has been completed.

458. Digital Scrapbooking

Digital scrapbooking involves the use of a computer and graphic design software to create visually stunning layouts of pictures combined with text and graphic design elements. It is definitely an easier and less costly alternative to paper-based or actual scrapbooking, but it still requires a good amount of skills and creativity. People love the idea of digital scrapbooks because it presents a fun and imaginative way to preserve their most cherished memories.

The first step to making money with digital scrapbooking is by creating your own digital scrapbook as your work portfolio. You can show that on your website. You can use sites like
www.kbandfriends.com
www.MyMemories.com to host your sites but other types of image hosting sites like
www.Flickr.com
www.Tumblr.com
www.Instagram.com would also do.
Another great site would be www.Pinterest.com, with its emphasis on DIY items.

Once you have your digital scrapbook available for viewing online, you need to start marketing it through social media as well as participating in forums dedicated to scrapbooking communities. You need to spread the word about your services, and one way of doing that is by writing short articles and creating video tutorials for popular digital scrapbooking techniques.

You need to create them in the highest resolution possible. It helps if you already know how to use Adobe Photoshop or Adobe Illustrator. That way, they'll turn out beautiful if your client chooses to print them out and use them to create an actual scrapbook. There are also digital scrapbooking programs that offer templates, which you can then save and sell online.

Scrapbooking kits often go for up to $20 (£12). More than that, the fulfilment is found in the fact that you're helping preserve memories!

Digital scrapbooking software:
Craftartist from Serif
MemoryMixer
Hallmark Scrapbook Studio Deluxe

Chapter 50. Sell Products Online

459. Sell Something

What about this for an unusual business idea: sell "something". That's what this website does: www.somethingstore.com. You send them $10 (£6) and they will send you "something". You won't know what you will get until you receive the parcel at home. You could start a similar site or sell something for $5(£3), $20 (£12), etc. We all love surprises.

460. Sell Your Own Products

I have already mention that you can create your own video tutorials in a certain niche and sell them from a tutorial website e.g. www.udemy.com. The downside is that the websites will take a cut of the selling price. If you sell a product with a one-page-sales-wonder (a one-page website that sells one product), or from your own website, all the profit will be yours when you sell one.
You can also create an affiliate page and let others do the selling for you. In this case, you will have to pay your affiliates. A few of my own one-page-sales-pages:
www.breakremindersoftware.com
www.dropshippingandecommerce.com
www.findingnichesmadeeasy.com
www.fromnewbietomillionaire.com
www.howtokeepmicropigs.com
www.howtoracepigeons.com
www.paininthethumb.com
www.printingyourscreen.com
www.designfreewebsites.com
www.peafowlspeacocksandpeahens.com
www.worldwideselfpublishing.com
www.micropigshed.com (a website selling my own product)

The downside of this is that you will have to set up your own payment processor. I explain this in full in my book "Drop Shipping and eCommerce".

461. Building Online Stores - R

You don't need to sell anything with this type of income-generating opportunity. Instead, you just need to help others sell their products and services by making online stores for them. Examples of virtual store hosting sites are the following:

www.allprofitallfree.com
www.ekmpowershop.com
www.goodsie.com
www.mystorexpress.com

If you create stores for people, you will be able to charge a monthly fee to maintain the stores, so this is recurring income.

Building a store is surprisingly easy. I've built one myself with www.ekmpowershop.co.uk. The store is www.liquorice-licorice.co.uk. It is one of my small eCommerce website, I stock all the products and the company is run by my staff. When I built it several years ago, there was not much competition for certain keywords, but there is now. However, it still ranks on the first page of Google.
I have intentionally built this site NOT to rank for the word liquorice on its own but I have targeted the keywords listed below. The site is shown on page one in google.**co.uk** for all these keywords:
- Double salt liquorice
- Double salt liquorice UK
- Triple salt liquorice
- Triple salt liquorice UK
- Triple salted liquorice
- Pure hard liquorice sticks
- Pure liquorice
- Italian liquorice
- Italian liquorice sticks
- Liquorice for diabetics
- Dutch liquorice
- Belgian liquorice
- Buy liquorice online
- Buy liquorice
- Gelatine-free liquorice
- Sugar free liquorice

Note: Searches vary, therefore Google shows different websites every day. At the time of writing this (December 2014), the site did rank on the first page of Google for the above keywords.

Here's a screenshot of my inbox, showing 25 orders in 14 days, that is almost 2 orders per day - on average. This website does not make me a millionaire but I love multiple streams of income, and this is just one of the streams.

From	Subject	Date ▲
chris@liquoricesweetshop.co.uk	ekmPowershop: There has been an order at your shop ·	07/12/2014 13:30
chris@liquoricesweetshop.co.uk	ekmPowershop: There has been an order at your shop ·	07/12/2014 17:28
chris@liquoricesweetshop.co.uk	ekmPowershop: There has been an order at your shop ·	07/12/2014 19:58
chris@liquoricesweetshop.co.uk	ekmPowershop: There has been an order at your shop ·	08/12/2014 10:21
chris@liquoricesweetshop.co.uk	ekmPowershop: There has been an order at your shop ·	08/12/2014 13:15
chris@liquoricesweetshop.co.uk	ekmPowershop: There has been an order at your shop ·	08/12/2014 13:35
chris@liquoricesweetshop.co.uk	ekmPowershop: There has been an order at your shop ·	08/12/2014 20:30
chris@liquoricesweetshop.co.uk	ekmPowershop: There has been an order at your shop ·	10/12/2014 17:08
chris@liquoricesweetshop.co.uk	ekmPowershop: There has been an order at your shop ·	11/12/2014 15:11
info@liquorice-licorice.co.uk	ekmPowershop: There has been an order at your shop ·	11/12/2014 20:15
chris@liquoricesweetshop.co.uk	ekmPowershop: There has been an order at your shop ·	12/12/2014 14:20
chris@liquoricesweetshop.co.uk	ekmPowershop: There has been an order at your shop ·	13/12/2014 12:49
chris@liquoricesweetshop.co.uk	ekmPowershop: There has been an order at your shop ·	13/12/2014 15:56
chris@liquoricesweetshop.co.uk	ekmPowershop: There has been an order at your shop ·	13/12/2014 16:20
info@liquorice-licorice.co.uk	ekmPowershop: There has been an order at your shop ·	14/12/2014 10:02
chris@liquoricesweetshop.co.uk	ekmPowershop: There has been an order at your shop ·	14/12/2014 12:16
chris@liquoricesweetshop.co.uk	ekmPowershop: There has been an order at your shop ·	15/12/2014 10:57
chris@liquoricesweetshop.co.uk	ekmPowershop: There has been an order at your shop ·	15/12/2014 17:58
info@liquorice-licorice.co.uk	ekmPowershop: There has been an order at your shop ·	16/12/2014 11:51
info@liquorice-licorice.co.uk	ekmPowershop: There has been an order at your shop ·	16/12/2014 14:11
chris@liquoricesweetshop.co.uk	ekmPowershop: There has been an order at your shop ·	16/12/2014 16:42
chris@liquoricesweetshop.co.uk	ekmPowershop: There has been an order at your shop ·	19/12/2014 11:20
info@liquorice-licorice.co.uk	ekmPowershop: There has been an order at your shop ·	19/12/2014 15:45
chris@liquoricesweetshop.co.uk	ekmPowershop: There has been an order at your shop ·	20/12/2014 17:22
chris@liquoricesweetshop.co.uk	ekmPowershop: There has been an order at your shop ·	21/12/2014 19:19

In my book "Drop Shipping and Ecommerce", I explain my experience with eCommerce or online stores.

A lot of such sites are free to join so you're again probably wondering why people would actually pay you for creating something that shouldn't cost them a penny. The answer is still the same: your clients can't be bothered to do it, but that's good news for you, right? When creating a virtual store, you need to remember the following objectives:

- Appealing - It must catch the attention of your target market and make everything look professional and attractive. A visually appealing layout always promises a better user experience, so be sure that the virtual store you create is the kind that your target market will feel at home with.
- User-friendly - There must be no ambiguity or confusion regarding what each page or feature of your store is supposed to do.

- Updatable - It must also be simple enough for your client to run on his or her own once you've finished your job, unless you charge them a monthly fee to do it. More to the point, the client must not have a hard time adding products and services to his or her virtual store.
- Secure - Remember that you'll be handling other people's money when receiving payments. It's your obligation - implied or expected - to ensure that none of your customers are wrongly or excessively charged.

462. Drop Shipping

One buzzword flying around in business circles is "drop shipping". Drop shipping in one sentence: You sell stuff, take the money from the buyer and somebody else ships the goods to your customer. Drop shippers buy items from a manufacturer and store them in warehouses. Clients are then allowed to sell whatever products are in the warehouse. They then pay the drop shipper the cost of the product and shipping cost, and they ship it to buyers. When people use drop shippers, they pay for the extra convenience of not maintaining the stock and the warehouse. They also pay monthly fees. Once you've established a good relationship with the distributor, you have the option of putting your sticker on the box to make it appear that the item being shipped came straight from you.

So, is drop shipping legitimate? Yes, it is, but you need to toe the line with this option. If you have good negotiation skills and goodwill with suppliers, you will enjoy success in this line of business. I am just mentioning drop shipping here as it took me a whole book to explain what it is all about. My book "Drop Shipping And Ecommerce" explains it all.

463. Last 3 methods

You could also:

- Fill in a lottery ticket. Every single week people who never expected to become millionaires become just that! You won't be one of them if you don't play!
- Marry rich. Find someone rich to marry! Of course, make sure you love him/her as money can't buy happiness!

- Hope. You can hope to inherit a fortune from your Auntie Pauline who you haven't seen or heard for over 35 years!

Needless to say, if I were you, I wouldn't count on one of these 3 to happen to you but hey, you never know!

Conclusion to Making Money Online

You are probably suffering from information overload after reading all these moneymaking ideas.

Maybe you are feeling excited and simply bursting with great ideas on how to get started! That's great because PASSION is the necessary ingredient that transforms IDEAS into REALITY.

So before I end this book, I suggest (when you've finished reading) writing down the first ten ideas that come into your mind about how to make extra money. Chances are, those ideas are what you feel most strongly about! Start with those ideas - one at a time. Work hard at each and every one of them and don't stop digging until you have found the ideal moneymaking idea for yourself online or offline!

Here are a few tips to get your creative juices flowing to come up with an idea that is not listed in this book.
Find a quiet corner and play some soft music - to help you think and ask yourself the questions listed below. Write everything down that you think about.

1. What are your best skills?
2. What inspires you, or gives you ambition?
3. What knowledge or qualifications do you have?
4. What would you do if you didn't get paid for it?
5. What do you want to learn more about?
6. If you could create your own job, what type of work would you do?
7. What are your hobbies or pastimes?
8. What do you do in your free time for fun?
9. What problems do you see around you that you might be able to give a solution to?
10. Have you had any experiences that taught you a lesson you could share with others?
11. If you only had a short time to live, what personal knowledge would you share with others?
12. Ask a friend if you were a good salesman, what would they buy from you?
13. What type of person would you like to work with?
14. Is there something you like to talk about for hours?
15. Is there a skill that you like to teach others?

16. Do you have collections of things at home?
17. Is there one type of activity you do more than anything else?
18. Ask your friends and partner what they think you are really good at. You might be surprised what they come up with!
19. Have you or your friends ever wanted to purchase something and could not find it? Perhaps other people are looking for it as well! Perhaps you could create the product and start selling it!

If you think you can't make any money after answering these questions, don't worry because you don't necessarily need to earn money in something you are good at or you are interested in. You can make yourself an expert in something you know nothing about.

A recommended book on this subject is, "The Zulu Principle: Making Extraordinary Profits from Ordinary Shares", by Jim Slater, available on www.amazon.com.

Although this book is about trading shares, the message in this book is very clear: you can become a leading expert in any niche or micro-niche in a very short time just by studying and analysing that niche. Slater applies his method by specialising in a certain type of share and situation surrounding that share. The book is about finding a niche and then attempting to dominate it. Slater suggests that you need to become a specialist in your niche, and your expertise will enable you to outperform the markets in niches neglected by others. The same principle applies to the web. If you can find a lucrative niche and specialise in it, you can make money. The ability to find a niche and dig deeper into that niche is an extremely good skill to have.

I have been in business for over 35 years and I have always believed in this principle: if you want to buy something and you cannot find it easily, you can assume that other people are also looking for it. Therefore, there is a market for it! I have set up businesses in the past based on that principle.

That is also the reason why I wrote the book, "From Newbie to Millionaire", because I bought lots of books and some things were still not clear to me. Therefore, I wrote the book I couldn't find myself. That book started my writing career and made me realise how much I love writing and sharing my knowledge with others. The book you are reading now is my fifth book and I don't think it will be the last one.

So you don't have to be an expert in your niche!

A lot of people I speak to tell me that they think they are not good enough to start a niche or a product based on what they know. Nonsense! You don't have to be an expert to create a product! If you know only 1% more than the people you want to teach, in their eyes, you are an expert, as you know more than they do. So, even if you think you are not an expert, in other people's eyes, you are, and that is what matters for your sales.

In business you get what YOU want
By giving other people what THEY want.

Remember - one good idea is all it takes to completely turn your life around
but
a good idea without a plan is not a good idea!

A Word About Taxes.

Just because you are working from home or selling online doesn't mean you don't have to pay tax. I speak to people and they tell me "I love my little side business". As soon as I mention the word taxes, they change their mind and all of a sudden it becomes "their hobby" instead of a little side business.

Whether it is a little side business or a hobby is irrelevant. You are earning money from your sales, therefore you need to pay tax on that income. You might look at it as a hobby or having some fun selling, but the tax people will have a different opinion on that matter! The rules are clear: you must pay taxes on all business and personal income if the income exceeds a certain amount. That also applies if you are selling on eBay or Amazon by the way. The money you are getting for your sales is considered - by the tax authorisations - as income, no exceptions.

In the UK, at the moment (December 2014), you have to pay tax on ANY income if it's higher than the limit of £10,000/$16,000 per year.

In the UK, you have to register for VAT if your turnover is over £81,000/$129,000 between any period of 12 months. If it is lower, you don't have to worry about VAT. You can voluntarily register if you wish to claim VAT back. Important: on 1 January 2015, there are new VAT rules for selling e-services online in the EU. Search "MOSS VAT" to find out more. MOSS stands for Mini One Stop Shop and the basic principle is that VAT needs to be paid on the product that you are selling, according to where the buyer is based in the EU. MOSS is pretty complicated and I know several Internet marketers who simply stop selling e-products because of this new legislation.

I am not going into detail about how much tax you need to pay, as that is different in every country and a thousand rules apply.

The most important thing to remember is: you have to pay tax if your income is over the tax-free limit. Remember this and always do everything according to the legal rules in your country.

Final Words

Starting a home-based business is an adventure. It can be scary, stressful and painful, but it can also be extremely rewarding on many different levels.

Just about anyone can start a home-based business. You don't need a lot of money; you don't need to be a financial or computer genius. Don't let the idea of starting a business intimidate you. While nearly anyone can start a home-based business, not everyone can succeed. Being successful requires a good idea, thorough planning, adequate resources, hard work, good execution and luck. Too many entrepreneurs think that a good idea alone will be enough but that's rarely the case; planning is an area that's often neglected, but which can give your company an edge over others.

Starting up and running a home-based business will give you a better education in all aspects of business—management, marketing, finance, accounting, strategy, operations etc.—than just about any other endeavour. Running a business will teach you about yourself, forge your character, and develop skills that will be assets for the rest of your life. In that respect, there is no failure for the entrepreneur who plans and prepares properly; the only failure is the experience that doesn't teach you valuable lessons.

Entrepreneurship isn't for everyone, but if you believe it's the right path for you, plan wisely, and good luck with your venture. If you don't want to set up a business but you just want to earn some extra money, I hope you've found some ideas that you like and believe in.

****

To be informed whenever I release a new book or product, simply visit www.FromNewbieToMillionaire.com, and opt-in. I promise I will not flood your inbox with crappy affiliate links—that's just not my style! My income does not come from sending affiliate links to my subscribers but from multiple sources of income of my own products.

****

As I am not selling some sort of automated software, there is no support line or support email set up for this book.
For any feedback about this book or anything else, you can contact me at:

christine@fromnewbietomillionaire.com

****

Thank you for reading this book. I hope you like what you've read. If you did, please leave a 5-star review on Amazon for this book. By the way, even if you bought the eBook version, you can still leave a review on Amazon, as you could have bought the hard copy in a bookshop.

****

I end this book with a few quotes that I like, believe in and practice every day:

No bees, No honey- No work, No money.

It's better to try and fail then to fail to try.

Winners are not people who never fail but people who never quit.

Excuses are your limitations!

Commitment is the key to success.

Kind regards

Christine Clayfield

Christine Clayfield.
www.ChristineClayfield.com

Author, Entrepreneur, Infopreneur, Internet Marketer, Book Publisher, Public Speaker

All Methods Together

For your convenience, I have listed all the methods together, so you can quickly glance through them. The methods with an "R" behind it, are the ones that will give you repetitive income: once you have a customer, you are likely to get repeat business from them. It is always a good idea to start and "R" business.

Part 2) Make Money Offline

Chapter 14. Jobs With Animals
1. Pet Sitter - R
2. Pet Day care - R
3. Animal Kennels - R
4. Dog Walker - R
5. Take Dogs To Training Classes - R
6. Pet Groomer - R
7. Mobile Pet Groomer - R
8. Animal Trainer
9. Mobile Animal Trainer
10. Professional Pooper Scooper- R
11. Pet Parenting Lessons
12. Animal Breeder
13. Pet Relocation Service
14. Pet Insurance Adviser - R
15. Dog Treat Baker - R
16. Gourmet Pet Food Specialist - R
17. Home Made Dog Food - R
18. Aquarium Maintenance - R
19. Pet Couture Designer/Seller
20. Pond Maintenance and Design -R
21. Pet Minister
22. Pet Grief Counsellor
23. Pet Memorial Plaques
24. Pet Cemetery
25. TV Or Magazine Advertising
26. Rent Your Land To Animals - R

65. Car Sharing - R
66. Become A Driving Instructor
67. Start A Repossession Service
68. Become A Driver
69. Become A Licensed Taxi Driver
70. Provide An Airport Shuttle Service
71. Rent Out Your Trailer

Chapter 16. Make Money From What's In Your Home

72. Rent Your Couch Or Rent A Room - R
73. Host A Foreign Student - R
74. Offer Storage Space - R
75. Rent Out Your Driveway - R
76. Rent Your Pool
77. Run A Bed & Breakfast
78. Make Your Home A Movie Star
79. Hold A Garage Sale Or Yard Sale
80. Rent Your Land - R
81. Rent Out Garden Allotments - R
82. Rent Your Stuff
83. Advertise On Your Fence - R
84. Photo Shoots In Your Home
85. House Swapping
86. Chop And Sell Wood
87. Host A Quiz Night Or Poker Night
88. Rent A Dark Room
89. Rent A Tanning Bed - R
90. Turn Your Home Into A Children's Playhouse
91. Foster A Child - R
92. Sell Soil
93. Rent Your DVD's
94. Sell Your DVD's, Games And CD's
95. Sell Your Books
96. Sell Your Old Jewellery
97. Sell Everything You Never Use

Chapter 17. Home, Garden And Outdoor Jobs

98. House Sitter - R
99. Cleaning - R
100. Natural Cleaning - R
101. Window Cleaning - R

102. Caravan Cleaning - R
103. Carpet Cleaning Specialist
104. Curtains And Blinds Specialist
105. Car Cleaning - R
106. Car Detailing
107. Boat Cleaning - R
108. Event Clean-up
109. Ironing/Laundry Services - R
110. Become A Housekeeper - R
111. Become A Local Handyman
112. Gardening - R
113. Lawn Care Specialist - R
114. Floristry
115. Vegetables & Fruit Growing - R
116. Herb Farming - R
117. Grow Plants And Sell Them
118. Start A Hydroponics Business
119. Become A Task Rabbit
120. Making Corsages
121. Rent Bouncy Castles
122. Do Chores For Cash
123. Care For Plants - R
124. Repair, Paint Or Install Fences
125. Re-glaze Bathtubs
126. Become A Gutter Cleaner - R
127. Become A Locksmith
128. Pool Maintenance - R
129. Festival Staff
130. Sweep Chimneys
131. Do Appliance Repairs
132. Clean Out Fireplaces - R
133. Tidy Cables
134. Become A Pedicab Driver
135. Become A Charity Fundraiser
136. Do A Street Survey
137. Clean Ovens
138. Become A Solar Energy Consultant
139. Become A Green Consultant
140. Upholstering

286. Hauntrepreneur
287. Haunted House Consultants
288. Fireworks Retailer
289. Christmas Overstock Reseller
290. Seasonal Ornaments

Part 3) Make Money Online - NO Website Needed

Chapter 29. Introduction To Making Money Online And Internet Marketing Terminology

Chapter 30. Make Money Using Internet Marketing Techniques
291. Become An Affiliate Marketer
292. Become An Amazon Affiliate
293. Earn Money From Recurring Commissions - R
294. Earn Money From Mobile Phone Marketing
295. Earn Money From Pay Per Click And The Smaller Search Engines
296. Viral Blogging
Chapter 31. Make Money From Social Media
297. Facebook
298. Other Social Media
299. Become A Twitter Manager - R
300. Become A Social Media Manager - R
301. Get Paid To Socialise
302. Forum Moderator
303. Video On YouTube
Chapter 32. Creative & Design Jobs
304. Drawing Objects & 3-D
305. Designing Shirts
306. Designing Fonts
307. Designing Logos
308. Enter Design Competitions
309. Make Art
Chapter 33. Use Your Computing Skills
310. Get Paid Using Your Computer or Smartphone
311. Data Entry Jobs
312. Designing Websites
313. Design WordPress Themes

348. Translator
349. Medical Transcriptionist
350. Legal Transcriptionist
351. Business And General Transcriptionist
352. Online Juror (US only)
353. Drafting And Reviewing Contracts
354. Digital PR
355. Event Planner
356. Accounting And Bookkeeping
357. Lending Money

Chapter 39. Trading Opportunities

358. Social Investment Networks
359. Gold Trading
360. Forex Trading
361. Day Trading Stocks
362. Trading In Stock
363. No Risk Match Betting

Chapter 40. Other Buying & Selling Opportunities

364. Domain Flipping
365. Domain Parking
366. eBay
367. Run An eBay Shop
368. Run An Amazon Shop
369. Become An Online Entrepreneur - R
370. Buy And Sell Coins
371. Buy And Sell Stamps
372. Sell Your Old Gadgets
373. Re-selling Online As An Amazon reseller
374. Pet Merchandise Seller

Chapter 41. Writing Jobs

375. Freelance Writer
376. Writing Business Plans And Financial Reports
377. Technical Writer
378. Grant Writer
379. Writing Resumes / CV's
380. Ghost Writer
381. Writing Press Releases
382. Article Writing And Article Marketing
383. How-To Writer

Part 4) Make Money Online - Your Own Website Needed

Make Money With My Products

Please visit www.christineclayfield.com/affiliates/ for more information on how to earn money with my products.

Published by IMB Publishing 2015

Printed in the USA
CPSIA information can be obtained
at www.ICGtesting.com
LVHW072159050124
768273LV00007B/151